G000046567

a Testament

of Grief

**ONE MOTHER'S STORY
OF LOSS AND SURVIVAL**

Jennifer Wilkin Shaw

Simone Bluestock Publishing

Devon Libraries

D 12763799 X 0100

Copyright © Jennifer Wilkin Shaw 2017

Jennifer Wilkin Shaw asserts the moral right to
be identified as the author of this work

All rights reserved

No part of this publication may be reproduced, stored in a retrieval
system, or transmitted, in any form, or by any means, electronic,
mechanical, photocopying, recording or otherwise, without the prior
written permission of the author.

A CIP catalogue record for this title is available from the British Library

ISBN 978-0-9955949-0-6

published by Simone Bluestock 2017
testamentofgrief.info@gmail.com

Some names and identifying details have been changed for the purpose
of anonymity.

For Charlotte

'All the natural movements of the soul are controlled by laws analogous to those of physical gravity. Grace is the only exception.'

Simone Weil

Acknowledgements

My thanks go to Peggy Vance for her help, encouragement and professional advice; to Bob Saxton for editing the book; to Manisha Patel for her cover design; to my beautiful friends and cousins, and to Frankie for always being there for me.

Note to the reader: *on Mary*

From time to time we all need specialist help. I needed a woman who was experienced in grief – extraordinary grief. I searched. No one.

Then it dawned on me: Mary.

Not inaccessible Mary the saint, or Mary the icon, but Mary the mother. Flesh and blood, a woman, a young widow like me, who not only had lost a son but had watched Him die the worst death imaginable: crucifixion.

She has helped me and will continue to do so. She knows.

The similarities, the answers, soon started coming. And finally the comfort.

My engagement with Mary's predicament is rendered in this book in italic type.

Prologue

We are all lovers. It's what we do, in one way or another –
part of our journey of discovery and creation.

The luxury of making another, of being a mother, is the
privilege of only some.

But what if you lose that status? And in circumstances
beyond your control.
What then?

Then the real choices begin.

The choice between rage and giving back in kind; or the
transformation of such bleak suffering and then
illumination.

It's a hard way that doesn't come naturally, and at times is
not even fulfilling. But it's a better way.

Something, that, if everyone followed this course, would
make for a better world.

I want you back. Nothing works. I'm crying in my car on my way back home. It's 3.45 a.m. Again.

I've had a good enough evening. If I say what I've been doing the critics will call this book too candid. Amy would call it life-affirming. But I didn't stay. I can't wake up in sheets that aren't mine, and I want to go home: where your cats are, where you last were, a place that smells of you, still.

If I go out, then I come back and something may have changed. I can never figure out what. Maybe I somehow hope that walking through my front door might walk me back into my old life. It never does. All I know is that I miss you so much. I miss your smell, your wet shoulders coming out of the bathroom, the way your teeth looked, the back of your head, your hair tied up. Do you remember what you said to me when I tied my hair back? 'What happens between brain and hands to you? Your hair's a mess.' Yours never was. You were immaculate to the last. And when it was loose and fell upon your shoulders, it moved on its own – other people have commented on that.

I recall odd socks: same colours, different patterns. I think about your feet under the computer table and I miss passing snacks up to you. I miss your perseverance, your pushiness and also your compassion. I miss your beautiful smile, but more than anything I miss that innocent childlike joy that I saw in you when you danced a solo in gym. That understated surprise that's so genuine in someone who can't believe they've won the gold medal. Someone like you who was so brilliant but never knew it. 'A bright shining light,' the papers said.

It's so hard to miss you, someone as big as you, as true as you. I'm not even sure if I'm doing it right. I'm in agony much of the time, a pain that's been physical, especially in my hands and feet and my poor heart. A pain that makes me cry in a deeper way than I ever thought I could. And yet, there's no mess here. It's what it is. I deal with it. It feels clean and pure. With the support of very good people and yet on my own, I deal with it. I do it for myself, for you and to show your friends that if I can do it, then so can they. Yet sometimes it's so hard, and I feel close to breaking, though I don't know what that would be like. But as my shrink says, not coping is part of coping, and when I feel like I can't do it I *am*.

I don't think I've ever felt as bad as I do today. Death beckons me. I can see my way towards it. I could get the blue rope that's tied around the wonky fence panel in the garden. If I cut it with the orange scissors in the kitchen drawer, then take it to the garage ... then bang! Same as Jonathan. I could do that. I could hang myself, there I've said it. It's outrageous; outrageous to say this out loud. I'm ashamed of these terrible feelings. But I'm afraid of this huge anger and the sorrow. I'm so afraid. And yet it isn't fear, it's only *like* fear. I have a panic inside myself, wanting to run, or hit out, dry throat. I just want to move in any direction, make a choice, because sitting in this feeling actually requires so much energy. It's all here with me now at 1 a.m. on Wednesday 20 February 2008.

And do you know the worst thing? It feels like nobody cares.

Amy says that I'm surrounded by death, so of course it beckons sometimes. And yet I hold on as I engage with bits of life, bits of joy, some of the time. I'm like a robot. Following a routine of sorts, a timetable, but sometimes it goes wrong and that's when it's dangerous.

I've had a particularly bad evening, falling out with the parents. George has been to the doctor. The medication he's on for his recently diagnosed cancer makes him at times understandably difficult. We know he can be like this, although I love them both now more than ever.

I'm there for dinner and am cautious. I resent having to steer yet another course. I try to engage in conversation to lighten the mood and he flies of the handle. Unusually I don't rectify matters. I put my jacket on, place my bag across my shoulder and walk to the door. With the usual hysteria and desperation, clawing at my shadow they both move towards me. For two ill people, I find their speed astounding. Mum (Grandma – she cries when I call her that now) barricades the door with her ageing frame, a lifelong response, which of course irritates me. I'm hell-bent on leaving.

'What about the dinner? I've cooked parsnips, what about the dinner?'

'I'm not tolerating his verbal abuse,' I say proudly and with new-found righteousness. 'I've put up with your anger for 30 years and more. Today it stops.'

'Can't you be more sympathetic?' comes the wounded, blaming retort. This is the moment when injustice and misunderstanding turn to rage. I feel that I'm about to lose my sense of grace. My rage feels like it's turning inwards. Then I want to strike, hurt, kill … but whom? Him, them, everyone, myself, God? Well, it can't be you can it? Charlotte Shaw is dead.

There. Keep repeating it. Repeat it! Bang your head against the wall, and bang my head on a rock. Bang it, bang it hard: a rock in a swollen river. Make me cold! Same as you. Make me dead too. Kill me. Fucking kill me, there's nothing left. Nothing left. Sympathy, yeah I got sympathy. You are nearly 80, one of you, the other over 80. I'm just over half your age. I shouldn't be this close to death. This shouldn't be happening, not to me, not this.

And guess what? I've seen death. It's silent. It's unmistakable. I saw you die, my Charlotte, without a sound you died and I died with you that night. My heart was scooped out, and my body left in the gutter, an empty shell. When your father hanged himself, also no sound: just me saying over and over, 'No Johnny, no.' And the sound of the rain falling and my small knife cutting down more of that famous blue rope, my hands shaking. So don't tell me that they are fucking sick. Nobody talks so much or moves so fast when they are fucking sick. You didn't, he didn't. I won't. Ahh! By the way it just dawned on me that I never heard you swear.

Actually I've just opened a packet of crumpets. Those orange scissors will never cut through the blue rope.

The funny thing is that I feel I've let you down because I haven't died. It's almost that I couldn't have loved you that much if I can still be here and function. Should I have killed myself like I said I would if anything happened to you? Now I'm transfixed by the thoughts of being with you. I'm premenstrual, low in carbohydrates, and overtired – a bad combination for a bereaved soul. It's also exactly two weeks till the anniversary of your departure and the longing to be with you increases as I remember exactly, helped by your diaries, what you did every day during this period last year.

As I look back, I see you vividly. I see particular clothes, especially a red vest top, places, stances, looks, expressions, smells. I'm hooked, drawn into your world, the world I shared with you, our world, our bond, mother and daughter, sisters, flatmates, friends. I can't stand the agony once again. I cry. It comes from deep in my throat and starts under my diaphragm. I've been here before. I sob. It stops finally, the emotional haemophilia clots. Until I open the wound again. Anyway, I can't die because I like scallops, reading the *Times*, oh, and the *Guardian*, eating chocolate and seeing lots of people. I also still love travelling. And I'm about to go to Rome. Are you proud of me? I'm going to Rome all by myself.

Remember our trips? The ones nobody knew about. Well, they do now. I miss them. Especially our little London moments. I haven't done a London trip since. It's the one thing that was ours. Do you remember our hotel, Flemings? In Green Park. We used to tell people that we stayed in Mayfair. We were so posh. And our wheelie bags? How we put them down immediately we got to the room and then couldn't wait to go to the sushi bar at Selfridges. We used to talk about it all the way on the train while we played Whoosit and listened to music. You even made a Hangman clue for me about how you were desperate for King Prawn Udon soup with seaweed. I still have that clue in your sweet writing. Again the thought of it makes me struggle between worlds. You can't come back to mine, even though I will it so and pull the hardest I can. It requires something I don't have to come to yours, so we're stuck. I have to acquiesce, the sooner the better.

Do you remember how many dishes you used to stack up compared to me and how reluctantly you shared your King Prawn Udon? I almost could touch you then. Then our round of ice cream tasting; and then, the sweetie area, those brilliant jelly beans and your triangular bag. Me saying, 'That's enough.' You giving me the look: then the off. 'Where next?' You say. Please, you say. You say it now, to me; pretend you're with me now, just pretend. You, my little Charlie, special girl: you say.

How about an exhibition? Remember them? My love of art, eh – you know I was a pretty good mother? Do you remember the postcard game? When I tell friends about it, they like the gentle introduction to art that I gave you. Sending you with five postcards round an exhibition to identify the work. You would find the picture and come running, so upright. You're bounding toward me. Oh, I see you again. Maybe this isn't such a good idea.

Anyway, you were a super sleuth like me ... reading maps, doing simultaneous equations on the London Underground.

You would have become quite an incredible woman. The only way I would have given these moments up is if they'd given way to something else. And they haven't. I sometimes remember you as that woman in the making. When we used to meet up with Uncle Jason and Mark. Cocktails at the Ritz, eh? How many 14-year-old girls do that on a mini-break? You wore your new green and caramel dress; no jewellery. You were stunning, perfect, and it frightened me. You were like an egg – translucent, perfect and ultimately breakable.

I eat and see that I can be calm. Hurrah for crumpets and tea. If I keep going in this vein, people who can't cope with it or me will start to send other people round. Let's all come and look at the petulant teenager – that's me now by the way, not you. It makes my blood boil that they have to pathologise this. They can't for one minute just see this as the manifestation of extreme pain. Fuckwits!

I look at a picture of you, the one of you with Anna on the gym trip in Barcelona. Your eyes fix upon me and I'm drawn in. I know you. You're mine. How can I be coping? How can I be carrying on? How can I do this, and worse, how can I not do it?

And yet so many around me have become managers: experts. Without experience and without a handbook, they've decided that they are in charge of me and my grief. And worse, have permission to judge me. The upshot is that I know exactly what to do and I'm trying to do it, and they haven't a clue. Let's face it, ability is born out of a hands-on experience. And no one can be more hands on than me.

They use words like 'time' and 'coping' and 'seems to be doing "quite" well' and 'after a year', and they ask me if I'm working. These experts know that if I cry, then I'm not in 'denial', another word, page 54 of the grief handbook (I'm joking), and that sometimes if I cry it's clearly too much and I'm not coping, because also on page 54 it says that a grief-stricken parent must only cry two inches of tears a week to be this side of pathology. And yet I know that my crying is already different to what it was six months ago. It's less desperate than it was at the beginning, and anyway crying seems to fulfil a function of release. After I do it, something lifts, things are brighter. If I store it up, it feels like layers of clingfilm forming one on top of the other and I can't breathe.

The truth is that the journey I make feels like I'm steering a huge ugly ship, without power steering, single-handed, through treacle, in the dark, blindfolded. All I know is that I seem to be moving, to and from where I don't know. The funny thing is that sometimes it changes to golden syrup, which I don't trust because I'm so used to the treacle. Coping is actually staying alive and not harming anyone else. Coping well is finding bits of joy along the way and giving myself permission to experience them. And for those who use the term incessantly, that's also 'moving on'.

The night before He died He took some bread and broke it, giving it to His disciples, saying that this was His body and they were to eat. He gave them wine and said that this was His blood and they were to drink it in order that they should have life.

What happened in the tent? Rumour has it that ten gathered about you. Did you really push banana chips upon their tongues? Were there raisins too? Was Yasmin your favoured one? Did you ask her to look after me? Did you know? Did you know that this was the last time you'd be together? Why did you ask them to look after one another? Did you know? Did you really discuss with them the options between death by fire and death by water and which they'd prefer? Did you really choose water? You spoke of the future that night, your future. Why? Are you in your future now? Where do you study? Is it like the dreams I have where everything's blue and white and there are stencils on the walls?

Did you leave us so that things would change? Is it me who has to carry through the change? I do feel I have a huge job to do. I don't know what it is yet, but right now I'm trying hold my pain with a kind of dignity, to transfigure my suffering into, I suppose, something else – in the same way that a chipper makes wood into fine dust. It's important to carry it, rather than unleash it, for then who knows where it goes? This is easier said than done. The most important thing now is to be open to it.

Mary ponders.

I'm standing at the bottom of the stairs. I've switched off all noise so that I can concentrate and remember. I imagine that you're asleep in your room. I can see you. One foot emerges from under the pale blue duvet in a colourful trainer sock. I try to remember which way round you might be facing. I can almost smell you and hear your shallow breathing. Wanting you to be there now makes the agony and shock return. The sorrow wells up in my throat, under my diaphragm, I shudder and my eyes prick as I fight back those familiar tears. I want to read to you from the *Winnie the Pooh* book. I forget where we stopped. I forget when I last read to you – I didn't need to remember then. Do you remember the cave man stories I used to make up? Alone in the dark with you, cosy, warm, bedtime, stroking your arm, loving you. All gone. I long to be in that moment of yesterday.

Suddenly I'm aware of the magnitude of the loss, of what has been taken from me. Fifteen years of love and joy.

Every life stage from the beginning, giving way to the next. But this phase exchanges with nothing. I've been cheated. I con myself that this compares favourably with you leaving for university or the army or a school for the brilliant. I pretend the loss would be the same. I take the hustle further, and tell myself that this way I'm spared the anxiety of you driving with boys, in fast cars, staying out late, and worse. I

8

repeat my mantra that says it was meant to be, it was your time to go, and who knows from what we've been spared. But the truth is, I'm a liar. I want to be anywhere except where you are not. I berate myself for loving the moments we shared and wishing for them to last forever. Because in any way they can't. Was it our closeness that makes this so painful? I cannot contain this. Once again the huge sobbing begins. I know that I'm alone, and as much as people care for me I know that not a single person understands this agony. Maybe what we had at bedtime was lovely but nothing lasts anyway. Tiredness trumps and luckily takes over the moment, once again.

I went to the school today. Your school, the only school you ever knew. Parking down the road transported me back into your life. I looked for you: your legs, your face, your stance in that familiar uniform. The way you wore your jumper, blazer pockets stuffed full of cereal bar wrappers, laden with shoulder bags. You see me and the irritation shows on your face: this is your place, not mine. I'm an intruder into your world, with your people, with your secrets and your plans. I conceal my joy as you try to conceal your annoyance behind a steely upright frame. I'm lucky if you speak to me.

But you are there. No! You *were* there! No joy today, just the crestfallen, sorrowful faces of your pals, who know minute by minute exactly what they were doing last year before and after the accident. They are broken and pieced back together and are so beautiful. I love them, we cry, it spurts out.

Is there another way of doing this? I don't know if I'm doing it right. I'm trying to take and give comfort in what's left, what you left behind. It amuses and amazes me that you don't know about life here now. People keep telling me that I'm amazing and I don't know what that is. In fact, I'm clearly aiming for sainthood, what with my stigmata and all, left wrist still bleeding, I feel that I can only be here for my own comfort and that of your friends at the moment, at your request. I'm looking after the most affected people in this crisis, as per 'your instructions'.

Today was about the trauma of the accident and how it has affected them. Did you know that Neil, whom you called Zinger, rescued you, but then lost his grip in the horrendous weather? Would you remember that? You fell into icy water. Yaz had fallen in just before and was advised to take her bag off, which dutifully you threw towards the bank on top of the weight of your own rucksack. You were the last in the line and fell in as a result. Do you know this? Do you know that the last person to touch your lovely hand was Neil?

There are no words now to describe our Neil. He's broken, strong, silent and on the way to becoming something incredible. Our Neil, your childhood friend, your oldest friend: the boy you might well have married.

Where are you by the way? Where are the history and mechanics and uniqueness that went into being you? Yes, Zinger caught your hand. He remembers it. It torments him. He replays it. He replays every moment leading up to it and every moment after it. He wants to know why he couldn't do it. He says it's his entire fault. A counsellor told him that it will be with him forever. I think the counsellor is an idiot. For what *will* be with Neil forever are many things, all taking their own space. New memories will be made to cushion this, and in time a balance restored.

I'm not having a Chinese with you tonight. It's noticeable. It's funny but I've spent a year's worth of Saturday nights mourning you, but tonight I notice that I've come back from Bideford without two things: you and a Chinese. We aren't going to sit together overfilling ourselves and watching crap TV, hardly talking, but just being each other's background in our familiarity. We aren't going to watch our agreed choice of DVD. And we aren't going to eat the chocolate we got from the Spar, whilst we waited for the Chinese to cook. Do you remember those days? If we got to the Chinese before 5.30 we didn't have to wait long. And you used to put the hot bag of food between your feet in the car to keep it steady. I can see it all and I wish I'd watched more closely and for longer, really relished it, but how could I? I didn't know what was around the corner.

Well, tonight I'm off to the Morse's for fish and chips. They live in Braunton now in a presbytery and are becoming property fiends, buying and developing holiday lets. Deb Morse has become quite the business person and is working very hard, you'd be proud of her. When I leave them I could go to The Joiners pub in Bideford to see Ranald's band, remember him? He does acupuncture.

It's the same old stuff, remember, we did it after Jonathan died, roamed around, unwilling to go home to the emptiness. Well, it's worse for me now, far worse. And yet, I always end up at home alone, so I may as well acknowledge that.

Ranald is one of my 'Holy Trinity'. Father Julian – remember him? – and Simon the shrink are the other two. I've allowed them with trust and certainty into my body, spirit and mind to help me come to terms with your shocking and untimely departure.

Today Ranald stuck a needle in my heart advisor meridian, really uncomfortable and sort of painful, but when it's over there's a sense of containment and smoothness of my barbed edges that allows me to roll along more easily. I'll get back to the Son and the Holy Spirit later.

Sometimes I'm terrified – like now. I feel left and forgotten, not by you but by other people. I don't seem able to catch any life lines and drag myself out of this pit. So I conclude that it's time to stay in the pit. This is when I cry the deepest and breathe and be, alone. It's a pit, it's the very bottom, but already we know each other, the pit and I. This friendship is vital. I've been here before, and before that. And will come here again. I'm reluctant. But the repetitive, even when so hard, becomes known, and then predictable, and then acceptable and trusted. In an odd way this appears to comfort. It's strange when something bad becomes one's comfort because of its predictability.

There's a certain relief in acquiescing to pain and sorrow and just letting it hold you. To embrace all is often to know all. And the worst it can be is only the pain you already know.

Stopped off at Zoe's on the way back from Rosemoor, just for ten minutes, to touch base. Sweet Zoe. If I leave it too long, then it becomes awkward again to see her in the street. But she wasn't there. Jane was cooking a risotto from a recipe with smoked salmon. There seemed to be a time limit and stress because she and Zoe were both working at 6 and it was 4.45. Zoe arrives. She sports a medal, a first. It was from the gym competition, your competition. I'm shocked at the timeliness of my arrival. Where's *your* medal? Where are you? Zoe seems ashamed to have won. Maybe she's not that keen on gym and has only done it to be close to you. She holds the disc around her neck and looks sad. There's such a sense of searching at times, for all of us, and I feel that it will never end.

There are crumpets in the bread bin and I remember that she has them for breakfast. My crumpets last longer now. You see I notice every detail and wallow in it. I have an internal narrative without fail about every bloody thing that's related to you, my Noods.

It's been one year one week and three hours exactly since I last saw you, and I desperately want to go back to that moment and change our future. You are with me, within me and around me all the time but there's little relief from the overwhelming loss of you. I wake up with it, go to bed with it and it feels like it's getting worse, but it can't be.

Everywhere I turn, there you are. Even when I write I can see the imprint of your name on the desk in your writing. I'm suffocating, going mad. And yet I forage for every detail of you, every blot of ink, and every hair, remains of chocolate in a foil wrapper, an earring, any piece of aliveness that was and could be you. I search and sniff and examine, like a hound bred for forensics. Nothing delights or pains me more than to find something new about you. It's compensation.

I drive myself into guilt-ridden frenzy, remembering how we argued and I'd push you away. I'd want you away, wish you were somewhere else. And now you are away. You see? I've got what I deserve. Be careful what you wish for! And yet when I'm kinder to myself, I know that this pure pain that I suffer cannot be borne from a loss that isn't real and huge.

Oh, but feeling intact is a dangerous thing. It means that my equilibrium can change at any minute. The OK-ness is so fragile. If someone falls out with me, if something breaks, or if a cat needs to go to the vet, then I'm reduced to that broken state once more. I then can't do 'it', whatever the 'it' is.

Custard has been ill, a virus. She wasn't eating, so I took her to the vet in Bideford. I'm not sure whether you ever went there. We sat at the cat end, away from the dogs. When we were called in, the vet asked, was I aware that Custard had 'fleas', in a very serious voice, like was I aware that Custard had 'death'? I burst out crying and had to be taken to an ante room for a glass of water. I explained that I was the woman who'd lost her daughter…. And … and as usual there were lots of 'oohs' and 'ohs' and 'of courses'. In the end I've milked it all I can, and I become intact again and go home. Only I can say this of myself, but I feel that sometimes I indulge in the role of grieving mother and the fame of what I jokingly call 'Torgate'. I sometimes can't separate real grief from wallowing (as C.S. Lewis says in *A Grief Observed*) – again, something only I'm allowed to say.

Custard meanwhile felt a heap better after her temperature reduction injection, legged it out of the box and gobbled up all the grub. She's now resting.

I too sit, with one of my famous cups of tea. I breathe. I sit. I feel things are fine. When I'm on this side of the line, of course they are. Getting through is enough, I don't necessarily have to like it.

Why are people so bloody boring? I find my head doing a circular movement when they talk to me. It's truly uninteresting. And I can't help wonder if this has always been the case. I suppose it's because I don't have the motivation to talk about Easter bunnies, and their virtues, because my life lacks the most basic of systems, a sense of belonging, so that I cannot engage in this way. After all, where am I supposed to put a pink and purple papier mâché Easter bunny in a life full of grief? It doesn't fit. My mind is filled wall to wall with grief and you – there's no room for anything else.

C.S. Lewis is far more polite about other people. He just wants them to talk to each other and not to him. I want them to fuck off all together if they can't stop talking crap. Still, it wouldn't do if we were all the same, would it? By the way, the crap talkers in question are the Aster twins, they are very yellow and white and 'critical parent'-sounding, and it's time to sanitise the hardship, the middle-class way. I'm beginning to wonder whether only 'common' people with their faces constantly in the dirt and people from warm lands can actually identify with me. It seems that the lighter in colour the person and the higher up the social scale they are, the less they are able to connect with immense, breaking grief. Perhaps I should do an experiment to prove my hypothesis.

I feel suspended in my nowhere place and time. The suspension takes up all my energy. It's like the emotional equivalent of treading water. All-consuming, yet going nowhere. I'm not in the past with you and Johnny and I'm still not quite in the future. But I exist in a space propped up by my resources which largely involve other people, most of whom know that I would rather be somewhere else and that by definition they are second-best. It's at least comforting to be with those others who suffer the loss of you themselves. Without labouring the point, I feel I'm surrounded by illness and death. It's like trudging through a minefield of decay. George is ill, chest pain and wheezing on top of the prostate cancer diagnosed eight months ago. Grandma has a second bout of polymyalgia. Now at this point I should (at least) be collecting a leaping you from a springboard into the rest of your life. But you're dead. How can I come to terms with that? Johnny is supposed to be middle-aged with me, mowing a lawn or opening a bottle of wine. But wait for it, he's also dead; Godmother, dead; Auntie Jean, dead; Sonny, dead; Enid, dead. Even the fucking hamster is dead. For God's sake what's happening here? Where is life? I'm it. From a Zen perspective Ranald would probably recommend that I worked in a neo-natal unit or with baby animals or seeds. Who knows? I'm going to start wearing a badge that reads, 'Don't do death, fuck off!'

However, we're all going to die, this and breathing is what unites us. These are undisputed facts. How we will die we cannot determine. I may well die of a heart attack or stroke or something, which may be painful or may not be. Maybe your death can be accepted. After all, what is there not to accept? You died, hopefully not knowing pain, doing what you loved with the people you loved. You went out on a high before life's traumas of relationship splits, financial worries and other problems got hold of you. Who would question this choice of exit? When I say it like that, it becomes bearable. And maybe it is, just for one or two moments in a day – is that progress?

Monday morning in the spring sunshine, full of hope and potential. But not for me. Am I wallowing in self-pity? I don't want to feel this empty on a sunny day. I don't want to look around me and see the remnants of a life that was. And worse, I don't want to imagine you in a red vest top looking vibrant and set for adventure and feel that I've taken that from you. I don't want to go to your room and wonder why you aren't at school. And worse still, know where you are, and that all the colour and life encapsulated in this space will never be more than this again. I'm cold, alone and frightened and no amount of wishing from this prison will make my dreams come true. The physical presence of you is not here.

On the day that you died, a baby was conceived. He's four months old now and called Hunter. Jilly, his mother, and I met in the painting group. Did I speak of her? She worked for West Country TV. And went off sick, and then took up painting. That's where I met her, at a painting group. That's where people like me meet other people. There's a bond between Hunter and me. He recognises my voice when he sees me and smiles and talks to me. There appears to be something of you that carries on in him. When I ask him if he knows you, he says he does. Now this is the moment I could change from being the mother of an incredible child and a career woman to being a crazy old bag who keeps cats and hears voices. But I do want to believe that something of you carries on in him, it feels good and alive. I sing to him sometimes. You know stupid made-up songs that appeal to little people? Do you remember the ones I sang to you? The one that began, 'Are you a funny little face, are you a little yellow bucket ...?' Remember?

Grandma used to sing as well, about the little green apples and showing her the way to go home. Sometimes I don't want to remind her because I'm afraid that if she cries, she may not stop. Would it be this poignant if you had left these days behind you rather than died? I wonder.

Sometimes I can't remember looking at you and really seeing you. It's almost like you were not there when you were there. Like you escaped my human gaze because it pinned you to the cork board of life. You seemed ethereal. I couldn't touch you. I hear this a lot about people who die prematurely.

I look at the photo of you with Anna again. I know the top you're wearing. I remember buying it for you: it was a size 8 from a shop in Atlantic Village. I remember doing it, being there with you. But I don't remember who I was. If I could just remember what it was like being me, then... I touch your face. Were those your freckles, your teeth? Are those the eyebrows you plucked? The hair you insisted on having in a French plait? There's your familiar smile, the one that made a reporter call you 'beautiful Charlotte', when you left me.

If I'm really good, will you come back? I mean *really* good. Am I being punished for a crime I actually committed? What was it? Was it the pen knife I stole when I was eleven from Catherine Dalton? Yes, I did steal, but only childish things. Am I to suffer so much over so little? Was I bad? I promise to be good if you come back.

Promise.

Where are you?

Tell me, Charlotte, do you play with other children there? Is Scarlett there? She's a girl from Hartland who died in Goa recently. Is that what happens? When a child dies, do they fast-forward straight to where you are. What a lovely place. I'm wishing for it myself. I do get so sick of missing you and not being able to do anything about it.

Truth and grace are uneasy bedfellows. It's easy to be truthful about feelings when you're happy and peaceful, but anger, who knows what happens when that's unleashed. It does seem to frighten people. Sometimes I really want to transmute my feelings of rage into serenity and at other times I want to kick ass, hard. It can feel so much easier to do the latter. Is it really more rewarding to hit out?

You see, Charlotte: my world now divides well into two sets of people.

First, the unafraid who sit with me in my entire world, both pain and joy. They don't try to change me or the situation, because they are limited in their abilities and they know it. They have full understanding of the hugeness and horror of the situation and never make false statements about time and differences and are well aware of my unique competence in dealing unpathologically with this unwanted crap that has entered my world. Amy is one of these affirming, highly tuned individuals.

Amy is careful. Sometimes there's a question of permission to enter this personal world of mine and she'll ask for it. Some want to come in and try to but sadly haven't the capacity and so they have to be humoured like children, which is irritating, but harmless. They half-know that they should keep out and maybe talk about the weather and they bumble along in a clumsy sort of way.

And then there are the ones who challenge me and my grace, and these are the people I'm beginning to remove one by one from the equation. Fundamentally, they don't know how to deal with this or actually much else. They are inadequate. It's so big for them that they try and make it smaller and me less than I am. So it appears that I'm not coping, a famous phase used regularly by the useless. 'Is she coping?'

They don't want this to exist. So they attempt to remove it, change it, are angry with me for having this thing, they have to make it better but can't. I just don't make their lives easier by 'moving on'. 'Well, Jenny, it's your choice whether you want to think about this all the time.' It's pointless to explain to these people what grief is like, because they will challenge everything. I can't tell them that this isn't something I can will away. I can't tell them that it breaks through the most impenetrable barrier, that it clings and bores its way through with single-minded tentacles. It clutches and gets hold of you in any way it chooses. It has will. They'll ask me if I'm a person in my own right, because then I'll suddenly be able to do it and thoughts of you will disappear as if by magic. Obviously they don't realise that my ability to be separate from you allows me to function at all and not be dead, but it never takes away from the contrast, or the sheer cutting pain, when I hear the words, brutally spoken, 'my daughter...' They also have not accounted for smell and where it leads. They can't see that this is not a state of mind.

You know, sometimes I smell you, Noods. Then I feel cosy, and I hurry to get things done before you come back. Then the wind blows through the hole within me and I slump to the ground.

The trouble with the useless is that there are so many of them. Like cheap deodorant, they linger. Amy is an expensive perfume, so happily I only need a drop of her.

When I was in the hospital, early on ... oh, you don't know that they carted me off for what's currently known as 'respite', to a secure ward ... well, when I was there, Jeff, a nurse, said that I need only talk about the weather. He made me a badge and pretended to put a note on my door to that effect. After all, the weather is a safe and familiar topic. Of course, even the weather becomes too rainy and wet and cold with poor visibility and what about icy rivers and then that girl who died in those terrible conditions the other day

19

on Dartmoor? This is when no topics are possible and I'm frozen to the spot. Charlotte, do all topics lead to you because I need them to? Although I don't want them to … or do I? This is the paradox of grief.

10.20 Sunday night. It's the moment of the week when everyone holds their breath. The time when we wait for something to end, yet nothing begins. For me it was always a time of anticipating a new week. The time when preparation is at its best, like before a first exam. A couple of outfits ready to begin work, your uniform sorted, shopping done; shoes polished, an iron cooling and waiting to be put away. Everything is as it should be. You wending your way to bed or even now waiting for a story or writing your diary. Maybe we'd have a row about whether you might do netball on Monday or we'd be peaceful and you'd tell me a secret. It was full.

When I go up now, you're not there and I miss you. There's a hole inside me like a tennis ball would leave if I was shot with one. It feels like you could see right through it.

I saw your classmate Jackie today. Wonder if she remembers the time when we went to the Big Sheep on your fourteenth birthday and spent hours watching that egg hatch. Do you remember? The three of us kept going back to the incubator to see if anything changed. It was slow, very slow. The bird never came out while we watched. So we left it and played. We had pizza and ice cream afterwards. Zoe and Yaz joined us then. I got each of you a virtual game from the toy shop in Atlantic Village. It was a great day.

I got to know your friends then, but I feel I know them so much more now. Now they have an enforced longing and sadness that we don't usually find in Western children. I like it but I feel that it shouldn't be there, contaminating them all the time. I feel responsible for their pain because you were mine and I gave you to them. But I know this is ridiculous.

I've decided to go to ping pong in Bideford High Street. As it happens, on the way I take a detour to have a brief interlude at Phoebe's. She lives near the High Street and I stop at hers for a cuppa. She's displeased to see me. The face cannot lie. I think she still feels I might steal Peter away from her, but I probably would rather ... well, date a date! He makes a joke about her, which lowers the already low mood. It's that his friends think that he's no longer dating, but in fact he's *carbon* dating, 'cause Phoebe is older than him and he's 50. I think it's funny, but pretend that it isn't and on her behalf I berate him.

It's an unfortunate thing that when a woman is jealous of me and thinks that I'll steal her partner, it becomes a no win situation. You see, if I say that he's attractive, then I'm that thief; whereas if I say that he isn't and I wouldn't touch him with a barge pole, then I'm insulting her taste. Another no win situation. Hurrah for those.

Anyway, back to ping pong. Of course, in its favour, I'm not bad at table tennis. I came second in the Friary tournament recently. Oh, I haven't told you, I've been introduced to a place full of men in brown dresses with holes in their wrists. They say, find where you belong, and be there. So from time to time I am. Anyway, I anticipated my reasonable game getting better and better if I played every week. In little socks and with a special bat, I'd soon be in a league of sorts, all eyes on me as I played the winning shot in a major competition. Fantasy is funny, isn't it?

I finally found the hall. It's behind the church we had your funeral in, of course, the Methodist church in the High Street. You were there last the previous Christmas, at a concert. I walked down stairs and you passed me. Things were normal then. I was just a parent. You were just a girl. It was before you were so important.

I tried not to let the memory affect me. I know by now that every bit of respite costs. I didn't mind being the only girl. But everyone else was brilliant, or else really hopeless and standing by the wall. Fantasy dashed. There was a really good player called Kevin and his effervescent son who did lots of wrist and leapy movements, which I found scary. Of course, Kevin paired me in a dreaded game of doubles, which probably because of me we lost to Chinese Alan and one-armed Dave, remember him from badminton? It's beyond belief. Of course, he knows and was really nice to me, very empathic. So I played two games and then lost my bottle. Suddenly I felt down about going home to no one at nine o'clock and not sharing this with you. The crying began inside me, and sick like when you're in the back of a car was about to erupt. Poor Jeremy got it full on. He must have wondered what he'd done, but someone will fill him in.

I legged it to Phansits Thai café opposite Woolworths for some corn cakes and sweet chilli dip: the only thing for it really. You would have loved the food. The restaurant is where that greasy spoon used to be on the corner where the High Street meets the entrance to the Pannier Market. Anyway I took the cakes home and thought about the days when Johnny was alive and I made the same journey later at night with samosas for him and me after I'd finished my shift at the pizza shop.

Instead of you and him, I find myself returning to two strangers in the shape of your cats, our cats, but I tell myself that this is the way life is now. It's not too bad. And anyway lots of people in the world would like to play table tennis, get corn cakes and go back to two beautiful cats and watch TV. And so I make it good. It sounds nice, doesn't it? If I try and look at what it is rather than what isn't, I might have a better time.

I'm off out tonight. Eileen from my art class and her husband Peter, who is 20 years older than her, have invited me to the theatre. We're going to see an Agatha Christie at the Queen's in Barnstaple – you know, where we went to see Richard Dawkins. Having dinner at Giovanni's first. I'm looking forward to it, but in equal measure I'm fearful. Make way for the 'queen of paradox'. The doom of seeing other people, those who wonder how I can enjoy, those who have wondered if I will enjoy and those for whom I'm a constant reminder of what can go wrong in life, and the fact that I'm dealing with it when they may not have been able to, burdens me. I'm already exhausted in anticipation.

It's the looks and the lurching head movements and sympathetic voices that they'd also use if I lost my suitcase at the airport or a photo of my grandma with her parrot. It's fake. It's as if they feel they have to make a sound, don't know how it's supposed to go and take the sound attributed to loss of purse and multiply it by 50. Oh dear, it doesn't work, does it? The question they want to ask, though, is am I doing it?

Am I dealing with it? Well, yes, I most certainly am. Though the range of emotion has me with a toe over the cliff, metaphorically, in one direction and with supreme joy in the other, I spend most of my time in the middle of sanity, structure, carbohydrates, and feel-good people and pursuits, trying to work it out. I am OK. If I separate from you, as Father Julian, 'Holy Trinity' member, said, you've given me the gift of separation; then I can reclaim my life, and space, even hoovering the floor is beneficial to such purpose. So here goes. The dinner is actually lovely and I eat well. Peter is very funny, for although we never seem to hear the punch lines of his jokes, the humour is in the speed or lack of it in his delivery, and the fact that he forgets the outcome, Eileen is patient with him and offers witty explanation. I laugh, which is excellent, but if I look around me and see someone I know, who knows about this, then I feel that I need permission to be happy, so early on, what rubbish. I'm beginning to feel watched and collated.

The trouble with going over the 'accident' in my mind is that it hasn't happened. I set and replay a scene that has a chance of a different ending. And to think that I could change it all hurts. In my story there is warning, method of rescue and no panic. I throw you a rope; you float along using your bed roll. You take the rucksack off slowly in the water, so that the weight of your body against the current doesn't change so rapidly. You use your waterproof top to float. I jump in and don't care if I live and rescue you, or die alongside you, so long as I'm with you. A force pushes from within me to work for you, to make it work for us, but it's gone. It's happened. It's over. I'm back here in the present. I am sorry I wasn't there. I'm in anguish that I wasn't there.

This is what the roller coaster's like. The perpetual mind games: it's like constantly being lured into a promise that's never kept. The constant blur between my life and your death or your life and my death. It's torture.

Now I'm in my bath with candles. The water is tepid and I wonder what that coldness was like for you. I feel like I'm cheating you by running the hot tap to make myself comfortable. I want to suffer like you did. I want to throw myself into deep, uncontrollable freezing current and panic. I want to witness. What was it like? Did you want me? Was there time? Was it shock straight away? Did you know that you wouldn't get out? Were you scared? As scared as I am every day and every night? How long before you hit your head? Was God kind to you? Did he show you mercy?

Did you know that I was in Morrison's, buying stupid shopping, when this was happening. I was talking to a couple, you know the woman, she works at the pharmacy at the Wooda surgery in East-the-Water. Whilst you must have been dying, even drowning, and I can't bear that, I was passing the time of day down an aisle. They asked after you, and after my response, she said, 'Well, at least you know that she's safe, no one ever dies on the Ten Tors.' I then had Swiss roll and coffee. This crazy irony will not leave me or her.

It wasn't until I got home that I found out what was happening to you. Ironically, at that time I was ironing for England and cooking. You never wore the clothes or ate the dinner.

The police came at 6 p.m.

Of all the bad parts of my life, seeing the two of them, a male and female officer at my door, was the worst.

Too much again.

Too much reality. Too raw. Can't do it, go back, back to the bath, another bath, a good bath. You are little and you've got the end where the water is cooler, and I'm near the taps. 'Mummy, I loveses you, you nog nog!' What did that mean, 'nog nog', and where are you to ask?

Ooh, back with the police. I want you again, madly, deeply. The searing pain cuts me in half, like a hot knife through ice cream. I feel the sharpness penetrate my heart.

Did you feel it too, Mary? Did Simeon tell you that a sword would pierce you to the core of yourself, right through you? Did you wait for so long knowing this pain would come?

I had a dream after you died. It was a scene like the Last Supper. All the men were sitting at the table with robes and watches. They were waiting for Father Julian, who was late. You were waiting on them with wine. Simeon asked you where Julian was and you went to look. The men were all holy. It was after the dream that I went in search of Julian.

I said to the police, 'Tell me it isn't Charlotte.' The right response would have been 'Who's Charlotte?' They gave me the wrong response, the words I didn't want to hear: 'Can we come in?' I asked if you were dead and they said that you were not, in a way that told me that you might be, and quite soon. It became obvious that every second mattered. And yet from that moment nothing really mattered at all. For I never saw you alive again.

The police car had to stop five times for me to be sick outside it, for I hadn't eaten and was probably in shock. We got to Derriford Hospital in what seemed like 25 minutes but must have been longer, with sirens blazing. What I remember is asking whether you were dead every time the radio went. They said no. But you were actually dying, and it was just a case of them delicately helping me with the terrifying realisation that the beautiful girl that I sent out to the moors only 36 hours before in what I thought were capable hands was never ever coming back.

I wanted to die. I've never wanted to let my wonderful, joyful life go until the moment I knew there was nothing they could do for you.

There's less than a 0.1 per cent chance that beautiful, brilliant, compassionate Charlotte will live to see another day. Nobody even said that you mightn't make it through the night, that the next 24 hours were critical. I couldn't even hope. There was nothing. You were gone. You had gone far away, leaving the flesh and bones that housed you to taunt me.

And yet like you, Mary, I was horrifically prepared for this moment – this time, this change.

Although it didn't seem like it immediately, I was prepared. The first time you broke your arm prepared me. The second time you broke your arm prepared me. But the third time of preparation was when you were missing just weeks before this happened.

She was not in her father's house, like Him.
You were in the supermarket instead of netball on a Monday. And I guess if a place to shop is a place of worship, one God steps into the guise of another. It amounts to the same thing. You prepared me. You knew. Jesus knew. You both did.

And now I know. I know that you're gone. I saw you leave.

It's Sunday midnight. Back to school tomorrow. Last term before people leave after GCSEs: very important. But not so for you. You've already gone on to better things. What are they these things you do? Well, you know your own worth. You had something else in mind, didn't you? No earthly pursuits for Charlotte. It's the reason I don't need to take flowers to your grave. And the reason I don't need to keep so many things relating to you. Because it's all about the spirit. No need for petty physical compensations. You and I, we had it all, we had so much, together. I know now why I made it so: why we had three lives in one, why we packed it all in, why you did so, so much.

We went to the Auschwitz Memorial, you and I. As we got deeper and deeper into the monument, you felt the oppression, the fear, you understood. We saw the *Nutcracker* ballet in the Mariinsky Theatre in St Petersburg. We stepped into clear shallow waters in Mexico. There were wolves in Budapest, where we also had Kürtőskalács pastries and mulled wine. And we licked ice lollies together in the hot sunshine in our garden. All this is locked in my safe and cannot be taken from me.

I can't help but compare my coping with losing you to other people's lesser problems. The fuss they make over my coffee in Good Gardens café. Double espresso with hot frothy milk on the side, why can't they do it without a song and dance, what's so difficult about it? It's not like they don't have an espresso machine or milk frother. From their expression one might imagine that I mistake them for a shoe shop and I ask for size 6 red high heels! And therefore the prospect of satisfying my needs is daunting. But it's a café after all, and it's a coffee I'm asking for.

The funny thing is that it's the same thing every time I go. It's not like I ask for an unknown, like a cortado or, like they do in *Frasier*, a semi-skimmed latte decaf, no froth, with extra cinnamon. Can you imagine? The place would come to a standstill, planting would cease and there'd be a minute's silence over the dwarf conifers and herb terrace. To make matters worse, Ester, my walking companion, actually goes along with them. 'Ooh, trouble, yes, she is, isn't she, where do you want the froth? – in it, on the side of it, on the saucer?' Do these people have no listening skills and, worse, no intelligence? If they did have such attributes, then surely they could achieve this without needing to make a woman who has lost her daughter and her husband feel like she's too much trouble.

Listen, world, please understand that it's all too, too much, please don't make it worse by making a big deal out of the little things. Just make the fucking coffee. And bring it over.

Sometimes I get confused with what part of my life I'm in. I know how old I am. But I'm no longer a proper mother, while still being a daughter, so that makes me younger rather than older. I'm separating in a way from my parents, which makes me anything from 16 to 35, but grief is exhausting so I feel about 60. That fits, because also I've done everything and there's a sense in which I'm retired.

Were you actually here? I go into your room often now with the purpose of confirming your existence. You see, I know you. I am you, and yet there's such a lot of confusion about where it went – not you or I but the stuff between us. Sometimes I have to check on the reality.

Julie said a funny thing. Remember, we liked her for the funny things she said. She misses you and cries. She comes round less now. I don't think she can cope too well with it. Anyway, she said that she could never imagine you doing certain things, like going to university. Or living as an adult in a flat. Or being married. It's like there wasn't a place for you here, only elsewhere. It's true. You were not fully here.

Was he, Mary? Was He with you? Could you touch Him, really know Him, appreciate an intimacy? When did He leave you? When was He too aloof, beyond, nearly gone, away, anyway? When did you know that the time was coming to let go? When did you feel Him slip through your fingers? With Noods it was happening towards the end of 2006 as the dawn of the New Year approached. She began to leave me and then she tied up the loose ends over January, February and March.

You told me you loved me then. You prepared me for loss. You scared me.

It's Monday morning again. I feel the sunniness of the day and the vibrancy of you and sport and flapjacks. And I'm empty, lost, sad, nothing.

I've got up three hours too late for you to begin your day. It's nearly 10 o'clock, I'm still in my dressing gown and I feel like a loser. Time for breakfast, high carbohydrates and *Ironside*. As I teeter over the year mark of losing you, people fall by the wayside. It's as if I've made it and there's no need for them to panic any more. Also, the interest value that was there at the beginning has vanished. This is no longer new or newsworthy. There's something for them about having been through all the 'firsts' that makes this all better now. But it isn't. It's worse. Now it's real. And I realise the impact that it will have on every aspect of life; and how long that life might be.

I want people to know the amount of pain that comes from this realisation. I want to show them. I want to go missing, to create a stir, to wake them up. And I realise why this happens to people at this stage and what prompts others to say, 'She was doing so well, I don't understand, why now?' No one is really that responsive and I have to beg for the crumbs off their full table. I want to have a tantrum, to be noticed. And my pride gets sick of it. I know I shouldn't have pride, it's not very spiritual to have pride. And if I really want to identify with the poor, then I do need to beg. Please let me come to be with you and your family tonight in your special celebration. Please let me tag along with you and your husband to the theatre.

I need to hold the rage of being apart, of being separated, unfairly. Do I shame them? Is that what I have to do?

Am I to be struck on both cheeks? Were you? When you were asked to walk a mile, you certainly gave two. Why? Can I?

I suddenly remember the evening that I would have been having with you. Beginning with you marching through the door. Latterly there would be a mixture of delight at seeing you and wonder at what plan you'd concocted during the day to interrupt my life. Always an elaborate plan and bargaining. Every night it was like being in a Persian street bazaar with you. And I'd sometimes lose my rag as you wore me down. You tired me and stressed me out and frightened me.

I'm relieved that you're not doing it any more, that my life is my own once again. For this is the only secondary gain here, my so-called freedom. And freedom is a big thing. It's absolutely lonely and without movement, but it's what we crave some of the time.

This freedom made it possible for me to go to Rome on the anniversary of your father's death this year. I flew there. After years of not wanting to move on this day, just in case, I threw caution to the wind and drove to Bristol Airport, without a soul knowing. I took spare knickers, a lipstick and a credit card and, of course, my mobile so that if Grandma phoned I could say I was in a café in Bideford, 10 minutes from home, and off I went. For a couple of days I rattled round outside the Coliseum in a t-shirt with a small bottle of water, and Euros in my back pocket for wine along the way. It was brilliant. I found the AD 200 house that my shrink recommended and I licked the rubble underneath the frescoes for good measure, and because I could, 'cause there was no one watching.

But for all the sun and liberation, I took you with me. Every time I ate an ice cream, you were there. Every time I wanted to bring a token back, it was for you. But there was another wound as well: all Italian teenage girls are long-legged with striking dark hair and pale olive-coloured skins. And they smile with a readiness the English may never know. I saw you every day, ten times, at least: around every corner, in every café.

As I was able to reflect, I'd wallow more. I'd think of what I didn't do for you. Pocket money I should have dished out, netball kits I could have said yes to without all that resistance. Demands I should have waived. I think of better ways I might have organised things, and priorities that might have been different. And so I spoilt my time with continuous berating.

Eileen is going to get me a stick to punish myself with. I replay events until I've made myself into an ogre and you a saint. Even though I know that's not the way it went. 'Must be punished more' is written on the label sewn into my clothing. I punish myself most for not being there to rescue you. I would have jumped in, risked death and done more than any one to get you out. But this is fantasy. This is what

I replay. I wasn't there. And, really, thank God I don't have that on top of losing you. So not only does every road lead to Rome, every Roman, or Roman girl any way, leads to you. And let's face it, if Neil couldn't do it, what chance would the rest of us have had.

Maybe if I was there I would have been hovering behind you and you wouldn't have been at the end of the line.

Do you remember when you rescued me? I was waving and unable to stay afloat on that snorkelling exercise in Cozumel, on the cruise we went on in 2005. I was panicking. You saw. You came. I wish you could rescue me now. I'm in a dreadful panic again.

Now I'm back from Rome, everything looms large. The status quo gets interrupted and somehow I have to reform my world. It's Saturday night and I'm about to go to the Morses and I'm OK with that. Same old routines that work. I forge forward, small steps, survival: one foot, moving in front of the other.

You know, I'm glad you're not here. There's no more worry for me, day in, day out, no more pain. I don't live under the threat of your departure any more. The weird sense that I knew I'd have to let you go. And how you seemed to go along with that. Always living on the edge, flirting with fate. I don't any more have that continuous anxiety every time you leave the house. No more phone calls, no more stress. It's so peaceful. I'm glad you're gone.

I'm no longer worried I might hurt you and lose control. You wound me up so tightly and never relented. We came so close to something physical. I almost hated you because I hated the person I could be when I was at the very end of my tether.
I can see the eyes reading this. They are on your side, you know. They can't possibly understand how I could say these things about somebody so precious, and now so lost.

Well, it wasn't all roses. It was hard, and there were times when I was sick of it and sick of you. In the summer before you left I went to Paris to get away from you and your schedules and your incessant demands. I left you and I felt relieved because you became Grandma's problem for three whole days and I was free. I never had the luxury of divorce because that man who could never tolerate pain decided at the first cut to hang himself, so I rarely had a proper break. But that August I scarpered. I rang you every night because I felt so guilty and I missed you, but I got away.

We didn't have a holiday that year, remember? We'd just got the kittens and had to stay here, so I suggested that we had two weeks when we did nothing, went to the beach, had days out and so on. But you made it impossible. First there was a trampolining course, then your job at the bakery, then friends you wanted to see. In the end we probably spent one day together.

You'd have made a rotten wife, never being at home, always elsewhere.
But you weren't a rotten daughter. And I lied about you making a rotten wife. And now I'm crying because I've hurt you and I don't mean it. On Mother's Day before you died you gave me loads of different Kit Kats and a city breaks brochure. The little card that had cats on it said in the neatness of your unmistakable writing, 'Have a break … have a …' I loved it. It was so simple and original. That was the last present I ever got from you. There was nothing for Mother's Day the following year, because I wasn't a mother any more. There wasn't anything for my birthday either, or for Christmas, and I was disappointed. I can never have those times back. I can never feel that cosiness one feels when one's in the midst of something warm. The unparalleled feeling of happiness that I had when I touched toes with Johnny at the bottom of the bed and you were little and in the middle. How stupid was I that I thought it would be like that for ever. How stupid and happy was I then? And how wise and forlorn am I now?

God, there are times when I'm absolutely sick of the drama of you: the pain of this. The continuous crying that's a symptom of my grief and all of it filling every cell of my life. Squeezing into each corner of my consciousness like a life raft that's been inadvertently inflated in a small room. There's no air left again. I can't breathe.

I've got a new shrink. She's very operatic. In fact, her name is Aida. Simon, the previous one, was very receptive. But his job has changed. He knew the whole story. Opera lady hasn't caught up with me. So she keeps talking about suicide. In fact, she just keeps talking and talking and talking. She has read 'every scrap of paper' (her words), and she doesn't know how I'm staying alive. Or *why* I'm staying alive, which bodes so well for me that I'm beginning to query this very point myself. She thinks I'm incredible. She doesn't know what she can do for me. I'm in a place, the loony bin, as an outpatient, these days, where most people are psychotic. I'm not on any medication and there's nothing really to review.

No madness here. She's quite right, for all her effervescence. So what now?
Of course, I feel like getting away from all this, who wouldn't? I had so much joy with you and because of you (I'm sorry I didn't tell you enough) that I'm bound to feel the agonising pain at the loss of you. And of course I'd like to get away from that pain, again and again, every day forever. So of course I think of my own death, because that would be a step. But removing the pain and seeking death are in fact two different things. Anyway, how could I do it to them, my parents, Neil, Yasmin, Grace, it's too much, then what, it's a knock-on effect, everyone in the world jumping off cliffs, it won't do.

But here's the thing, what if it wouldn't harm anyone? What if it was definite, with no risk of side-effects? Would I do it then? You know, I don't believe I would. What's my motivation? Well, I enjoy the little pleasures of life too much. And I believe that I have a job of work to do that's very important.

Did you, Mary, have a job to do? To make things better in some way for some people? Was that why you hung about throughout the pain and rumour? Did you carry the world's pain so that they wouldn't have to? And, importantly, did they see? Did they trade anything for this unseen advantage? Did they give you some reward (not cake, I guess) for continually being alive and carrying the burden of death, so that they could be spared?

And so I begin to try to change people's lives. Although sometimes with a little playful berating and naughtiness, I confess. When I was in the aforesaid Rome, recently, I sat at a pavement café to enjoy a coffee – an espresso, in fact. You know, the ones that the Gardens can't produce. And I ordered a tiny little custard-filled and fruit-topped pastry to go with it. This item is called a 'mignon'.

Now upon its arrival two things came to my notice: a sad and dispensable coffee bean in the saucer next to the cup and the couple adjoining my table looking aghast at the 'mignon'. They seemed to be saying that I was obviously in cahoots with the management and, what's more, a local and therefore preferential treatment was afforded me in the shape of a delicate-looking, delicious mini fruit tartlet.

They were wrong. But to wind them up I ordered another coffee and whispered in the waitress's ear a request for another 'mignon'. The second offence appeared to cause a great deal more pain and presumed discrimination than the first, as the singular coffee bean on each of their saucers seemed ineffective. They ordered two more coffees.

What sorrow, two more beans? Life certainly was treating them unfairly. What with Sally their eldest not getting into Cambridge (I overheard snippets of their continuous moaning), and the fact that that very morning the woman had lost a freshwater pearl from a necklace. All in all, they were having a bad week. So I couldn't resist. Another coffee and this time the whisper requested and secured three more 'mignons' which I duly lined up like tequila shots ready for swigging.

She keeled over. And then I afforded them the punch line. 'As you can now tell, it's not because I'm Italian that they bring a "mignon" with my coffee and it's not because they like me more than you, although they probably do. After all, you've been moaning quite a lot. It's merely that I can read a menu and articulate my wishes. These,' said I, pointing, 'are called "mignons", third page in on the menu. And these two are for you in the hope that they will add some joy to your life. It certainly works for me." And I told them what I'd lost. They were speechless.

Was I helpful? Maybe not? Come on, Mary, don't judge me from your sainthood, I bet you slamdunked the greedy occasionally. Didn't you?

I'm pretending tonight that you're nearly 15 and still here, Johnny isn't dead, but lighting a fire, and there are a brother and sister playing games. I get really excited. Then I don't. I wonder how people take this scenario for granted. I know, Noods, I can see your face telling me that people have their own problems within every situation, and just because it looks good on the outside, it doesn't mean that there aren't issues on the inside. But you know, I'm jealous – there, I've said it – I'm jealous of people who have a nice family comprising husband and children, and you know what, it's the first time in my life that I've really experienced jealousy, and I don't like it. It makes me paranoid that if people knew, they'd use it against me. I feel that maybe they'd talk about their families more, rub my nose in it or, worse, say the word 'daughter', over and over, and then again.

Am I surviving this because I didn't really care that much? Am I ruthless? Or is it that I have the capacity to bear extreme pain and discomfort? I didn't realise what an investment you were. That sounds so calculating, but it isn't. I put into you time, love, consistency, effort and sacrifice. I gave these to make a platform from which you could be all that you could be. And you were. Sometimes I was a little comparative in my thinking – that you had it all when in my own life I hadn't, and I wanted a little thanks and recognition. And a week before you died, when you were under the weather, you gave it all to me.

'Mummy, I loveses you, you're a good mother. You care about me a lot, thank you for going to the shop and getting me my special ice lollies and tomato soup. I love you.'

I wonder, am I worthy of such love? Am I a good person? Will there come a time when I like being who I am now so much, even with all I've suffered, that I won't want to go back to before? I ask Neil the same question. No, we know the answer. We'll give anything to go back to before and not let you set off on the Moor that fateful day. If I could, I would without question change that at least. But I'll watch this space, to see what unfolds.

Remember you and Zoe used to call Jane and me 'the parents' on the cruise? Well, I'll call Grandma and George the grandparents. And today they aren't half bad. Instead of berating them and not giving them a chance, I have of late been listening. And there's a lot of wisdom there. It's a lesson in opening myself up to all things and embracing what is – which makes life more bearable and more of a continuum. And I mean this in all ways.

Maybe we're all wiser since your departure. Neil has become so big in order to deal with this, it feels like he's a man overnight. So he can no longer be small and managed, when required by his 'superiors'. He's in a position of suffering that he doesn't want to be in and is angry that he's on show and people think they can enter without permission into his intimate world. How clumsy they are!

He's leaving the school after the exams and going to the college to do A levels. But he, like me, is afraid of forgetting. As life goes on, you're sealed in a deep part of my heart, but in order for life to go on I have to engage with other things and with people, and sometimes for a moment I realise I haven't thought about you and I feel ashamed, guilty and yet a little relieved.

Can I really think about you all the time? Would I, if you were at college? Am I allowed to forget you for a moment, to be distracted for just a while by something else? We won't forget, just as we don't forget to love and to breathe and to give, but sometimes I feel like I'm letting you go. And it's a little frightening.

There's no reward for Neil, no compensation. He's given something up and there's nothing for him instead. There should be a 'Pride of Britain' awards show, not only for brave people who succeed in a rescue, but for the bravest of those who don't, and have to live with their unsuccessful attempts. For the same courage is put out and often has to be sustained for longer. Neil should get that award.

If he were older, just maybe he'd understand that holding this experience is reward enough.

I realised how annoying parents can be when I was with them. How Neil's relative spoke of his trousers getting shorter. How people feel entitled to enter our intimate world, even strangers.

Sometimes I'm almost angry with you for leaving.

It's Crumble dashing up the stairs. After all this time he hears the computer and looks towards your room, crying. Is he expecting you? Would you come back for a day just for him? If I asked you, would you have something better to do?

There are times when I actually feel quite crazy. I'm driven to crazy by lack of care or by misunderstanding. The landlord of the house next to Sybil's, Harry, is having the roof done. The workmen he's employed are banging every day and balancing their apparatus on my fragile kitchen roof. Nobody has had the courtesy to inform me. So I feel violated. The work has also led to parking changes outside my house. Sybil – remember her, she's about 83 now and still lives alone – has positioned her small blue job next to my wall. I have no space to park, apart from up the road. This is a very different story to when you first died and Joss and Matt, neighbours, a few doors up, needed my one visitor to constantly re-park, because they were edging onto their side boundaries, stealing their 'spot' (that all-important word) when they had 21 shopping bags to drag into the house. Oh, to have that many cornflakes!

Oh, to require that many, instead of making a cereal bar last for days. So it's double standards. I'm angry on top of being misunderstood.

Your son felt this, didn't He? Was it one of His wounds?

Certainly it's one of mine, as well as being grief-stricken. So I'd very much like to select each of the pink bottles of Zinfandel in Marks & Spencer and drop them. Following this, I want to smash every single bottle in the shop and see how far I can get before security arrives. But I won't, because I know that if I do I'll be arrested and detained and examined and labelled and sectioned. Then I will be crazy, and all because of someone's bad parking manners. So what's the point?

Of course, it's a Wednesday, counselling day, and of course dancing behind me and helping me towards 'crazy' is my mother, and of course I'm, wait for it, pre-menstrual.

And then I take it out on her because she gets it wrong and then I feel like I'm 15 and then I'm you but you were better, and then I feel worse and guilty and bad and mad and angry and I'm back to being tempted by the bottles of Zinfandel. Then I stop. I'm exhausted.

Smashing up has no place. And it would break my record of grace. I must maintain. I must contain. I must stand.

Of course, the truth is that I'm well past tiredness – danger! danger! – because yesterday I went to London with Amy.

We saw *The Year of Magical Thinking*. This is a play with Vanessa Redgrave as the only actor, elaborating incessantly upon grief. She was playing Joan Didion, the woman whose memoir it was, who had lost her husband and daughter. How many points does she score, I wonder. It must be what, one point for losing a hamster? Three at least for an ageing granny, seven for a husband. It must be twelve for a daughter at least. More if you and she are under the acceptable age for death. All in all, Joan Didion scores 19 but I win. I score 50. Why? Well, because the house wins every time.

I am the house. I win in all games. You were nearly 15 and not an adult – taken away before time. Double my score. Any extra for the hanging and the finding part of the Jonathan death? Well, maybe. Only that woman in Darfur amid the shelling and having the threat of constant invasion and starvation can win this round – yes indeed, let's play 'How much does your grief/misery score?' Obviously I chose wrong. I did wrong. I am wrong. I don't play right.

Are you wallowing in self-pity again? Wait for proper grief. Wait, there it is, the nice jab of C.S. Lewis's 'red hot' poker, it's you in a brown vest top on the train. Thank God. I thought I'd avoided any real pain and there you are. Of course, you're backing me, so the first sighting is your dark pony tail, perfect length, there are tufts which frazzle out of the sides, a bit greasy and vulnerable and unbrushed. You've scratched a spot on your shoulder again. I can see the blood from here. You look pale, have you been eating crap again? Your hat has a Krispy Kreme logo, from that doughnut shop in Harrods. Oh my goodness, I can't believe how deeply the knife is going in. I'm swelling up like a sponge in the bath. Turn round, let me see your face please, so I can get out before I panic.

I don't want to play any more.

I wore your coat yesterday, the brown suede one that Uncle Jason bought you. Do you remember the last film we went to? It was *Music and Lyrics*! I found your ticket in the pocket. There was a pack of cards in there too. And your last London Underground ticket from December 2006. I look at the film ticket stub. We saw the film on the 23rd of February at 6 p.m in Barnstaple. If I'd known that 11 days later you'd be dead, would I have changed anything?

We saw Beth and Sara at the cinema. Sara remarked on it today. I went to see them both. I hugged Beth. She smells like you. I was shocked and cried. I can't replace you. There'll never be anyone who comes near you. And I wish I'd appreciated you more, but I don't know how I could, how that would have been. I thought that you were beautiful, brilliant, sporting, and I told you so and tried to support you. You needed a lot and sometimes we didn't agree. And you weren't namby pamby, so we fought. When I remember you standing so tall over me, I want to grab you and hold you close and smell your hair and neck and feel your muscular frame and never let you leave me again. But I don't want to cling, and I'm confused by my overwhelming need, and what you would have made of it.

Mothers can be quite ugly, can't they? Having lost their lustre, they cling on to what might have been through their teenage girls. They look at the bloom and wonder. I remember the first time I saw an adult man look at you instead of me. In the lift of the Flemings Hotel. I was afraid for you: you seemed so vulnerable and little. In a way I was also flattered that I'd made you and that you were such a source of attraction and, I have to admit, a little jealous that I was older than you and a less vibrant version all at the same time. It's funny how so many feelings can occur simultaneously, so that one doesn't know which one actually takes precedence.

Tell me, were you angry, Mary? Did you feel second-best? Was it all right to give Him up even with warning and preparation?

On the night before He died, He shared supper with His friends.

So did you, Noods. Did you really gather them to you? I can't believe it. And did you poke banana chips and raisins into their mouths. Did you draw them together so that they'd have each other when you'd gone, like you insisted on getting the cats for me? Thank you, by the way. This came to me at the Friary when Benedict started the Eucharist. I realised that in fact you'd had a moment with your friends before you left.

Fears are growing for the safety of a woman in her 40s. Jennifer Wilkin Shaw was last seen at her home in North Devon last Friday evening. She hasn't been seen since. Jennifer has been suffering insurmountable grief since both the death of her husband in 2000 and her daughter Charlotte on the Moor seven years later.

Then there'd be a whole host of assumptions about me, my thoughts, my mental health and the fact that I cry. People would be questioned and an incorrect profile drawn up on me. Don't worry, I'm still in my cage. But I do realise that my emotional balance needs to be redressed: it's somewhat askew.

The problem is that nobody comes to the house for long enough these days to share the regular pain of my world. Nobody knows what it's like to pass your room every day and wonder whether I want to open the door to let you out or myself in, to smell your smell and relive that life for a moment, nobody at all. It's required that we have witnesses to share not only life but also death. And I have few if any of those in a real and deep way.

There are the girls again, the legs, the pink, the dark hair, the walk, the bag, the arms, the pace, the you, the you, where you, not you, is you, why you? Why not? Too much, crazy, where not? Never.

There's a single moment in most of my interactions when I honour someone with the purity and openness of my heart. At this point they show me whether or not they're afraid. Amy isn't. Amy isn't afraid of anything. She has given me permission to die. And also to live well. Does this outrage? Some people may naively think because she's said that I can die that I'll be obsessed by the thought, and suddenly be found face down in a river, oh no that's you, but it's no more likely, if someone tells you you can kill yourself, that you'll do it. If anything, once explored fully, the concept of suicide seems like a poor one when there are so many experiences to be had and so many uses to put one's skills to. The thing is, perhaps I'm not courageous enough to do it. Or do I need more courage to live with all of this, than to die?

I've licked the detritus of my own misery, I get sick, reach rock bottom and then I want something better. Amy helps, she steers. Who did that for you? Was it Sophie? Unafraid Sophie. She permitted you, didn't she? She was the one who said: whoever you are, I will love you. All that you are I delight in. Was she the unconditional one in your life? She hurts so much now. She doesn't smile in the way she used to. She doesn't beam: it's as if something has died within

43

her. You see, giving permission for life doesn't mean not having pain, if you lose something precious.

It means bearing it.

Respite costs. I don't take it for granted. Gardening and reading in the sun was so lovely today in my world. I went to Rosemoor to walk and buy some plants I had my eye on. Lovely. Payment one, a sighting of Jackie in summer clothes; and payment two, Zoe's stepfather, Botting, walking Molly the dog, smiling – that's him, not the dog. They are all still here and going strong, without you, how can that be? Then I'm in your world, missing you, longing. I'm shot out of my moment in the sun. In a short space of time everything changes. Nature and people wound by being indifferent to my suffering and they don't mean to be.

Amy gets this and will affirm it. Most others begin their response with 'Well, Jenny, you can't expect...' And actually I don't, you stupid fuckers ... I don't expect, I'm merely saying what it's like, just how it feels to be the only one. I just want them to share it, to know it, or even nod gently, not necessarily to change it.

I don't understand why Johnny continually mowed the lawn, when he was going to leave us. Why did he bother to lull me into a false sense of life, only then to go without warning, suddenly?

Because you aren't here any more I don't feel that I have a place. And I don't feel worthy. People talk about their children and I've nothing to contribute and it makes me cross because there was a time when I understated you, because you were too great and I didn't want them to feel overshadowed. Anyway, now I can't break into their world and I can't keep myself out. There seems to be no place for me. I search.

I slip back to the very distant past when I was 15 and remember my mother's roast dinners on Sunday nights. Her roast lamb and parsnips were to die for and she always made a curry accompaniment, a kind of East-meets-West thing. The flavours were incredible. I want to tell you about me walking round my local cemetery on those Sundays feeding the ducks and eating American hard gums. I want to tell you lots about the way I was. I want to share with you the fantasies I had and tell you about my long grey coat that I found and when I pretended I was an aristocrat from *Brideshead Revisited*. I sometimes think if I'd been different or if I'd made roast on Sundays and hadn't married a vegetarian, then you might still be here. Is there a link?

But you had a brilliant appetite. Do you remember the meals at the Han Court? We three don't go there now. That's Grandma, George and me. The closest we've got is a takeaway from Mr Ho's. November 1999, that must have been the last time all of us ate together, all five happily. You wore your black and cerise velvet dress and knitted waistcoat, plenty of beads and you insisted on bright red lipstick. I have photographs that remind me.

Oh my God, Mary, I've just realised that when Jesus went you must have had no image of Him whatsoever. There was nothing for you to keep Him alive in form like I do. Did it matter, was this the way of it then, people died and it was a given that the image of them goes also? And yet He's probably the most painted figure in the world, though you couldn't know this.

We must have had prawn and noodles and you would have had mushroom foo yung until you started branching out and ordering chicken and cashews and prawns with ginger and spring onions. Johnny wore his green suit and looked handsome, but to no avail, for he seemed no longer interested in me or any thing for that matter, and was determined not to get help. It's horrible to watch people slip away without being able to do anything about it. That was the last time I took anything for granted. That was the last time I observed my family. That was the last time we were intact. It was the end of what was and I had no idea of the changes that were about to occur.

You said it would be all right. You said nothing would happen to you. You said I was paranoid and neurotic and if I wasn't careful I'd become like Grandma. You lied. It isn't all right.

Miss Wilson said of you when you were quite little, maybe six or seven that you'd fall off a cliff and expect someone to be at the bottom to catch you. Was there anyone there? Were you caught? All I want to know is that you didn't suffer, that's my only concern.

Your room torments me. You're there but not there. If I change it, then I get rid of you. But keeping it the same brings you no closer. It's weird to be able to touch your things without penalty. To wear your clothes, read your private thoughts and get to know you in an intimate way. I'm wearing your red top. It doesn't suit me. My mind wonders and I'm gripped with the thought that it's been nearly two summers since you frolicked on the beach at Westward Ho! I'm sure that your friends miss that. After the bakery with your tuna roll you'd meet Sophie or Zoe and get in your wetsuits and into the Atlantic Ocean. Then I believe it was spring rolls and chips and back to Sophie's house to play computer games whilst of course remaining in wet clothes. Aren't I boring? I'm glad you did it all, it sounds idyllic. At the time I was worried for your safety. There were so many variables: strangers, people watching you and becoming familiar with your pattern, and you being trusting, in the sea, getting lost, but you were always fine then. I collected you and you were there.

Of course, I too am fine now. If I don't scratch the surface, life is great. And I wonder if it's not the same for many people who don't seem to want to look below the cracks at what's really wrong. Most people live in the fear of what is my daily experience: separation, the death of very significant others, multiple loss and being alone and left and unattractive. But you know what, if you stop clinging to everything, then what emerges is a kind of security in the insecure, a home within oneself that's strong.

Feeling relaxed, just had acupuncture and massage and what Ranald calls 'Buddhist mask removal'. So to fuck it up I've decided to go for a coffee. And here it is. I'm at Atlantic Village, in Presto's with my voucher. I see Steve, an acquaintance. He's a one with the ladies and presumably is with a new friend. He introduces us and she smiles through gritted teeth, I suppose it's flattering. She even covers her mouth, maybe she is stopping herself from saying, 'Pretty cow, piss off', but what intrigues me is the metamorphosis when I return from the queue with my goodies, for then she looks at me openly and with care. He has told her about me, would you credit it, Noods, and I can just imagine the conversation. 'Who's that, Steve?' 'Oh, she and her husband had the pizza shop when it first opened. Her husband committed suicide, in the garage, with a rope, she found him hanging, just like that he was. And it was her daughter who died in the Ten Tors practice a year or so ago on Dartmoor.' It really is a conversation stopper, isn't it? Well, I assume that when she got her head around the fact I had a husband, so no threat, now haven't but am hugely grief-stricken, so still not a threat, she presumably felt a huge sense of guilt-ridden pity. My predicament obviously makes certain women have more pity for me than they do jealousy.

I also see around me beautiful men and beautiful children. I see two girls, both like you. One is very like you, spinning round, with long dark hair. If you asked anyone what Charlotte was like, they'd say long dark hair, always smiling. This girl doesn't smile, not today anyway. Their father is like yours was, maybe a little taller, serious. And I look for the mother. Is she like me? Will she lose it all? Have they lost her? They all go. It passes. Then another family appears, each member carrying an appropriate suitcase, going away together. The adults seem bored with each other, so I'm not missing much.

There's a school bus in my wing mirror. It has stopped. Will you get out? Why do I think that's a possibility? Why don't I stop torturing myself?

Sometimes people say the wrong things one after the other. George seems to need to relate all the mistakes I've made. Grandma talks about her worries for the future. And I met an ex-work colleague called Jill, who told me that my life is the worst ever. And although her daughter is odd, at least she's alive. According to this collective view there's nowhere to go. You would make one of your dry jokes or you'd say, 'Don't talk to her again. Don't reward bad behaviour.' Do you remember how I used to say 'Note to self'? Well, note to self: leave everyone except Charlotte behind, go to Atlantic Village for a coffee and a ginger dunker and be cool. My life is like a board game; my starter square is number 1. If I land on square 2, it's potential suicide, so I stick to the squares from 3 onwards, although there can be other squares that challenge. But don't feel smug ever, because there's a snake's head right up to square 59, which leads me back to number 2 and potential death. That snake reared its head on the Sunday just gone. Judith's husband has left her and her little girl. But she has very few people to support her and she pushes them away with her abuse and intolerance. So you might wonder why I'm surprised that she sent me a text which read: 'What a fucking useless friend you turned out to be. I hope this message causes you incredible pain *bla bla* ...' Even in my worst moments I haven't treated even the strongest people like this. She's caused me pain, which is very dangerous. But once again it's my decision as to whether I roll the dice again.

I made it. I've bitten the bullet and done something different on Jonathan's 'bad' day, 2008. Yes, I told you already. No need to protect this day now. Far worse has happened than the death of your father. I'm in Rome. Here I am, brave, alone and excited. I feel mad but free. Spending the anniversary of your father's death in a different city. Of course, now his death is neither here nor there. When I tell people about it, they produce one deep 'aah', but when I tell them about you as well, they sink to their knees, and there's usually a penetrating look (presumably because they can't believe that I'm still alive), a grip of my arm and at least one 'my God!'.

As I let go of safety and reputation, I begin to know myself. I see my own weakness and strength. And there becomes an incredible security in the not knowing, in the drifting, in the following of heart. But to a degree I've always known this. I've never needed the picket fence and the small dog. My security is in waking up and smelling the air. Holding a tea cup that's hot. Knowing that we are in fact part of a bigger thing that protects us, that blood is not the only strength, that we can live well and competently even if we're in the familial sense alone, for if we seek to give as our way of receiving, then it doesn't matter anyway that family are not available.

Wasn't it Jesus who said that His brothers are those who feel the same as He, who preach the same words?

Was I enough family for you, Charlotte?

You'd be proud of me, going to Rome. I was so proud of you, my brilliant girl.

You know, I nearly backed out between booking and leaving – so scared and anxious, I felt I couldn't do it. But I'm here. I've said that three times, haven't I? 'Yes, Mum.' Well, it's 10.30 a.m. Roman time and I'm heading for Vatican City.

Would your boy have hated the reputation He has gained then? Should we fear God? And is there such a thing as blasphemy if God is everywhere in everything? He is surely in all language. At least this is what I tell myself. Yet none of this represents true Christianity. Would He have been ashamed at what He saw today, Mary?

Charlotte, you'd be proud of your disciples and the way they operate. Yasmin is so giving, Sonny is as his name suggests, and Neil ... well, amazing Neil.

When I'm in the supermarket I fantasise that everyone's looking into my trolley. They find that I'm buying for one. It's confirmed then that I'm lonely and they can feel sorry for me ... and, worse, suggest an untenable course of action. Hopefully not. I select a smaller smoked salmon, a trial pack of cheese, the ones people buy to see if they like the flavour. I ask for half a water melon and put two apples instead of three hundred into a bag and then I disguise it with a giant bag of salad. And, of course, the two boxes of cat food, the saving grace of my shopping. The truth is, nobody stops long enough to notice that I'm there at all, which could possibly be worse. Although are they wondering why I haven't got a hand basket, rather than such a large cumbersome family-size set of wheels?

I begin to wonder whether many people hate the word 'family' and all its needs and connotations, when they aren't privy to its wonder. You see how paradoxical my thoughts can be? Am I going mad, or is this part of the self-obsessed neurotic thinking in the magical world of grief?

So I lug the shopping home, Bridget Jones-style. Of course, it's only in three bags, and that's the whole week's worth and includes cat clobber and wine. I want to get it into the house as soon as possible, because I fantasise again that people look at your shopping to ascertain how close to death you are. The cat food is high-calibre, anyway. That means I have company. The wine always means that you're an alcoholic even if you drink less than the average observer, and the salad, 'Well, she has to get her vitamins from somewhere, especially if she's drinking that much wine, on her own.'

Oh, I didn't tell you. In the supermarket two women were reading about you, something to do with the Ten Tors. They were feeling sorry for the girl's mother. I walked past twice.

I wondered about you then, Mary, and whether anyone knew that the boy was yours after the event.

Crumble and Custard are full-grown now and they seem to have a little routine of sorts. They go out all day until dinner time and then return to eat and have long unbroken naps until morning. I had Custard done after you left, so no kittens, I'm afraid. But she's turned out to be the feisty one. And quite a *femme fatale*. Sybil Shepherd, remember, her next door? Well, now *she's* having her roof done and Custard is very involved with the comings and goings and lunch boxes of the tilers. She sits watching them bang, pull and scoff with a sweet gentility and ever so slight ginger tartiness that only she could pull off, and they give in and throw her a morsel. If she were human, in a red dress and high-heeled shoes, she would have finally won the equivalent pint of stout, I feel sure. She's certainly not deaf as you feared, and not as timid as we'd have liked her to be. She was made to be pampered, but with that rough rusticity that some of the lesser royals have when they get a bit bored. In fact, one of them has a ginger overtone as well – I hope I won't be sent to the Tower for saying that, but this is England, 2009, and the country's famed for its freedom of speech, as my solicitor says.

Why do I need to torment myself so much? It's 11.12 at night and I'm not ready to go to bed. I think back to previous 11.12s because I want to know what's different. I want to know what it's like without you, and I can only do that if I know what it was like with you. So I open your

51

door. I press my nose through the crack and I can smell the familiar sweet but now stale smell of you. The familiarity and safety of you cuts me and I feel punched in my womb, in my deepest core, that no one can see, beyond the lie that is my smile. I think of you in the room, and now I feel those lost times and I begin to yearn for your movement. I want to see the concentration on your face, preparing for the next day, and your unwillingness to interact with me. I want to get you into bed and know that everything is all right with the world this day. I want to hear your breathing and imagine your secrets. But you're 16 now: you've grown up and gone. You aren't in this child's room with the stars on the ceiling and the kitten calendar. These are not your knick-knacks, your story books, your pink CD player and your funny earrings. This is not your bear from Copenhagen and these are not your medals on the wall. This is not your blanket; these are not your thoughts. Charlotte Shaw, the name on the certificates, is yours, though. There are Christmas cards on the wall from 2006 – I told you they'd would bring bad luck if you left them there.

The stickers, the games, the conversations, the magnets, the pot noodle. Every little thing tells a story about the person who lived in this room before their tenure ended. But you're 16 now and you're not here any more. And yet I can't find you. I can't find you anywhere. The volume is turned to max on the computer, because I know that no one's trying to sleep. You're 16, remember, and you're up late these days. I'm going to bed now. Please turn off the light when you're done. Please don't disturb me, don't play your music too loud, and don't leave anything on. Would there be anything else I should say? Don't say good night. Don't kiss me. Don't die. Too late. All too late.

Everything is second-rate compared to you and your father. The dates I go on, the conversations I have, the children I meet, nothing compares to you, and I feel that it's all such a waste of time. I can relate superficially as long as I don't have to think or feel too much or too deeply, and then I want to leave people who can't possibly, with all the will in the world, relate to me.

It was your 16th birthday yesterday. Sunday 18 May 2008. You were born on a Monday, like me. Monday's child is fair of face. Thank God, if you were born on Tuesday, then I wouldn't be able to drop and step on all the birthday cakes in Morrison's. Don't worry, I won't. But wouldn't that be a therapeutic thing to do? Well, why should anyone else have a cake if you can't? I didn't do it. Although I can see your face if I did, that disapproving look of utter disappointment in me and then you'd walk away. Well, no cake, no presents, no party, only sorrow. How could you judge me anyway, Noods, how could you tell what's it's like to lose you on top of Johnny? I can drop birthday cakes face down on the floor of the supermarket if I want, and I might, oh and I can hear my counsellor asking me what ego state I'm in. I'm 10, Jo, I'm a child. I want so badly to smash things up. How do you say 'Happy Birthday' to a beautiful girl who isn't here. Where do you put it? In fact, I can't. Last year I could, when you were 15, just after it happened, but this year I can't. Because this actually marks the beginning of the future that I'm not going to have with you. It reminds me of the distance that grows between us. The distance that makes Zoe worry about forgetting you. The distance that will soon contain driving lessons, being 18 and then 21, going to university, having relationships and children and work. All of which I'll never witness. All of which has been taken away from me. All of which died with you.

So on the 17th I saw a film with Amy and then had a little wine and then didn't know where to be or why. So I stopped trying and went with the miserable flow. I just carried on. I saw Zoe on the 18th, which was a gift. I burst into her house crying. She looked a bit stunned. But I'm done with pretence. She was wearing a very sweet pink and white spotted dressing gown and was half way through a chocolate éclair. I knew that she knew why I was there. I wonder if people think that I open the wounds deliberately.

But are they ever really closed? And what is opening them anyway? Isn't it just feeling what is? I wonder how many of your friends have let themselves reach the bottom more than once.

I spent the evening playing with baby Arthur who is now nearly three, at Jayne K's house. Exhausted, I finally went to bed. All in all, as expected, an unbirthday, crap.

Christmas is a funny time. People in our world take it for granted. They look forward to it, spend too much and completely forget the purpose of it. I know that we spent years trying to work Christmas out. Do you remember the first one after Johnny died? We had a stocking each, but I'll tell you a secret, Charlotte, I wrapped everything in them both, the chocolate games, gel pens, I think there was a soft toy for you, I can't remember what else. I pretended mine was a surprise. The funny thing was you thought the stuff in mine was better and felt somewhat hard done by. It was so long since I'd wrapped my gifts to myself, they came as a surprise anyway. Such irony.

Lots of stockings, that's what you wanted, maybe five, one for each member of our imaginary family. I wanted that for you, and for years we were on the lookout for successful potential new members of our unit. Weren't they crap, though? You were right, I really do have bad taste in men. There was the lazy Catholic, the mini author, the drunken stockbroker, the controlling millionaire and the semen-free bald git. After you died, Father Julian said that I thought too much of you to let a man into my life. Too right. Anyway, which one would he chose for me? There's really no point in doing for doing's sake, because then the wrong things happen. So Christmases came and went and we developed a lovely routine with your grandparents and the rest of our extended family. It was fine and then really good and the year before you died you wrote that actually at Christmas you realised how many people you had and it was the best Christmas ever and we had the cats with their own stockings. We went to London. We went out in Bideford on Christmas Day. We were there. We were OK.

The four of us had lunch in Tantons, overlooking the river. You began with tomato soup, and there was a carvery. We drank pretend Champagne, I wish people wouldn't do that, and you got a skeleton in your cracker and I got a fish. Death and water! How ironic. You gave me a beautiful top and long afterwards I found the receipt in your room and cried. I gave you a magnetic game that I'd bought for a pound, which you played with till March. You wore your old brown waistcoat and asked me if it looked babyish. I said you'd look beautiful in a paper bag. I nearly wore my night clothes. We all had fun, the four of us. We belonged to each other. I felt safe.

This year I didn't celebrate. Nobody likes Christmas any more.

On the day, the first one after you, I was at the grave, yours and Johnny's grave, my husband and daughter, lying on top of one another, and me only 44. But I did give a very surprising gift. Well, I wondered about Neil, and what this day was like for him, whether he was a child celebrating, playing with his toys, feverishly unwrapping surprises, or whether he was a man in torment, wondering when this is going to pass. When will he get his life back, when will Charlotte come back so I can annoy her? So I sent his mother a text. I wondered if he wanted to join me at your side. He didn't but I went round there. It felt like he was carrying this heavy weight. As if he'd stopped breathing for nine months. As if he'd died with you. He fell at me and we held each other, only a boy and carrying so much. He said it was all his fault and I asked him what your response would be to that. I put in all I could to turn this brave man's life around. It's so easy to live with winning but so hard to do what he did and have nothing to show for it. He replays those moments and hopes, they are agony. I know that pain. He was wearing a dressing gown and a necklace and reminded me of a holy man. The definition of 'holy' is that there's an apartness – like the strange coming out of the familiar. And to see this intensity of pain coming from our Neil, he is that – holy, I mean. I stayed with them until it was proper to leave.

What will it be like if I have a new family and we have a tree and stockings and the children are excited? Where does that leave you? Will you be upset? Will I hurt you? Or will it not quite happen like that? Or will it never happen again for me? Maybe I'll run an orphanage and there will be 20 dismaying stockings by 20 threadbare beds. What's going to happen to me, Noods? Will there ever be a Christmas again?

Did I know that you were going to die?

Mary is now as she has always been for me, remote, quiet, still, ponderous. Little was known of her, and yet I feel now that I know so much.

What was her reality? She stood in the background, by the side. With no alternative, powerless, knowing that this moment would come. Knowing that she had to wait in silent agony for this the ultimate in human pain, the loss of Him, her child. She knew that this day would come. She alone knew it and bore it like she knew and bore Him, as I bear it now. And yet what did she do to prevent it? Nothing. But there's nothing to do. She doesn't even ask herself. It's inevitable and unstoppable. She knows that even to involve herself in preventing His flogging is to risk Him suffering more, if He sees her being beaten and thrown to the ground. She knows, as does He, that His death and suffering are written, and will happen, and that she's powerless to stop it.

What of the suffering? Jesus must have suffered such sustained, severe, physical pain, but for how long? When does the body take over, the flesh die and nothing more can be felt. Does the pain become predictable and acceptable? Did He invite it into His body? If we acquiesce, does it no longer exist? We can know that at least for Him, it happened once. And for Mary, what of her pain? For her it happens more times than she can count. She relives it, reworks it, until every detail is gone over, and worked to death, like His flesh. Does she work in a different ending? With no mark on her she bares a silent witness. So difficult to do. But what He would have wanted? She watches the child she'd smelt at bedtime bleed. She may well have seen the same blood erupt from his torn back that she wiped willingly from a childish knee. She stood crying silently, not wanting to add to His suffering by letting Him see her pain. And yet this pain is to last forever. Only broken by sleep and sometimes not even then. She wakes with it and sleeps to its beat, analysing every stroke of the Roman whip, wondering if His suffering ever ceased. Putting it in a box of bearability. But for Him it was bearable. For Him there were recompenses. He was to be the saviour of humankind and have the great compensation to ascend. For her: a lifetime of human suffering, morning to night, set apart from other mothers, left with nothing but an intangible energy, which is generated into sainthood. Whatever that means.

And what is Mary's prize. What does she get? His is the glory. He gets to suffer, to be a martyr, to teach the ultimate lesson. He gets, through swollen eyes, to see His punishers wonder why? Wonder what has made Him and then what has made them. They have nowhere to go in their own badness. But she witnesses, as she has before, so much energy for such little return. The adventure has never been hers. She the mother, the hand washer, the clothes bearer, the one who probably cleared up the wood shavings after His latest project. What is her prize? Does she wake up in their house the day after His death and still taste the blood? Does she hear the crowd calling for His execution? Does she quietly look around His room and remember when He made that box and ran towards her to show it. Does she smell His sheets and look for traces of His lips on the water goblet by His bed. Does she find His hair in places and wonder if it's hers, and half-written passages and letters to remind her of the boy she has lost. How does she separate in her mind the beautiful, compassionate yet ruthless leader she produced in flesh from the hated, bloodied, battered corpse that leaks above her? The man who was your king. The girl who was your gymnast, your dancer, the one you made the hero to the Mariah Carey song. Music that always for all of you is a reminder of the joy and pain, of the life and death, of your Charlotte. *Does Mary howl with unbearable pain, the cry that's only heard in a mother who has lost a child?*

When I looked at you in the hospital, I could no longer see the child I knew. I saw only the shell of a heart and life full of vivacity. A joy that you gave out, like bread shared. I was that mother, as I sat by your side wondering what led to this. I witnessed you pass from life to death and I willingly gave you up without a fight. I talked to you, because a nurse said that hearing is the last sense to go. I wanted the best for you right to the end. And when it was over, I left and didn't go home. You weren't the one I knew. I could see the scars from your previous broken arm, and knew it was you. But this was a different time. If I'd thought more, I would have asked them if I could hold you without all the tubes for the last time. But I didn't. There was no Pietà for me. So I left without the reason I breathed. I, like Mary, had nothing to go on for. All the pomp and circumstance of the Magi and the star, and now nothing. Just an empty room that begins now to smell sweet and stale. Pyjamas that vaguely smell of you, and your last entry in your diary, fingerprints on your lip gloss. Things touched so much now that maybe they are *my* prints I begin to see.
Nobody yet knew what died that day. They didn't know the impact of what was to come, and probably still don't.

I live a parallel life in a parallel world now. Which is acceptable some of the time. Until the little haunting of past times scratches away at me or stabs me like C.S. Lewis's 'jab of red hot' poker.

You were pierced in the heart, weren't you, Mary? Was that to remind you just in case you forgot? It feels like it.

Hey, don't go around complacently being above your pain, because I'll wound you again in the same place, and then again, and then some more. Let's call it a reminder.

I got three jabs today, only three that I can recall. The first was when I had coffee with Phoebe, and you were there in the café. Wearing your blue hockey top with white lettering with your dark silky hair tied back, you were there. I walked up behind you and as always asked myself which seat near you would be least painful. Of course, I settle on the one from which I can see your face. I stare. The hockey player and her companion are uneasy. I stare more. They wonder. I'm angry and don't care. They should know better than to look like you in a café where I come for respite away from you.

Second sighting was when I parked my car back home. A school bus stopped at the top of the road. You got off like you used to. I watched you walk down the road in my mirror. You carry two bags and are in gym shorts, even on a crisp day like today. I cry and look at my lips in the mirror. They look beautiful. I look like you but older and now my hair is shorter. I begin to become dishonest in my wallowing. I can see that it isn't you. The person is blonde and her gait is different. I'm angry again. These are angry tears. You've been torn from me and I so want you to walk back into my life.

As I begin to write for the evening and switch on the computer, Crumble goes mad. He's such an intelligent cat. Custard is the pretty one, although Crumble is a head-turner in his own right. He runs up the stairs as he hears the machine's familiar sound and miaows loudly. He then begins to scratch at your bedroom door. Does he associate the sound with you? Is he looking for you? It's the saddest thing to see. Can you see us from where you are? You know, when this first happened I didn't want to see the cats again, or our home for that matter. But both, funnily enough, offer me comfort now. When I'm tired, the cats accompany me to bed about midnight. I'm glad of that. When you begged me to get them nearly two years ago I'd no idea how important they would be to me now. I'm quite dependent on the routines we have together and the safety of those in a way. As I read, I now have a very cosy chair by the bed. Custard lies on my lap and gazes at me lovingly as if I'm the best thing ever. Sometimes I think she's right. I can see you raising your eyebrows at that, Noods. But you know, it might be true, at least to her.

As I sit at the computer table, I imagine what it was like being you, with me downstairs. Your secret world of study and communication. When I passed you snacks through the banisters, what thoughts went through your mind? What did you think of me? Did you look forward to the dinner I was cooking? Did you want to tell me things? Was it nice being you? I remember you asking me that once? And I said yes, because, funnily enough, even now it is. I look around me and I'm glad of my education and taste and the qualities and morality I possess. It's cool being me.

I'm having a bath in a minute and then trundling over to Trevor's for dinner. It's the best I can do today.

Sometimes I wonder if things happen for a reason. Like your death. Am I to go on doing something that hasn't quite unravelled yet? Am I imagining the signs that come to me and the people I meet? They seem like gifts. A few months after you died, when I was back home, I began to go to Rosemoor Gardens as part of my 'weekly walking and feeling better' structure. I figured it would be free with my RHS pass, local, and raise my endorphin levels all at the same time. One day, I think a Sunday, I was there with Grandma, who doesn't like to be called that any more, and we met a family. I still don't know quite what inspired me to inquire after the little old man sitting on the bench by the fountain, maybe the incongruous bright redness of his jacket, compared with his overwhelmingly stricken soul. Anyway, I asked him if he could tell me a way of getting through this pain, because he looked like a survivor. Just like that! He showed me numbers etched into his arm, told me he was Polish and spoke of the war. Then a little Chinese girl ran towards us and called him Grandpa. Her name was Ming. She's adopted. I'll leave it to you to give this encounter meaning and make sense of the extraordinary.

Last night I had the weirdest dream. I gave birth to twin boys and had a husband. It was mediocre. Well, it wasn't my life, not compatible with me. There was no lustre. I suppose the fear is that I'll never have the incredible relationship I had with you and you with me again. But life isn't like that, is it? Actually bringing someone into the world or even bringing them along can only be wonderful. I have such an incredible amount of anger coursing through me. It's like little bubbles moving through my blood stream, which are steadily getting bigger and I wait for them to burst. It's partly a sick feeling, which increases, probably to do with my liver and storing anger, and the recent lack of acupuncture. My guess is that the grief has stuck somewhere down the digestive tube and I really need to move it on to the excretion bit, but I'm actually wanting to throw it up. However, apart from my attraction to puce-green, that's it. Oh no, wait, also fuelling my anger is, of course, other people, nothing specific, just their tendency to talk and interfere in stuff they clearly know nothing about. The Morgans keep telling me to eat more and they constantly make me feel bad about it, when I'm the perfect weight and they're as big as a house, both of them. And Phoebe has called me 'bonkers' once too often, when I'm dealing with this in a non-pathological way and in my opinion doing the best anyone could. She, on the other hand, drinks to excess, smokes to excess and takes Prozac, also to excess. I'm misunderstood. One of the most painful of Christyboy's wounds, I'd say. Wouldn't you, my Noods? You knew what it was like to be misunderstood, as young as you were. You tried to find your way in relationships, only to be betrayed, like him, by a good friend. You confided in her and trusted, and instead of being honoured by sharing in who you were, in a sense she sold you out and ripped you verbally to pieces with another tormentor on the netball court. You know who I mean, don't you, Charlotte, because you wrote a poem about her from your pain. Well, it sort of backfired, if you can call it that. Sad were they both when they heard of your death, so angry with themselves and no idea of how to resolve the torment. For the lesson is, we never know what's going to unexpectedly happen. We don't know, as we sell our soul, what the price really will be. So they try to make good by talking to your second-in- command – that's me by the way. They confessed to the terrible things they'd said to you, and I listened, a very painful but necessary thing to do. It's really changed me. I feel so alive with the sadness. I can taste the metal of the metaphorical blade as it slides flat across my tongue and sharpens to go down my throat. Then I taste the same metal of the blood from my body. They are still happily alive, as am I. Does that sound like a strange thing to say? Well, they are young, and tormented by guilt and wrong, controlled by what they did. It could have been unmovable. I had to help them. I had to make a path for them. It was the right thing to do. They will now go on to be the best people they can be – hopefully, extraordinary.

There's another 'How could we let this happen?' in the paper. A little girl in Birmingham has starved to death, or shall we say has *been* starved to death. She could have come to live at ours. I'd have given her a gingerbread man as a treat and milkshakes for her bones. I'd have packed her lunches with all the things she liked and put her on the school bus in a clean uniform. I'd be waiting at the end of the day and we'd have cosy food and TV and prep and baths and games and stories and moments, and not misery and not fear and not death. Mind you, look who she's with now. The most interesting people are there. Probably Pavarotti and Judith Beer, my old boss, have you come across her? What about Madeleine McCann? Please tell me that she isn't there. Her parents are in torment. Her father says that they're living in purgatory. And in another way I know that hell. But you're there, so that's good. Will you look after her, in case? Like I need to ask.

I'm at the Friary in Batcombe, Dorchester. This is my fourth time to stay this year, so I feel like an old hand. I'm probably one of their most regular visitors. And I have to say that I've come up with a couple of revelations about myself. The first is that I settle and bond easily, which is handy, although these days my circumstances move people to look at me in a funny way, which is extremely difficult. Either with awe or with pity. Secondly, when I awake here, there isn't the same pain. Now this is the question: is it being at the Friary or just being anywhere other than home? And is it also dependent on time? For when I woke up at Amy's on your 16th birthday I was in a lot of pain. But then it was your birthday and I was about to go home. I think that being in a place of community and silent gentle care is perfect to cushion this. The Friars mill in the background and are non-invasive. And because there are other guests in pain and project workers, there's a balance linking to the outside world. It does feel like a stepping stone towards acceptance, recovery, freedom, choice. It feels like the perfect unconditional home that I can return to time and time again. I fantasise that in due course I might go to Oxford to study Theology or Venice to teach Art History, or America to drink juice and have eggs easy over. Isn't that what they do in America?

The upshot is that I don't want to be stuck in my home environment forever. For sometimes the comfort is overridden by pain and loss. It's almost as if your childhood had ended now in that room and it's time to change to a more adult mode and to begin my separation from you and from Grandma. Like that's likely! However, the truth is that we don't play Dash for Dinner any more, or Whoosit, or cards. We don't colour and we probably wouldn't do simultaneous equations any longer either. You are not my companion and now at your age you'd probably have a boy friend. You'd also soon be leaving to go to university. It would have been difficult for me – I don't know what I would have done without you. When I saw Father Julian, he said that you've given me the gift of separation.

I love it at the Friary. I feel cut off from the world and yet part of it. The brothers aren't silly people in brown dresses: they are incredibly useful people living by a flawless code, which seduces me. I like them a lot. Here I study kitchen gardens, tame sheep, learn of projects of global significance, eat well, five times a day, sleep and walk and pray. And I want to tell you all about it. Today is Friday, my second day, fish and chips in a minute. Blood pours from the wound on the wrist, I write, and I still wonder about its significance, but am afraid to ask. It smells like rose water. I'm having funny trance, like moments in the chapel and sometimes at the lunch table too.

I can't imagine other people handling this as well as me. For instance, if I died, would my mother come to a Friary and smile and wear your red top for bed? Would your friends' mothers' garden if any of them died? Or is it universal that once you decide to live, you do stuff like this? I'm going to investigate other widows who have lost only children and see what progress they've made. *Not you, Mary, because you went around healing people and avoiding nasty priests, so you were great.* But it would be interesting to look at the patterns of women's lives after they lose particularly single children and are also widows. When I write this, it sounds hard to do.

I'm pretending that I'm 34, which means that I had you when I was 18 and not 28, if any one asks. But, of course, they won't. If I'm 34, or even 29 at a push, then I can still study, or leave home, whilst having had a contained experience of husband and child of 20 years in total. Is that enough? Wow, a bit exciting to reinvent myself in such a way, I think.

I'm experiencing what it's like to be free. Doesn't that sound weird? Very few people really get to have that, so it makes me feel lucky. But on the other hand, look what I've had to do to earn freedom. I'm trying to enjoy times without the worry of financial issues, neurosis on the part of you know who, and there are times I take off, for a night or three. It's what's possible, and I'm taking it. When I do it for longer, I expect someone in charge will have the initiative to change the cats' poo tray, so that Crumble is not a frequent defecator in my bath.

I don't know if you knew that word. There are so many things that you hadn't moved onto. I realised that you'd never had a filling at the dentist, which can only be good. And also, this is presumably a testimony to enough calcium and vitamin D. Anyway back to my tripping. I think this is the first time in my life that I've been free and in some ways I'm loving it. Bad. I must be bad. You gone and I love it. Getting used to sunny weather now without you. New life emerging and I love it. No one to please, no deadlines to meet, fabulous. Leaving me completely free to regress and fantasise. At the Friary I pretend I've gone back 20 to 35 years. I'm a cowboy again riding to new pastures on my horse. I find a suitable stick with a face and mount it and I'm off. Giddy up. I ride through the secret garden wishing this was a real beast, and I'm on a Spanish beach without a saddle. I make believe. I've just dismounted and left my steed in the secret garden eating pine cones. What would my counsellor make of that?

At the Friary I meet lots of interesting people, like us, Noods, well-rounded travellers and erudite members of the human race. People who do crosswords and equations for fun. People vacuous individuals would call nerds. Ben is a typical plump middle-class chap, going to stay with his aunt and cousins on Lake Geneva, after a few days with the monks. That sounds like my cup of tea, and then there's Liz who tells me about Mary who has lost two sons and a husband. Lots of points there. But I can't help but think that, as a woman, losing a daughter gets you more points then losing a son. But then having a girl in the first place must surely start me off with more to lose.

I also met a guy called Simon, who's a cleaner at Asda. He has a girlfriend with mental health problems, whatever that means. He keeps saying, 'You gotta keep going.' I wonder what it would feel like doing this without my friends and without a home to return to.

I'm in the bath feeling crap. The water is cool again and I think of you in cold water and think of you not upstairs and feel unusually full of despair and angry at those adults who let this happen.

Is this right? Did you have to die to make a difference? Is something big going to happen? Could you have not lived and things be altered still?

If your son had said sorry, if He'd denied He was the son of man and the son of God and gone back to reading the paper, then what would have changed? We wouldn't have had Christianity, but would people still know what it was like to love and be good? Did you die because we've lost sight of this? But then nothing seems to have changed so far. Since you've been gone, knife and gun crime seem to have reached epidemic proportions. Seven teenagers have been killed in as many months, often being found in doorways with fatal stab wounds. It's terrifying. Soldiers are also dying every day in our current war in the Middle East. It's the norm now, what do you think of that?

When I was incarcerated in Williams ward at the hospital, after you left me, I had a really surreal experience. One evening when I was thinking I was the only one in the world to whom this was happening, I was desperately seeking the company of another poor bugger in the same position. So I prayed for an angel. In the middle of the night, in the shape of a larger than life, raucous, limping, figure, she descended. Her name was Heather. The first time we set eyes upon each other was over lunch the following day. And I knew at once she was the cause of my sleepless night. And once again, for some reason, I attempted to respond to her need to hear my story. You know, the one about you, on Dartmoor, falling in the river, hitting your head on a rock and dying. And she said, quite casually I thought, well, Williams ward is fundamentally a mental health unit, now renamed "Ocean View", a rose by any other name and all that. Anyway, then she said quite madly, 'I had a daughter called Charlotte, she fell into the river on Dartmoor and died.' I flipped my lid. I stopped chewing. She must have read about it in the paper. How was I going to sit next to this person for weeks while she talked crap? Luckily a staff nurse, Jane, was sitting with us and, without breaking confidentiality, went to check out the 'tall, injurious tale'. You know what? Nothing Heather said that day was a lie. She too had lost a daughter, the same name as you, and in a river on the moor, although she was on a horse. As Grandma would say, 'How do you like that?' We became friends. I'm so sorry that I doubted you and this magic, Heather. A year on, she sent me a postcard from her house boat in Instow. She lives there sometimes when she's not on the ward. She gets through. She has a son she vaguely sees. She has an estranged husband, and when her little girl died she was already under the mental health services and was therefore unable to go to her Charlotte's bedroom, to do whatever it is I do in there. A privilege that I don't now take for granted. She lives with the grief and so can I. Was she sent from you or Him? Did I pray so purely that my prayers were answered?

By the way, I've chosen Amy to write my obituary and Trevor to edit her, considering that he so enjoys making corrections. And is so worthy of the task. It's a bit of an in-joke, because Amy wrote the foreword to his book and he seemed to feel the need to correct it, not the content but the grammar.

My relationship with Amy has changed a little. And I can't help but wonder if the same thing happened to you with J after your father's death. When women like us suffer trauma that's too hard to bear, we find solace in the emotional company of woman. This can result in a psycho-sensual confusion about the nature of the relationship. The tenderness that's displayed to me in my agony by Amy has resulted in my having feelings of wanting to be near her more than is realistically possible. Amy, unlike J, has dealt with this well. She remains in her own words 'unfazed and admirous' of me and will always love me. I'm sorry that your confidences were met with such betrayal and harshness and torment. But we could say that J was too young to step up to the plate. Life is never easy. And sometimes people are too immature to know what they're truly doing until too late. *'Forgive them, for they know not what they do.' Did your son say that? Did you see Judas's body, Mary, after he hanged himself? Did you feel bad? Is there anything you could have done?* Within weeks I sought out the children, like J, to enable them to go forward. The purity of the joy that came out of this was amazing. To listen effectively to how another child treated you so badly before you died that your last moments might have been miserable, and to forgive that child, is a triumph in my spiritual life. I feel good.

On my wedding day I got married in a second-hand dress that smelled of fags. Hilda, our neighbour at the time, kept the dress in her house for me until the big moment. Remember Hilda? She was with Keith, who had a stoop from driving too much. Well, I wonder why I didn't want the proper stuff – why I made do. Why I didn't want a posh dress for a big wedding, why I didn't have a deluxe buggy for you with matching nappy bag and stripe, and why therefore I didn't buy you brand-new boots for the walk and air your sleeping bag – mind you, I did buy you a huge rucksack and everything else on the list, so that doesn't fit. Make it fit, must be a reason, must be my fault. The question remains, 'Did I do it right?' The answer always comes back, 'What is right?' If I ask whether you died because I didn't provide you with something necessary, then the bigger question would be, does everyone, without the necessary, die? The answer is a resounding 'No!' There are children sleeping near sewers for warmth, who don't die, there are infants without any maternal protection who lie on the streets, who don't die. Look at you, strong, well-fed, interested, laughing, humble and bold. You just died. You just died. That's all. And that's when it's OK.

People always seem to need the proper stuff. They need routines, but that doesn't establish long life. It just establishes a way through. Something we're all looking for. Even as a child I'd rather play with a stick and a broken pot than with a new toy. Was I never worthy of the new toy or is it merely that manufactured playthings are generally plastic and boring as fuck, whereas things you find are long-lasting, unique and no one gives a monkeys when you break them.

Can you imagine what it's like to smell you, taste you and realise that you'll never come out and never go in. I touch the keyboard that you touched, my fingers on your prints, seeing the indentation of your writing on the desk, the impression of you without the being of you. Feeling your shadow, seeing the cats you brought here and watching them grow and be funny. And knowing that as everything changes, you witness none of it. My heart is brittle, I can feel it near to shattering and sometimes I wish I could enable that fatal crack. It's surely worse by a thousand times than the pain of an unrequited love. But I go on. And I go on, and I talk about going on and I even bore myself. I must bore other people – maybe I need new people to wear down.

I'm at the hairdresser's – not Anton, but Kenny, in Braunton. You didn't know him but I think that you would like each other, in fact, possibly too much. I begin to wonder what you'd be like now, what your emerging maturity would be like and your tastes. I picture you. Am I annoying you? I'm sensitive too, you know? Anyway, Kenny first cut my hair on Williams ward. When I looked like a shadow. He massaged our scalps and cleaned us and made us look like princesses. After I said 'I want to die, I want to die,' a thousand times, I became engaged in activities and indulgences, for pleasure, and one of them was being touched by Kenny. He literally goes on to the ward to touch people. A lot of people don't get that but it's so important when you're suffering. You and I were lucky, we were lovable. We got touched. Everyone loves Charlotte.

Anyway, today I'm a proper person and I'm at his posh salon. Of course, there's a girl whose hair is being cut square at the bottom and I think or pretend or want it to be you. I'm back there at Anton's and you are here and you're tapping on your phone and not liking my unwelcome glances. You're private and I can't ask any questions. And I want to cry out in pain and ask what if it were the other way round. Supposing I died, would other women look like me and would you tell anyone about it? Would it be too much to share with Sophie? What happens when she leaves to go to university soon, would you go too? Would you want to live with Grandma or Jason, or Zoe? I can anticipate some rivalry for your affections. Are you somewhere? Is it right to keep your stuff? It's your bedside that I can't alter, the time when everything is all right. The end of the day when the fires are lit and you can take stock and say 'All is well in my world today.' Do you remember the caveman stories and rubbing your arm in bed? Have I asked you that already? I loved those moments best in all my life. When she came round, Grandma used to sing 'Catch a falling star'. It's the theme to a TV advert now and it makes her very sad.

Oh God, how I keep repeating myself. Maybe if I keep doing that, it becomes more real.

'Catch a falling star and put it in your pocket, / Never let it fade away.' You were little then and Johnny was here. You're big now. What happened to the characters in our play? Where did they go?

Anyway, I'm having my hair cut. That's it really. I'm being made into a new person just for a while, someone different, with different hair and a different life, someone who hasn't lost you.

They are canoeing again, or setting off for canoeing. Why isn't your head in one of those yellow helmets, and your beautiful body in the maroon and blue life vest? And why don't your eyes meet me when you turn around? Why can't I find you? Why do I relentlessly search, like a tramp for her hidden biscuits and tobacco? I forage endlessly for scraps, signs, pretence of you. Why doesn't this ache go away? It pays not to be hungry and tired and fall into this pit. People say that I don't have to think this way. But I wonder what else is there at this point other than you in everything, either by choice or accident. In fact, for the benefit of those unaffected and uneducated by grief, let's assume that I just go about my business. Well, there are two ways: defending against what I might see; and entering into it. I can spend an inordinate amount of time trying to avoid certain places and sensations: all my energy goes into avoiding being dragged into the whirlpool, the black hole. If I go up the road slowly, if I don't look left, if I by pass the Eden shop, if I don't look at the girl carrying the bag, if I don't pass Subway, if I don't go into the Leotard shop, then I'll survive the journey today. Exhausted but surviving. But will I survive? It's usually then that I see you full-on, no protection, nowhere to go. Finished. Dragged in, too late. In grief, the hole has a force of its own, so don't bother trying to escape, it only seems to add to the madness and energy loss. So I go with it, I face all of it, I even search for it, I hunt it down. I desensitise myself. I rub myself in it, roll in it, and cover myself with its scent. I have become grief, we are inseparable. We now have a lifelong bond. We're partners, lovers, intertwined forces. So when they tell me to avoid it or to deal with it, or to … erm, what else can there be, I wonder if they've really thought it through. Don't you? I seem to be dammed if I do and dammed if I don't. It's here, welcome her onto the stage, ladies and gentlemen, if you don't know her now you will soon (drum roll) … Grief.

It feels like my body has been blown to pieces and the world wants to paint my toenails. I'm trying to keep my spirits up, but I wish they wouldn't ask me which nail polish I'd like. Should I humour them, 'cause after all they only want to fucking help? And it's my duty in life to make them feel better and not the other way round.

I know that you're looking at me with those stern eyes for going on and on. In fact, although there's a great gaping hole in my life, I do feel grateful. I'm glad to be doing this here, in the West, not under shell fire, with a little money for my needs and not having the strain of bringing another through it. If I look at this as adventure, it saves me from quite a lot of unnecessary suffering. I also know that I owe it to all those women who surely make up 80 per cent of the rest of the world and who have lost a daughter but can't go for a coffee and read a paper to find momentary relief, but have to undergo rape and shell fire instead. I know that I'm privileged. I do.

When there's movement and I'm fulfilling a task, something changes. There's purpose for a while, I'm doing something worthwhile, and I remember this from when I cleared the garage and sold the Land Rover after Johnny died. But when it's over, then the fall. First the 'I've done it' feeling and then the 'Now what?' and finally the 'Where are you?' And, of course, now the 'Where are you both?' Where's my reward? Is he back yet? Is she here? Then the disappointment that once again, whatever I do, nothing changes. I tell myself that 14 years of your life is nothing. I only knew you properly from five upwards so that's only nine years, so I can get over this really. But it's a lie, an 'un-boxable' lie. But then I think, well, I had you for a good 16 years including pregnancy, a good long time for a relationship of any kind really, and I was lucky to have had it, and you. So many contradictions yet again. Well, I could think of it as a chapter in a long line of chapters, forever varying. So what's next? – that's the question, where does Jennifer go next? God's not helping, by the way, and I'm confused.

I remember being a star in a warm sea. It must have been 1998 or 1999. You and Johnny were on the beach and I was in the water. It was St Ives or St Just, or a place in England that could well be Côte de Something because of the non-chill factor and super-tropical sense to it. The sun was blazing and everything was held in a glow of warmth. It was perfect. The sky was as blue and clear as a baby's laugh. I remember feeling that life couldn't get any better, and I was right.

When I go into your room now, I seek that sunlight, that aliveness, you, so much more vibrant that anyone I ever met. I realise you're gone and I can't link the two. There's no connection. You see very sick people die, not well people. Especially not very well and fit people. Where's the justice?

Mary represents these contradictions in my world. As nothing and everything, she pervades my thoughts.

Our neighbourhood is full of building work at the moment. Sybil is still having her roof done and we're having our list of jobs done at last. The Morses' builders are on a 'secondment' to our house and they're doing fences, a wall, a little shower fitting and a new step into the bathroom. It feels so good. They're like locusts, in six hours they ate the garden. Now I have a third more decking than I did before and everything has clean lines. I love it. I can't wait to sit in your hammock with a gin and tonic and a twist of lime, nibbles and a straw hat. Now that I'm emerging, I feel like a teenager on an adventure again, and people resent the excitement. My day is so enjoyable that some people are jealous. I get up, have breakfast with the cats, reading and listening to the radio. Then I begin to write at about 9.30. At 11 on a couple of days a week I'm found at The Plough with a good coffee and something oaten or fruity. Then I shop for healthy lunch doodles and return to write before lunch at one. After lunch I do my last writing slot before afternoon tea and a film, during which I nod off maybe for a second. When I awake, I dance and do pull ups for half an hour and then a shower before dinner or cinema with a friend. This is hugely variable, but I like it. Of course, I've begun to break certain routines and emerge out of potential madness and have even been on a date. So it looks like we're moving forward at last.

Lately I was taken to what Devon calls a posh restaurant, Dusk in Bideford. My date spent half an hour giving me a detailed commentary on how he booked the table, which I found fascinating. I humoured him with flattery for his choice, even though the service was less than best, with the canapés remaining on the table until dessert and the remonstration he received, for using an extra fork from another table. Also the waitress's admission of her inability to produce a proper coffee. 'I've not done this before' are words you don't want to hear in surgeries or restaurants. However, my date made up for this by somehow casually getting past what would have impressed me as a conversation topic, such as theology, theatre, grief, Picasso, or even food. His unusual choice of after-dinner banter included anal sex and the preferences of women he'd known, followed after a time by lady boys and red underwear, no, red and plastic underwear, the subtlety of which was above my head. Sometimes when I'm mortified, I find that I inappropriately smile and nod, whilst buying the time for an appropriate response. There was none. Am I seeing him again? Why did I see him in the first place? is the question I ask myself? Is there any merit in putting yourself out there? I guess I know what I want sometimes from what I don't get. So many learning experiences are by elimination.

I bring a plate of dried fruit and biscuits and good coffee to my desk. I trip up to the times when I brought you breakfast in bed, maybe four years ago. I tried so hard to get it right and wonder where I failed, or *if* I failed. I miss you again and can smell you and feel you, are you there? I feel you there again. Will you look after me please, Noods, 'cause I'm a bit scared. Now gulping and a bit tearful. A bit naughty for wallowing again, it's a choice really. Custard has come in. She smells of two types of aftershave – interesting. She seems to have received the advances of two different roof workers, after all who can resist such a flirty lady in red? She's quite stunning. And she's now quite the marauder, you'd hardly recognise her. She's bold and risk-taking – remind you of anyone? She seems to be out the front more than the back, and can scale unimaginable heights to get there, with her little tiny legs. Again she seems quite reminiscent of a certain other athlete.

People keep telling me to be careful. It really irritates me. What am I to be careful of? Death? No. Loss? No. Pain? No. Heartache? No. And aren't they all the same thing? The crisis has happened. It is. Do they think any more will send me over the edge? Over what edge, and what will it take? I have, after all, lost all members in my immediate household. And I get up and clean myself every single day. I want someone, somewhere, to say, 'Live your life to the full, don't take any care at all, and be completely spontaneous.' After all, when you want to die, it doesn't matter any more, does it? That's the bottom line. So if you're above that line and are lucky enough to feel that you have a second shot, why must you make it safe and neat? Can you see me as someone who works in a bank at the counter 9 to 5 and then comes home to TV soaps and tea?

Maybe you can, but I'm so much more. I'm no longer afraid of leaving anything or anyone behind. And as a result I can risk completely. I can adventure. I can be anything I want to be, which makes me Simone de Beauvoir's dream.

I wonder what people are afraid of at these times and why they don't display that fear. I feel more broken when I'm alone at night, or awake at three in the morning, wondering where you are, or when I'm inches away from the nearness of you. It's the continuous emotional discomfort that bothers me and the fact that it will never go away. But people don't seem to mind that. It doesn't register with them at all. They see me smile, they see me do things, and I'm all right, but they give me a warning if I'm doing something that's beyond their emotional remit. They can do that, you see. Be careful of meeting that man. Be careful of getting involved with him. Watch out when you go there. But you see, the things to really be afraid of are not living or dying, but the never-ending prospect of nothing. And that, after all, is what makes us all shudder.

I went to the Ten Tors challenge yesterday. It was a huge thing to do. Zoe's mum came with me. Mainly to show me where to go. The night before I was really scared of the change that would inevitably happen when it was all over, and I couldn't sleep and I wondered what the hell I was doing it for, or for whom. But I knew that not going and watching it alone on TV would be worse. It was a matter once again of showing myself, making it all right for your friends to do this now and the next time. So off I went. I took your Jack Wolfskin rucksack that Johnny gave you when you were six. And I put a packed lunch in it and thought that I was doing it for you. Confusion, that's the main feeling. When I got there, confusion. There were thousands of people waiting for teams to return and probably 2,500 children on the Moor. And yet I felt that if they knew who I was, all sympathetic eyes would be on me. Yet no one knew, so no one looked and that wasn't right either.

The atmosphere with your schoolmates, their parents and a few teachers was comfortable and actually gentle for me, but then the pain set in. If Neil and Zoe and Sophie were there and I was watching, where were you? You must be in the team on the Moor, so I waited. Your shape, your tilt, your vibrancy didn't come. I was still waiting for your team, wanting you to be with them. Waiting! It's so me. Neil waited. Zoe waited. And I understood that they were not part of the team this year, whereas Charlie K and Lizzie were, and Harriet, with a new three who were not on the practice when you fell, including your lovely Kathryn from gym, who's now at the school. After the pain then, the guilt – wishing I had these in-love, longing feelings, appreciation feelings, wanting to boast, that's my daughter – feelings before. But the reality is that I suppose I did have all these feelings, but you flicked me away because I was an ugly embarrassment. We are, aren't we, as parents? We are unrequired, hangers-on to our teenagers' secret dreams. So I waited. I was lively when I wanted to be and cried when the hurt came and then I saw Sophie. Your Sophie. Your beautiful, broken-hearted, torn-apart Soph. How I long to draw her to me and let her cry over and over until she sleeps. How I wish she can find comfort in me, even though I'm second-best. She sits alone and looks inconsolable. She's wearing the funniest T-shirt. It reads on the back, upside down, 'If you can read this get me out of the snow.'

I go over to her and tell her I want to cry. I don't know if I'm invading her space. I tell her I don't know why I'm on the Moor today, that I'm waiting for you. That all I do is wait, or so it seems. I tell her that I have a sense of comfort and familiarity, being with all your friends and the parents and teachers, and it feels that you must be there somewhere, but where? Maybe you're in the team that's about to come over the brow of the hill. I tell Sophie that I fantasise about this. I expect your frame, your tilt, your tiredness, your robustness, you … I expect you. I can now see you. Still waiting, gripping on, it will happen. Lies. Waiting for nothing. Always waiting for nothing. Longing for something, getting nothing. Why don't you ever come? From waking till sleep, the all but nothing of you. I ask Sophie whether it's like that for her. She says 'Yes', she looks down, she says 'All the time,' she cries.

I think about Sophie a lot afterwards. I think of how important gym is to her and how the thing she loved so much is now so full of the loss of you.
I show Sophie the whole of me as I laugh and joke with Zoe's and Neil's mums. I realise how irritating and flippant they can be to their children. When another mother asks Zoe a stupid question I want to cringe, and I realise that I identify more with your friends at the moment then with their parents. This could be a threat to one or two.

The team are coming over the hill. I see the banner. The words 'Edgehill College' make me historically proud and happy and desolate all at the same time. I follow the crowd and the team see us, but not me. We move on to the photo-taking stage and Charlie K and Katherine see me and they fling themselves at me, cry and say, 'We did it for her.' That's you, by the way.

Time moves on and sometimes, happily, I get lost in the moment. I looked after Ritu and Marc on Sunday night. They were thrust upon me, which is the best way, since planning makes for panic. Gen, their mum, you may not remember her, well, her car broke down and I was required to take the boys back to my house. For a short time other people were a nuisance, ringing me continuously, because at last I had a job to do. The best and unexpected thing was that your room became a cupboard, a store of useful goodies that I could entertain them with, rather than a shrine full of untouchable, immovable memories. I realised that if I throw myself into something, it may make a difference. It's the commitment, the moving on, the establishment of new roots that's spoken of without care. The testing of the water in jobs, movements and relationships. I can't help feeling guilt with every fresh step I make. The idea of having fun without you having your share too is still abhorrent to me. I miss you now more than ever. Time has passed and time does soften, time enables newness and coping, but time also makes for new clarity and you exist now without clutter. I see you clearly. I can separate you from everything and everyone else and there's a frighteningly strong path that connects us. I can access you quickly, and as usual you're vivid but transient. Like rice paper, you melt before I've tasted you.

They ask if I have games and I send them to your room. It's like a treasure trove to them and I just know that you don't mind. Ritu loves the Tomb of Doom game but the loud noise the skeleton makes frightens Marc. He picks up the huge bag of Lego and drags it down the stairs, it's nearly as big as him. Ritu remarks they should have looked after you better. He knows. I agree but don't want to spoil their time with sadness. I feel at last that I can discipline myself and almost, not always, select when to be unhappy as a release.

There's a price to pay for everything in our lives. Living life in the way that I am living it singularly now and without commitment or involvement means that I'll feel at times that things are vacuous and shallow.

I went to Edinburgh recently, don't tell Grandma – remember, same rules apply. If you're gonna tell, you have to answer the phone and therefore the continuous, relentless questions for at least a week. Oh no, you can't tell, you're gone, can't say 'dead', well, that doesn't sadden me at least. Well anyway, Scotland, I stayed in the Royal Terrace in what appeared to be a pretty gay area of the city, I drank champagne, went frequently to the art gallery and watched kilts and other dress codes going by. I talked to anyone and everyone about all sorts of things, went to a play about children leaving the Scots' social care system and going out into the wide world, and ended up half-deliberately going into two unusual night clubs. I believe I'm now a gay man, there was such eye candy there. Just more fantasy, when reality is too hard.

Saw Zoe today. It's lovely and uncomfortable at the same time. And as with every other bloody thing, I don't know what to do. I suppose I'm coming to the conclusion that this is all a minefield and to get through it at all is enough. And we're doing that. You would be proud.

Zoe is 16 soon and she looks it. She's becoming the woman she was always meant to be, funny, glowing, slender and sensible … well, thoughtful. Of course, I wonder why you're not going to be 16 and I feel cheated. But I feel cheated about a lot of stuff and the sense of the waste over you is confusing.

This evening she's wearing a black dress. She glows. Her childhood for the moment left behind. She calls to me from across the road. I notice Jacky, Yaz and Lauren Priest are with her. For a moment I get caught up in it and I search for you. Not there. No surprise. Consciously I wonder what you'd be wearing if you were there: your gold dress perhaps, the one that Auntie Rockie gave me, then I gave you, beautiful. That prompted the question of the scar from your erstwhile broken arm. How would you have hidden it? Surely not with one of your tennis armbands, not with the gold brocade dress. Speculation, again.

They run across the road to be near me. I'm glad but I know how it will end. They have bags of gifts. It's someone's birthday – maybe someone else is 16. Zoe fills me in: they are on their way to Barnstaple on the bus for a Chinese. It's a netball friend's birthday. I tell them I'm collecting a Chinese and having a friend over. We agree that it's a Chinese moment for all, and laugh. Then the second after the laughter: the shadow, the discomfort, the reality, the pointlessness. The moment of recognition, which I can roughly translate as: 'We can do this, but we shouldn't. She's not here, who are we kidding, we're miserable.' But what else is there now? What else indeed. Zoe's face falls.

Here's a typical day in the life of me, your mother. I got up at 8.30 to the sound of builders on Sybil's roof. I felt sorry for myself. I lingered in bed and had a moment of thought. Then I got up thinking I was having coffee with Phoebe, but she's none too reliable, so her text never emerged. Then I started writing. I'm really disciplined about that and aimed to create 1,000 words this morning. Then I had coffee. And then a nap. I made excuses to myself that I was traumatised, so I took 40 winks. On to more writing and then lunch, usually alone or with TV or reading. Like you I'm reading about five challenging and interesting books at the same time. Always my nose is in one or the other, apparently. In the afternoons I can manage a walk with a friend or alone round Rosemoor or Good Gardens. It's familiar, comforting and exhilarating. Then that uplifting cup of tea and home.

It's good to go out and come back in – there's a shift in energy. I try always to eat with people. They cook for me. Even Trevor, a couple of times a month, cooks a three-course meal. It's very impressive.

I saw Yaz in Safeway's. Actually I saw someone who would have been Yaz, if Yaz was mine, and I'd lost her. Now I'm fantasising about having other peoples' children and losing them. More madness?

I felt a bit lost and feint at the checkout and once again kept mulling back to the food that I'd given you on the Ten Tors walk. Was it enough? Was there enough protein, given that you didn't like cheese. Should I have given you peanut butter or a veggie pie? Was it my fault? Could I have done better? Did I let you down? Did I clean your boots enough? Should I have given you more breakfast? Could I have let you have the ice cream you wanted from McDonald's the Thursday before the tragedy, after netball? Should I have said no to netball? Was I too good a mother or not good enough? You were brilliant, beautiful, courageous and happy. Haven't I done my job then? And done it well? Was the fact that you were always more special than everyone else, had more needs than anyone else, a contributing factor in my madness and frustration? And what now? What do I do with the empty space? What do I do with the box? Now that the present has been taken.

I must be dying. How I could be living with such pain. Every morning the same, never the respite of seeing you. No change. Not today, not next week, not in ten years' time. I just don't know what to do. I mean, I know how to get up and how to feed the cats, and breakfast, and wash, but I don't know what to do with my energy, my interference, my power, my closeness, the family bits, the neck sniffing, the inappropriate, silly behaviour that you used to glare at, the in-between bits that link one thing to another. I feel lost.
Dribble falls from my mouth when I nod off. I'm conscious of wiping that away now and appearing proper. Probably because if I don't, then people will stare more and come to conclusions. I saw her today, she can't control her saliva – that would make the headlines of the *Echo*.

I wonder if a small part of you wanted revenge, Mary. Whether you fantasised about waiting for His killers at nightfall. With nothing to lose, did madness push you towards the need to make someone suffer, did you want His torturers tortured? You must have been a little older than me. Maybe 47ish, probably reasonably healthy and wise. So what did you feel and think? But then how long does it go on for? Someone has to draw a line, somewhere.

At the moment rarely a week goes by without a teenager being fatally wounded by knife or gun. It's terrifying. I see the faces of the mothers. They live in the most inhospitable conditions still, with continuing fear perhaps for their other children, and I wonder what their days are like, what their expectations are. What they have to get through, how they cope.
I feel that it's important to draw a line under the suffering that has already happened. Somebody has to draw limits. And that somebody is me. I think that higher thoughts and

pleasures help to restrict the wish to inflict pain on another. They help me find a way. It's important to find pleasure. It's an antidote to sorrow. A film, a trip, a good coffee, the touch of a friend, laughter and wine. They make moments pleasant despite everything and they feel good. But not everyone is lucky enough to have that environment. Lack of it can only double the unbearable pain and discomfort. I'm lucky. As Grandma keeps saying, this happens to everyone. All people have troubles. But I feel unusually lucky to have the resources that I do.

She thinks I'm amazing in my difficulties. She says, 'Look at your face, your skin and the way you speak, how young you look, no one would know how much you've suffered.' She tries to make it smaller, though, so that it's bearable. Of course, she still remains, ironically, in desperate need of hearing my voice every couple of days and tells me so. I haven't heard your voice exactly 17 months and two days. Two days is too long for the old lady.

But I remain OK if I keep moving and if, when I take a rest from movement, it's in psychological safety. This is very important. This is when it can be safe or go very badly wrong. If I get very disappointed and look for comfort but things just get worse, then I face emotional danger as night falls, and it becomes important to have other things that work – the bath, the cup of tea, the book, the call to the Samaritans, and bed. For tomorrow is always another day, with new chemistry.

It's the little things that distress me. Looking in the airing cupboard and seeing the expanding flannels I bought you year after year for your Christmas stocking. They are never used now. Looking at the hat we bought you in Russia because you left yours behind. When I picture you falling on the skating rink in St Petersburg, I see you clearly. I shouted at you. You were only 10. I wonder if I kissed you enough, if I was warm enough to you, if you knew enough that I loved you, that I still love you, that I'll love you until my last breath even though there's no physical presence to whisper to, no hair to smell and no you to scoop up and squeeze tight. The summer is at its height now, and although you remain everywhere, the deception is big. That girl isn't you. I remember Christmases when the world was clean and my heart strong and the only bad thing was tiredness. I remember eating the reindeer's carrot because Johnny wanted the mince pie that went so well with his fourth sherry. Just as well we didn't leave all that for Santa or we'd have found him face down in his own vomit in the morning. I remember Johnny filling up my stocking and me doing his and each of us trying to outwit the other. There was a little champagne on Christmas morning. Then a ton of chocolate and dinner later at Grandma's with games and presents.

They don't want anything now. It's her 85th birthday on Sunday and we're going to Rosemoor, for a cuppa and a walk. Little steps. How sad, but how amazing to keep going.

Crumble sleeps. I watch. He murmurs and opens his eyes in protest. I remember your eyes, they shone. And when I opened your eye at the end, I saw that you weren't in there any more. It had burst and you had gone. I'll wish forever that I don't see that image at night. I cry for you again and I don't want to be here. Not without you, not any more, not now, again. Nobody knows the full scale of this war, the atrocities I suffer and overcome. I do feel that if they let themselves in, they should be prepared to witness it all.

Today all mothers have daughters, today all mothers love their daughters so much. Where are you? Why aren't I loving you? Why aren't you here being loved?

I just don't know how I could have watched my sweet husband hanging in front of me and barely seven years later see the blood on my dead daughter's head and then be here now eating chocolate biscuits and drinking coffee, reading in my conservatory with a sleeping Custard cat. But if I don't, then I too am dead, and then who next and who because of them? And then? I have learnt that I have to throw myself into things sometimes and then try to enjoy them. Otherwise thinking about whether or not to do them becomes heavy. I wouldn't do anything. I wouldn't get out of bed. Then I wouldn't go to the wedding this Saturday and take Grandma out for her 85th birthday.

We are going to Rosemoor to see the new gardens and have a cup of tea. I'll present the birthday lady with a bouquet of beautiful flowers on arrival and I'm taking a surprise cake with candles for tea at the café afterwards. Maybe I'll include a mini bottle of champagne as well. I'm sad you won't be here to see it all, but maybe you do! Then on Tuesday I'm taking her to Padstow to lunch at Rick Stein's and stay the night in the Metropole Hotel. I like family. We might play a game together, maybe do a crossword. I miss those things the most with you. Although the 'dynamics' – Grandma hates that word, and also hates the word 'hate' – were sometimes strained, we had fun. It was real. We did so many things. The trip to Bristol for that trampolining competition, when you left your leotard behind and we had to go all the way back for it. We stayed in the Marriott Hotel and had chocolate cake, late. We couldn't find the place without panic, and you still won.

You loved these treats and times: we were sisters, flatmates, friends. I was flattered when once in a while you wanted to be like me. When we stayed in the hotel in Portugal – you know, the one with two names, with the amazing buffet – you copied the way I ate the food in different courses, a seafood starter, then salad, then main, pudding and cheese. We rolled upstairs for coffee and dancing. You loved the tiny chocolates. Grandma can't do such a trip now, and in any case to go without you would be fruitless. There are so many changes. We're all a little older, and the changes that might not have happened just yet are happening too soon. I long to make new family and have ownership, and I get very scared of being left completely alone. I want to do things with my family and feel that warmth. That sense of belonging. Even though they are both reluctant, there's a sense of peace and well-being in spending time with the old ones and then coming away, a sense of being expected and looked after. Like when we all went to the Big Sheep together, or maybe it was Crealy Park, and George bought fruit pastilles for you and me. Sometimes when I see teenagers, I see you too and wonder if you'd still be eating fruit pastilles or whether death has called time on your snacking.

Grandma's birthday came and went. It was the best we could do. You must be proud of me. She was 85. I arrived with huge orange and lemon flowers and champagne, a lovely gesture. We went to Rosemoor for a walk. When we sat in the café, they gave Grandma the cake with gold and silver candles on it, I'd pre-arranged it. I keep thinking that you know Lou, in the café, but Lou is after you and because of you. We ate cake, George got confused over a scone and I burst out crying. I feel so sad and hard done by and tired. I kept feeling you and seeing you and wanting that cosy, settled feeling. I was inconsolable and kept saying sorry ... but they were OK with it. What is this? What am I supposed to do? You may not have been here anyway, so what have I lost? More 'It's not so bad' stuff. You didn't talk to me that much really, so what was there? Help me to put it in perspective. No, we can't. It's only now that I've realised the full extent of what I've lost. No one compares to you in brilliance, beauty or compassion. Why didn't I look after you better, make things easier for you, behave better towards you, here we go again. Didn't I do it well? Please tell me I did it well. It's confusing again and I can't remember the reality.

Right, you died. At the time you were behind everyone else and threw a 'bag'. You were being you, helping, in charge, leading and spontaneous. What could I have done to prevent it, to stop it? How could I have stopped it? It was a few seconds in time. The wrong conditions for the wrong steps with no lifelines, which made you fall. I'm so sorry that this happened to you. I wanted to say 'goodbye'. I didn't say 'goodbye'. Three different times in the hospital after you broke stuff, the anaesthesiologist had said: 'Say goodbye to her.' As you lost consciousness, I said 'goodbye' and kissed your cheek. I always felt that this was the last time, that I'd never see you again. And yet I did. Then there was a reprieve, three times a reprieve. But not this time. Has my luck finally run out? You seemed always to be in hospital. I couldn't stop it. I was always preparing to lose you, like Mary with her boy. Aren't we prepared to lose anyway, though? Don't daughters go to Australia, to marriage, to life? Don't we lose them to adventure, to the world, aren't we lucky if they return, even sometimes? But this loss, this loss, with no compensations, is more than any kind of preparation can withstand.

Did you kiss Him goodbye, before He went up there? Were you allowed? Did it fit? Did you regret it if you didn't? Funny, isn't it? That if we can't have them alive, we have to have something, to know that we've had something, a last kiss, something, a lock of hair, a piece of flesh. There's always something about a piece of Charlotte that maybe, if I blow hard enough, will become her.

On top of Grandma's 85th birthday, I watched Hannah Langdon getting married. It was a Saturday thing and 12 hours long. I felt privileged to witness this and wanted it to be you. It wasn't so bad. Because it was in a Baptist church in Appledore, it was low-key and understated. Guess who she married? Tom Overton, Trevor's son. The groom made the ceremony very amusing, so it was easy for me. There was a cream tea on their farm and then a hog roast with quiche for vegetarians. Plenty of dancing with my old doctor school friend Sara Herriot, and Trevor of course, who by this time in the proceedings had his top two shirt buttons undone and was a worry to us all. Although I'm glad I'm not a vegetarian, quiche even at its best is so dull.

When it all goes wrong and I want to know where you are, I wonder how you came out of that tiny room. Then I stop, and I see that you came out of so much more, all that was me, us, your grandparents, your fellows, and so many experiences that were premature for you. I feel that I want so much of you and there's nothing left to take.

I forgot you died. I was thinking of the word 'peripatetic'. I was cleaning our bathroom and was thinking about why that word was constantly on your school fees bill. And I wondered if it was there again now, this term. And suddenly I'm back with you, you're six or eight, and then I realise, you're dead. But it was OK, because it was slow, the realisation, like when one comes to wake from sleep. It's gentle, and I'm aware, for all those who want to put me right as if I didn't know, 'Charlotte isn't six or eight, Jenny, she isn't here any more, she's gone, you know she's gone and she isn't coming back, don't you?' It's not prudent to have an existential moment in front of fools, you know? Because they step in doing the only thing fools can do, put me right. I know that you're dead. But sometimes I just want to make believe.

Violence is difficult to compute. If someone makes me angry and I want to hit them, then what more should I do to the people who were responsible for your lack of return. There is, after all, no point in hitting someone who says or does something trivial if you don't hit the people who left your daughter on the Moor, to the worst fate. I mean, choose well where you strike. Luckily I'm very compassionate. I know there's a choice of response in all things and I chose the adult one. And I know no one killed you. But you are gone. And no matter how hard I try to get away from you, you burst through and I explode. And then I feel that you're judging me with your steely glare. I feel so guilty for leading what seems at the moment to be a hedonistic lifestyle, even for a moment. You were so straight and perfect. You steered a course of truth and compassion, and I feel like a fake in comparison, feel that

I've no right to be in your space, I'm a pale substitute. And yet didn't I make you? So there must be something good about me.

I'm sick. Eighteen months after and I'm feeling sick, with a cold, flu, whatever. I just feel crap. Cosiness and pampering calls, but never you in the background. I reminisce about the times when I was ill and you were little and we called Grandma to rescue us. She came. She attended to us both. I was your sister then and for a moment had few responsibilities and played.

When is the inquest? When am I going to know the truth? And who did what, and for whom I need to have compassion? And with whom I need to try not to be bitter?

I'm stuck. It's all been taken away. Getting you to a level, to adulthood and choices, has been removed. I don't know who you would be, become, and I resent the loss. I'm missing the huge cleverness of you and I'm disappointed with the others. No body replaces you, and I can't find solace again.

You know, I took a taxi to my first O level. I was afraid of being late. The taxi was late. We panicked. Grandma was the same then, worrying aloud about everything whilst I just let things occur. I had all the equipment in my pencil case. Maths stuff, everything sharpened and refilled – you know, high standards when it's the first time. You didn't get to yours. I'm confused about time and sometimes mixed up about who did what. Everything goes on except me and you.

I found some dark pink shoe polish in the cupboard. I remember buying it and thinking, will I ever polish these little shoes before you grow out of them. We went to our pizza shop, and you showed Johnny your new pink shoes. That was the life I had then. When I didn't know how horrendous things could get. I wonder now if I could have made it different. If the shoe polish had been all used up, whether life would be OK now. Is it because I didn't clean your shoes with it and kept it in the tin and still kept it for years after that, and then for years after Johnny died to go hard in its case? And still kept it and forgot it was there, so long after the shoes, so long after Johnny, and long after you. It has shrunk, cracked in the tin, with gaps in it, dehydrated and lifeless. Is that why my life is like this? There are no pink shoes any more, no little Charlotte to wear them, no Daddy to show them to, no big girl to remember: just me and the tin and the hard pink polish. Is that why? Tell me not to dwell on this. Tell me not to wallow. Tell me to live my life to the full, to get on with it. But with what? Will it get better if I find some pink shoes, or a little child who needs pink shoes? Should I go to India where there's currently an earthquake and rescue a child and give them pink shoes? Will that make it better? Pink shoes are special in India. No, nothing makes it better. Nothing at all.

It's the ponytailed head, to be precise, that distresses me most, the almost central ponytail. The skin by the ears, the shape of the neck and the hoodie. I can nearly always smell you and then I start longing. The anticipation of the turning round of the girl who isn't you then gets to me. I miss. Closer and then closer and then nothing. Torture. The giving of something which isn't.

Your boy had it as He died, Mary. He thought it was water, must have imagined its taste, longed for the satiety of that pure life liquid. And then not, something else. Something hellish, vinegar, torture.

Back to school and sixth form they go, not you, and therefore not me. I'm so sick of being without you day in, day out. No one's here and no one knows. They don't know what state your room is in. They don't know what it smells like. What any of it means. What relevance every item has and what its history is. They know nothing of me, you, us, and it. I'm alone and sad.

I move further from the 14-year-old that was you, but no closer to the 17-year-old that you will become, next year. I'm stuck in purgatory, in suspension. I wait and am caught between wanting you and letting you go. This place has no movement. It just lets me sit and rock and breathe.

'The Services have let Jennifer down. Nobody picked up the signs or heard her cries or listened to her pleas. She is now missing 19 months after her daughter's death and fears are growing for her safety.'

Sometimes I feel excited and I don't know why. It's as if I've chosen to be a different me. I'm nine and looking forward to Christmas or even 39 and excited about a holiday with you. In fact, there's no reason, it's about movement and feelings that are just there. Maybe a smell. It's just a feeling triggered by a sense. The repeated happinesses, now empty.

I'm in your room looking for evidence. In books I search for you. Something that I haven't seen before, something that you've left for me to find. Something to prove you were alive. I think almost pathologically as I seek moments to capture. Then I flit to another place. Maybe our last trip to London two years ago was captured on CCTV cameras in Fortnum and Mason. Maybe if I asked. What would be the question? Do you have CCTV footage for 26 October 2006 please? Is she connected with the police, is what they'll wonder, and then I'll tell them. 'I want to see my daughter again, as if for the fist time. I lost her, you see she was 14. You might have heard. Maybe her DNA is on the glass covering the chocolate counter. Maybe she dropped something once and it's still there.' Maybe someone remembers you. The manageress of the sushi bar, she'll remember you. Then she'll be upset and too busy to express it.

What should I tell your friends about how you are? What do I say to them?

I want to feel good about just me. Be able to get up and embrace a new day, feed the cats, work, play, wash, just for me.

I feel cosy. I can't tell why. I chop peppers for a salad. Are you having some?

'Jenny, Charlotte isn't coming for dinner. She doesn't live here any more. Only the cats live with you now.'

'You mean Johnny has gone, I've lost him and Charlotte has gone as well? I saw her eye go, does that mean that she won't be coming for the peppers today?'

You torture me, never here, never going, never fully gone. I'm suspended in a nowhere place, trapped, hoping just enough. I'm caught in a shrine of longing, a prison, where I can't leave and don't want to stay.

Is my cosiness all about going to the school tomorrow and feeling that you might be there. Will you be there tomorrow, Charlie, will you meet me, please meet me. You can bring Johnny too, please.

You never come, even if I'm good you never come. You tantalise me, never there, never going, never fully leaving. I'm suspended in a nowhere place. A shrine of nothingness, a prison.

I'm not getting enough relief for my suffering. I have to try really hard to get my needs met. I feel really needy and I'm getting sick of it. I wonder if people are getting sick of me. Maybe I shouldn't complain any more, after all it's been 18 months. 18 months after nearly 15 years. Does anyone understand? Is there anyone out there who can carry just a little of this for me?

I do feel that I want them to know that it does keep going on for me. That you don't suddenly return and then it's all right. There's no end to this. God, am I going to have to have a tantrum after all? I can understand how a person like me could jump off a cliff in despair.

Was going to the prize giving a mistake? They were a little distant. It feels like my unwanted celebrity status has gone. The focus was on how wonderfully everyone is moving on. Eighteen months, no time at all, considering that I brought you up for nearly 15 years. I put in all that energy and work, and just as you were blossoming, taken, gone. Nobody has said sorry. And I'm angry about that. I'm so disappointed that you weren't there in a suit representing the sixth form.

I'm angry, resentful, jealous. They have more than me and they don't deserve it. These other children are alive and performing, and you who were at the school for so long and gave so much are not here. There isn't even permission for you. There is no acknowledgement of your life or death, and it feels like the injustice carries on.

I tell myself that we had quality and it doesn't matter about the amount. You are upset with me for not valuing what we had. But you see, I'm greedy. Yes, Charlotte, I'm greedy. I want more. I want you. I want you now. I want you forever.

Should you have left and gone somewhere else anyway? Were you more than they could handle? Should you have given your brilliance to another place?

Went to Atlantic Village after the bash for a pasty with Gracie and Helen. Grace had scooped the junior gym prize. We spent two hours there until Grace was itching to buy some specific tracksuit bottoms. Remember that? You should have been there once again. Clarice and Win and I went for a Chinese after and we saw the new film, *The Duchess*, about an antecedent of Lady Diana. A lady with similar sorrows and choices. Keira Knightley has come a long way since we saw her in *Bend It Like Beckham*.

It was a long, long day. I ended up in the Joiners discussing 'chiaroscuro' with William, a printmaker with no teeth. My life, what a whirlwind, eh? Is that good or bad? Should I have gone to bed earlier, instead of roaming and roaming?

I had two glasses of white, nothing to write home about, but this morning I'm significantly down. It can't be the alcohol or the late night, so it must be the 'no you' again. Somewhere, within myself, I expected you. That's it – after all that effort, you'd come. I wait. I eat a high-energy cereal bar. Charlotte or cereal. Daddy or chips, remember that advert before Johnny died? Too confusing. I drink my morning cup of tea. Cats are out, I'm still in my dressing gown.

I breathe. Once again, I breathe.

I take comfort in a lot of people and places. It's the looking forward to them that's good. I've adopted layers to my day, which helps with motivation to keep going. They call it a 'structure'.

There wasn't a photo or a mention of you at prize day, and I felt affronted. It seems so wrong. But you're there so strongly in everyone who loved and worked with you. Where is your brilliance remembered? I begin to read things into the lack of you. Have they thought about mentioning you but realise that this could go on forever? By the way, school, it *will* go on forever. She's gone forever, acknowledging that eases things. But she's here in everything. I feel that once again I've let you down, because I haven't shouted this out loud. But then they wouldn't invite me again and I'd be a bad example, showing a lack of grace. It is better in the main to do the harder thing and suffer in silence? *Yes, Mary?*

The school has got it wrong. At first we all got it wrong, because it *is* wrong and the only way of getting it right was bringing you back. But then there's being open. The school must include your friends and me in all decisions. They must be transparent, careful and not prescriptive. They are not. They have not asked us what we want – neither me nor the children, and definitely not you. I seemed to have little status, I'm being phased out. You're being phased out. There's no acknowledgement of you any more. It seems like your time is up and they've concluded that enough is enough. This doesn't fit with the fact that you were there for 12 years or more. There seems to be a lack of honouring you and me. Maybe they feel this is not your moment now but theirs, and they separate you. But the snag is that the children think about you constantly. They can't work it out, the mystery of your sudden death, and the life that was before, and they need the adults to bring you up, all the time. It's the only way. If they don't, then you'll find your way back in and it will always be shocking. You are breath and life and blood. You are stamped so indelibly upon us all, you cannot and won't be removed.

This was a time when people were celebrating, not only the end of year results, but also all the times before. You were absent, removed, but present upon every face. Do they really think that if people don't talk about you, you'll disappear? Is that even what they want for their children?

It's as if they are afraid to speak your name. Ironically, soon there'll be a bronze memorial to you in front of the school, which is breathtaking and so does you complete justice. You'll be looked at over and over, but for how long? Will you eventually become a fixture, part of the background, static? You aren't in that sculpture or in your grave. You're inside all your friends who are bursting to say, 'Do you remember when and do you remember her and do you remember Charlotte eating all those stupid banana chips. I'm thinking about her now and it hurts.'

'Jesus, the Christ', how long Mary? How long before they could utter His name without guilt and shame. And then how long before they could say it with pride? Every second person seems to wear that cross now. What does it represent? Worse, what does it mask? That memorial to the man who died that day on the hill. The girl in the water, the man on the hill, one memorial seen by few, the other known by all and worn by many. But when does it become just what it is and nothing more? When does a cross just become a pendant, a jewel, a decoration, a shape, an accessory, a forgotten truth, a piece of landscape behind a lie?

Is it a memento to a betrayal? Are that cross and that bronze sculpture our archetypal 30 pieces of silver? Are they another way of going to church? Tick the box, wear the crown, buy the gown, accessorise with 30 pieces and tomorrow we'll be right. No need to do what's right today, we have a get-out-of-jail-free card. We wear a cross for all to see. The bigger the better. You see, we're Christians. If it's really big and heavy, we can feel it wearing us down but even then we get used to it, and we don't remember who we are or who we're supposed to be – sacrificial, loving, good, that's always tomorrow's task. All our tomorrows are filled with the good intentions of the cross. All our tomorrows are filled with the good intentions of the bronze memorial. Tomorrow I'll visit Jennifer, and I'll see how she is, tomorrow. This becomes all my tomorrows, and all my tomorrows become all my hopes and all my hopes become nothing and the nothing is dust. And the dust is death and then it's too late.

Charlotte, wake up, darling, and have some cough medicine and honey!

'What, Mama?'

You're coughing. Here, have some of this. There, go back to sleep.

My life feels like it's been suspended. It stopped the day you left and I'm waiting to continue when you return. Am I aware that you aren't coming back? I wonder.

I don't miss you being such a hard taskmaster. I found the coloured dividers that I bought for you and got wrong. Remember, the ones that don't cover the page properly? You looked at me as if I hadn't listened. I fantasise about taking them back to the shop. What would I say? Supposing there was a fight about it, would that be the last straw, would I overreact? What if I grabbed the shopkeeper by the scruff of the neck and all my grace suddenly slipped away? All the anger in my life might suddenly shoot across the stationery counter at Smith's. And then I'd be up for assault, and not because you died, but because I didn't get 97 pence back for some dividers. And that would be incongruous.

I'm forlorn again today. Why? I've entered into a little phase of new behaviour and I'm tired and feel that it may be too soon. I don't know why I feel so bad about it but counselling will make this clear.

I wonder if this is now all straightforward stuff about my emergence and living my life and it's actually positive rather than negative. Nothing can stay the same, however much I try and keep things static, I'll move and then it gets complicated. I feel I need a routine to be immersed in, but then I also want to live for the moment. More fucking paradoxes. I find the integration difficult. Sometimes I feel that it's all a kind of madness. And I wonder if there are ways of doing it that normalise life better.

I'm wearing your Bench black and white jacket, you know the one. You'd have a fit if you were here. I want you to be here. I want to argue about it. I want to annoy you and see your face. I'm wearing it without asking. I'm the child. You're the parent. Whichever way, you're still dead. For such a slight jacket there are, unusually zips, on the pockets.

I undid one. I was curious to see what the last thing in it was. I found crumbs. In the darkness I smelt them, but nothing identifiable. I immediately thought, cereal bar or chocolate, but it felt more like biscuit. Today I look again. It's sand. I puzzle. Where is this sand from? Did you wear this when you went to Barcelona with your gym club, on the beach? Is it Spanish sand? It has to be from the summer of 2006, in any case. Because that was your last summer: so hard to say these words. That was Charlotte Shaw's last summer alive, before she died in spring 2007. That really stabs me always. Barcelona was in June, but it could have been Devon sand up until August. I dwell, I think, I wish, I torment myself. It's always the detail which encourages me to drift and also makes me so alone. You see, Charlotte: it's always stuff I remember about you and, worse, about us, this makes me lonely and it's continuous. That's the pain, no one to share and too often. So what am I to do with this sand? If I lose it, am I losing you again, or what I have of you or traces of you, or any of you?

I recall the beach. The times we played tennis in Westward Ho! And tucked our socks into our trousers and hired rackets. The ice creams we licked whilst looking out to sea. The bingo we played and the daft prizes we won. The sand is now under one of my nails and it falls upon my leg grain by grain, unidentifiable. I can't remember the colour of the sand in Westward Ho! And it's too sad to go there at the moment, maybe Sophie will help me. Maybe I could show her the sand.

I'm at the Friary. It's a year since I first came to stay, and I do feel quite different. I speak to Brother Vincent about isolation and freedom, and read the Dalai Llama's guide to meditative thought which engenders positive mental health. This is possible. I ponder on the huge challenge of taking upon myself the suffering of those on the walk, so that they're free of it forever and I carry it. Will this be too much of a burden for me? Will I be more alone? The pain does have a way of being glorious, though, like a raw precious stone, a thing that's pure.

Separation is the vital clue to surviving this. I need to be, to emerge, to leave home, and to let you go. But what then of integration, of togetherness, of joining. Don't tell me, it's another fucking paradox. Anyway you're dead. Remember you told me to get a life of my own? I think of you as an individual who actually did everything she could have done. Suddenly this is possible. If you had got 10 GCSEs and then As and then university, there may not necessarily have been any difference to the outcome. What if you went to fight in a war, away for months, me always wondering? Still there would be no children as a legacy. The state of grace to which I aspire is that I steer my course right now regardless of what was or what is.

I need you. Like I need a mother and a life-line and comfort and blood. I want to share stuff with you. I miss our little exchanges. Now I'm in my room at the Friary and the light has gone. I feel low. I miss you, and where is anyone I might tell? I feel that no one expects me: no one knows that I exist. I could go out now, and come back at 8 a.m. or not at all, and nobody would know, but of course we all die alone, really, and somebody has to be last. And anyway I hugged Neptune, one of the two Friary cats. I think he loves me and I am on sandwich duty tomorrow at the Stigmata Festival. When I was last in a room like this I was at university. I wish I'd been more organised then and knew more, and got everything right. Maybe it's time to stop wishing and start living. Maybe I should become the strength that's required by another person somewhere. I shower and look forward to dressing again. It's a little bit of change and movement in my world, alone. When I'm out of the room there's a chance that something might happen. The mobile phone might go. I might receive a message. I want to talk to my parents, tell them that I'm here, and feel connected to them, to people who care if I'm alive. But I know if I do, then the price is that tomorrow my mother will ring the Friary and then Sunday and then every time I'm not at home. I can wait to talk to them. All I've ever wanted is togetherness without condition, anxiety and neurosis.

On the days when I feel alone I really have to try not to fear. I must try not to sink. The Friary is my place, just me, you were never here. This, Rome and Edinburgh, all my places, my time, my future. The Friary is spiritual, Edinburgh cultural and Rome, both. There are no memories of anyone. The Friary is fresh, a home from home, full of uncles and grandpas and brothers. It's peaceful and energising. My favourite Brother is Kevin. He's compassionate and funny and pissed off, and I like the combination. I suppose because it's real.

I'm back to the same old way of thinking too much. Jayne came yesterday with food. She does that on Sundays, it's so reassuring. When she left, I kept Friary rules by going to bed early. It was comforting. The cats and I and my latest book, but things were whirring around in my head as I thought of recent events. I get up and rush around with plan after plan. I'm only doing it because of you.

Crumble has pooed in the bath. He is such a sensitive cat. Any change and he does something demonstrative. I use toilet roll to clean it. There are two empty carcasses of toilet roll lined up for the bin. Have you been here whilst I was away? I wonder, because this is what you used to do. I steal into your room, just in case, and smell and remember. The familiarity is huge and heavy and empty. It hurts so much once again. I used to stand in here and wonder what it would be like when you were gone, not if, but when. Is there an answer to anything? I flit to a bigger picture. At the Friary there's a sense of beautiful reality and lightness of how things would be if we all contributed to a simpler kind of life, then I'm back in this world, needing to spend more on parking than a family of five spend on food in one week in certain countries. Needing to spend more on coffees out, more on a newspaper, which tells me about those families, ironically. I think about it. A lot of people spend £5k a year on two rounds at the pub and 20 fags a day. That's 20 families fed for the year. Can we change anything? Charlotte, you can give me strength to help, to be of use.

I'm so glad that I didn't look at you again after you went. I mean in the funeral parlour. If I had, then I feel that I would have died twice. If I'd seen you hard and cold like I saw Johnny, I think that would have been it for me. I wouldn't have recovered. And yet grandma saw you. Incredible. People have such different types of strength. You know, sometimes I feel that I really can't keep going like this on my own. But then I feel that compared to a lot of other people's crap it's actually got edges and is not an ongoing trauma – these little compensations! I find any way to talk myself out of the horror. You know, it's sort of happened, gone, and I know what I'm dealing with. I definitely have a God complex now, though. I think that I'm something special. I bear this overwhelming sorrow. I have delusions of grandeur.

If they couldn't cope with it 2,000 years ago the first time it happened, how are they going to cope with it now? History doesn't change stuff. People make identical mistakes. If I said I'm someone they could follow … No, Noods, it's not like that, I just have a lot to teach now.

They won't believe Charlotte's mother as they didn't believe your son, Mary. If I try to help or lead them, some will say I'm mad, they'll mock me, they'll fashion me a crucifix and say that I'm a crazy blasphemer. And then one of them will shoot me. And this is the word of the Lord, and I'm afraid. Or am I?

Grandma and George came to the house this afternoon. It's 24 September 2008 – 18 months and 19 days since you left. George wanted to ride a bicycle and Grandma fell up the steps in the garden, and I wondered if these problems and abnormalities that we have as a family are what lead to death. I wonder why we're outside and not taking tea in the warm living room, which would surely be more fitting for two people in their 80s. But there's a strong sense of *What's the point without you?* There seems nothing central and nothing peripheral any more. Maybe I'm looking at it the wrong way. It's sort of good that both of them want to be moving. It's good that they're out of doors. And it's good that they're still alive, relatively well and 80 odd. Let's raise a glass to that, rather than associate everything that's wrong with our wrong choices.

Crumble is trusting. I bend down over him and he doesn't stir.

The shock of something new makes me cry. I get to know you, more, through your friends, and I'm moved. Katie is 16 and one month. She's an adult now, with breasts and a mature countenance. She carries files and says hello. She hardly recognises me with my short hair. You don't know that I've had my hair cut. She still calls me Mrs Shaw. I like that. We're at The Plough. I book cinema tickets in one long wave of entertainment and escapism. She's talkative and unashamed. She says you were lovely. You were a very good person. She misses you so much. She thinks about you every day. She thinks about me a lot. She'd cry but she doesn't need to. I cry. She tells me you said that she was beautiful, when others called her 'fat'. She said that even if a person was unlikeable and not popular, you'd help them if they were down. I believe her. I believe this of you. Who were you? Why can't you be present?

Katie has been doing something theatrical and I walk her to the bus stop. She copes well with the huge gamut of emotions erupting. She can't imagine how it is for me. I feel restored by the knowledge that she and so many feel for me.

You are missing. I notice this. Sunday night again. I maintain a big routine for Monday. Bathing, candles. I'm tired. I listen for you, but there's no energy there. Your door is shut. Crumble cries again. He rubs his hot nose against my eyebrows. His mouth is dry. He combs my hair with his teeth, a nervous thing. I can feel you moving around me, getting stuff ready, but I don't want to cry for you, not again. I'm too tired. It's been an emotional weekend since the heart advisor pin in acupuncture. I've been pre-menstrual, tired, and low in carbohydrates, and I've seen Katie at The Plough. Enough. Am I being too repetitive with my sorrow? I can't get out of this, I wish I could, but the pain is always unset, still wet underneath. Always seeping through. Did you really tell Katie she was beautiful? You were something else. I'm finally fencing on Mondays! Maybe it will help with the anger.

I'm sitting in the ironically named Palace Club with Phoebe, you'd have laughed. I dread the moment when Nick, Andy's dad, will come over. He's clearly working here. Andy has split up with Joss and has been expelled from the school. Also he's done badly in his GCSEs. Now let's console him and completely miss more irony that a very interested and clever student like you is dead and Andy is still here. Also let's begin the stifling show of comparing Phoebe's children to Andy, in a really 'Did he, yes, she does that as well, it's good, isn't it?' manner. Whilst the mother of the dead but interesting child has nothing to contribute and feels explosive. I have no status, no reputation, surely then I'm holy. I want to be verbally cutting or cry at the wound of injustice. But I know that's not the way. So I try another tack. I tell the truth. And funnily enough, it humbles them. In fact, when one is real there's nothing stronger. So here goes. 'I just don't know what to say to you both. There's such talk about all your children and my one is dead. In my position would you keep silent or offer what was, in a 'Yes, Charlotte used to be this or that' kind of way, or would you do something else all together?' They realise, and are thoughtful. It's not that I don't want people to talk about their hideously boring lives, of course I do, I just want permission to include you.

I collect dead people. Well, I must do, mustn't I? And I'm not even on my way to a complete set.

I'm having such fun. Fencing is great until I see you across the badminton court. But you know, I've allowed myself a reprieve. I say 'No' to the indulgence of self-pity sometimes now, and get on with the lovely task in hand. Just me being happy, doing what a 'me' does.

Of course, it's the first time I've been in a gym with lines and walls, high walls and markings and rubber shoes and people with sports stuff and and sweat and stench for over one and a half years. It has strong links to collecting you three to five times a week. It confuses temporarily, because it's me doing it and I'm without you as always. There's something else. I don't feel worthy. I don't think I'm good enough to be here, I think that somehow, because I'm less than you, I don't deserve it. But then I think about the amount of effort I put into staying alive, and I think, yes, 97 percent. You deserve here and now, Jennifer.

I was looking at old photographs under my bed. I'm transported back to Portugal when you were 9 or 10. And Grandma was 78, maybe. You're in the swimming pool with the little girl Annesh and her parents. Who remembers? And then there's you in Israel at the Herod Hotel with that sweet waiter. There are so many memories that are only mine now. This is why I sometimes feel old, because I'm the last man standing, though this usually happens when one is 90.

So I look in a box, reserved for people who only have memory. When dreams have gone and weariness takes over. Your father's watch still works when I wear it and the photo of you in the school magazine makes me smile as you flirt with the camera – no one has as many poses as you. Why do I make the time to do these things? Are they really necessary? Why is it I torture myself? Custard is beside me. She's made a warm spot in the sheepskin on my bed. I remember when Johnny left a warm shape in the bed. There'll never be a warm spot in your sheets again. Your pyjamas still wait. I'm punished, kept away. It was your school, my school for 12 long years. Now it's different. They are here, but we are not.

Penny for the guy, spare some change. A thought for a dead child, sir, madam. Can you spare a thought madam? Please come round to my gaff and bear witness at the emptiness of my life. Penny for the emptiness.
Everything is such a big deal. A joke is always in bad taste because I see your face when it's made. You're angry with me?

I'm surrounded by men in the Joiners. It's like a big sea, when you're thirsty. Not a drop to drink. Of the ones that are single, not one is suitable. I'd rather sleep with Felicity, my friend who's helping out. Bick has done a Masters in sand erosion through pipes and likes to tell you about it. Euan has just been to New York on a shoestring. He buys a round. I asked for water and he hopes it's tap water. Harry is a dentist who fishes for entertainment and is too immature to know how to treat me. Scat, or Andy as he's called, is the only box ticker. But I'm not attracted to him. He's witty and educated and considerate, but sadly there's no chemistry. So what now? Another night in bed with Custard, Camomile and a book, could be worse. How?

I listen to that song, 'There'll never be blue like that again.' I park the car. I look over Saunton Bay. It's after midnight. It's pitch-black out there. It's dangerous. It's just me and very dangerous. I play the music loud now. I relate the blue that there'll never be again to you. There'll never be you like that again. I feel sorry for myself. Danger, danger, careful, Jennifer, careful. With all my life hopes dashed, I want to be in the water. With speed I want to celebrate life and beckon death and fly into the cold water. I want something to end, is it my life? I teeter on the metaphorical line. A part of me wants to go. I am going, oh! It mustn't end on this note. I must keep safe. I mustn't let people have this as well. I am the glue. It isn't difficult to pull myself away. I just wanted to see. I drive away, I knew that I would. I'm home now.

Did you die a long time before you died? Did they humour me, so that it would be gentle? Did they know that the shock and speed would be too much and in fact I needed to fight for you, not too much but just enough? They did the right thing. At the hospital in Plymouth, they did the right thing.

Nobody knows where I go. I have your dressing gown at the bottom of my bed. I wore it whilst mine was in the wash. I smell it. There are sweet, stale memories on it, and probably Marmite. Now there's a meld of you and me. It hurts and comforts. The bitter sweetness co-exists; the joy and sorrow intertwine like two necklaces that cannot separate, knotted, irritating, won't separate. Never one without the other. I want to rip them apart. Why? People berate me with many whys? But I say 'Why not?!'

Edward from across the road is mowing my lawn, so kindly. It's brilliant, but I feel sort of guilty. He's 70 something. But in a way people want to do stuff for me because I carry the sorrow for us all. Although both he and Velva have had challenges of their own. They too have lost a child.

People should give me at least a sponge soaked with vinegar and gall for my trouble. *When you learned of this, Mary – or maybe you saw it happen? – did you suffer more? I wonder what your pain was like. Did you break, Mary, did you, break? Did you dream? Did you scream? Did you cry? Tell me what I'm allowed to do.* When I heard that the scout helping your group told Yaz to take off her bag whilst crossing the river and told you to chuck it across, I was devastated. I broke. I saw it.

I cleaned the car today and renewed my passport. Two major things in the life of a domestically unmotivated individual. Whilst these were things were happening, I was positive, but now I'm flat because you're still not here. Is it that I was distracted and want to come back to my favoured reality? Or that I've achieved something and want the reward. Who cares? It all points to you. But I haven't done them for you. It's not about whether I'm capable of doing something for me. It's like this in our families: we never fully do something for ourselves. For the stupid among my advisers, all that we do is because our children are here, because we have base. The knowledge of their existence acts as a reward when the job's done. A sort of symbiosis.

Transfiguration is fucking hard when dealing with idiotic people who think that they're in charge of my life. It's difficult to be graceful and steer an appropriate course. Being misunderstood is one of the most painful of Christ's wounds, but why? Why does it matter what another person understands? After all, not everyone in the world can get it.

The times when I've switched off that light, ushered you to bed, been irritated after you've pulled another must-do assignment out of your academic hat. I watched you concentrate, go into your lovely, cosy little room. You lived in it for 14 years. You wrote the poem about it.

Mum came home, a smile on her face,
She told us all the news.
'We're moving guys,' our faces fell,
Blackened like a bruise.

A change of scene, a change of life,
Who cares where we will go?
The others said OK, why not?
Not hearing me say no!

Packing boxes, cases, the lot!
While memories fill my mind,
I can't believe they still want to go,
All the good times left behind.

Somebody new, living in *my* room,
I cannot bring myself to the thought.
We haven't even a place to go,
For somewhere new, we have not bought.

I've lived at this place for all my life,
Don't they understand the gloom?
But alas, it's now time to go,
To leave the emptiness which is, my room.

We drive away, the brave gang,
While tears prick my eyes.
Moving slowly further away,
The house, my home dies.

I watched you cosy and I kept you warm. I was near you. It's all gone now. I try to remember the feeling but I can't get close. Your room, does anyone know? The glass, the magnet, the egg light that changes colour, the pink CD player, the photo of you and Zoe, the one of me and Johnny, the star earrings, the five-pound note and the new cash point card. Why can't anyone share this?

You're in the paper again. Your trampolining team have had their memorial competition in recognition of their team mate who died. That's you, by the way. Did you know you died? Well, you did in the Ten Tors practice, last year. Twenty months on, I'm still afraid to open a newspaper. It still hurts to read the words and I still come home alone.

'Time is a great healer.' That's the third most popular greeting for me. The first being, 'Are you working?' and the second, 'Are you still in the same house?' At least they are neutral questions, and not intrusive ones, like the other popular openers. 'Have you lost weight?' Not there aren't a variety of fantasy answers to this, one being 'Yes, I'm dying, slowly,' which I find a bit of a conversation-stopper and mildly funny, but the classic top fantasy response has got to be, 'No, I just appear to have got smaller because you're bigger. You are, aren't you? So therefore it's an optical illusion. You've got extremely, hugely, excruciatingly, fucking fat, enormous, big!' This clearly can only be used to allay the fear of my demise, via starvation, when a fat fucker asks, and it's usually only such a person who brings up the worry. You're laughing, Charlie, aren't you? You always have a sense of humour!

It strikes me as being irreverent, how people give themselves permission to be so personal, without invitation, and attack. It's not like I ask them if I look all right. So let me put them out of their misery. I'm currently 133 pounds, which is bang in the middle of perfect weight for my height of 5 foot 7. Do you know that actually, even if I say this, there are some who look at me with disbelief, take in a sucking breath, look me up and down and then humour this mad skeleton by rubbing my puny bones in sympathy. Maybe a right hook will separate illusion from reality?

Time heals. Time, there's very little healing about it, actually. Yes, I learn to accept, to ride the storm, know that I've lived through it and therefore can live more. I know what works, behaviourally and from a structure point of view. And so on. I move. But actually, as I enter into new things, I move away from you and I don't want that. It's terrifying. This in turn makes new life terrifying. Not only that, but the old way no longer suits and I find myself spending a lot of time in-between time zones. It's like being in quarantine or even purgatory. I have to move forward if I chose to move at all ... I need new, I want new, but new means old fades. You fade. You stop and even die again. Exhausting! See, time sucks.

Sometimes I'm sure things happen for a reason. I needed to go to Morrison's for cat biscuits and water melon and fabric softener, it's a bit like *Ready Steady Cook*, isn't it? Let me see, let's make cat biscuit and water melon stew with fabric softener dumplings. Oh and yes, for five quid. Well, guess who I saw? Completely out of the blue. Mrs A. Remember, your junior school head at Edgehill. We really liked her. She was in the coffee shop with her secretary Mrs G. They had that expression. I suddenly feel like a saint. They look at me with wonder. I feel like the person that others want to see and touch and gaze at, but never be. I look suitably together and they agree that I look really well and I'm incredibly strong to survive. By the way, I do look very hot at the moment, you'd be so proud of me. I've died my roots, I do a bit of exercise, 'bit' being the operative word, and I look good. They want me to join them or keep in touch or something. It's all a bit above me. And I have so many good people already I just can't fit in or maintain any more. Maybe I'll bump into them again.

I look at the muscles in my hands and know that yours don't move like that. I look at my skin changing colour and I know that yours doesn't. I remember. I wish people could respond to where I am in the sorrow and realise a little more and not look for pathology. I don't want them to think that they're continually doing me a favour. I want to see this as an opportunity, more than anything else. Yes, an opportunity, to let myself into the world of the 80 per cent of women who have this and nobody bats an eyelid. The woman somewhere on Earth who has lost a husband and daughter and maybe more but now is under threat of shell fire, physical atrocity and worse. I owe it to that woman, whoever she is, to do this in my world and do it compliantly.

Just because you died, does it give me the right to sneak a lemon curd tart into The Plough to have with my coffee? And if it does, then for how long?
I burst into The Plough today. I've taken on the explosion of another, guess who it is, I'll give you a clue. She betrayed you and now she's so sorry. She thinks about you every day. *She has nearly got the same initials as your boy's betrayer, Mary.* And I've been somewhat careful with her. Can I help her resolve her issues and ease the burial of grief and guilt, and if I do, how will it impact upon me?

110

How much pain will it cause me? Anyway, I've been rightfully told off for eating unlicensed pastry as a result. The lady behind the counter is not happy. I'm humbled by her comments on the fact that she's trying to make a living. I say 'Sorry.' She is softened. Sometimes an apology is all it takes, and eating humble pie, but not in The Plough and not if you buy it from the bakery opposite, boom boom! Sorry, Noods, not funny.

Feeling very low again. Sometimes things are so difficult, so bad. I guess it has to be this way, and there's no reason.

It's Saturday. You'd be at the gym today. I miss you ... had a late night last night. Went to the pub with Phoebe. She hurt me. Maybe it doesn't take much. She's the only person I know who seems to seek out the topic of daughters with everyone we meet. Of course, everyone alive has a teenage girl today. She went on and on. 'How's bla?' 'Oh, is she, *bla bla bla*, well, my Rebecca, *bla*.' 'Shut up, Phoebe, shut up, OK?' I go out to forget, not to have my face slapped by it, OK?

I get up, and there are muddy paw prints on my duvet cover. I don't clean it immediately, my first thoughts are that Grandma will come on Wednesday and help out. She doesn't come any more, though. There's no need, for a start. I'm not at work, so I can do my own cleaning. Secondly, Johnny has gone and you're not at school. So there's no real mess. Anyway, she's 86 nearly, and things have changed. No one is looking after me and I'm terrified. All is lost and all is irreplaceable.

Everyone seems insensitive. 'I'm so glad to hear the sound of your voice,' she says to me. That's Grandma again. This makes me furious, jealous, like a knife that's already stuck in me is being twirled around for more amusement. I feel angry at her and ashamed of myself. But I verbalise. 'Yes, I wish I could hear her voice, just once.' 'Oh sorry, yes, what to do' and then it becomes her pain. What am I supposed to do, I'm running out of ideas.

I look through the newspapers whilst lighting a fire. There are some before and afters now. I look for evidence of you being here. 'Gymnastics team wins gold medal at competition. Charlotte Shaw got a top score.' Look, a picture of you, want to see it?

Our mental health is measured by our connectivity to others. I currently feel isolated and alone and it becomes dangerous. I'm in your room getting a T- shirt for fencing. I chose the Liverpool Ministrada one. It smells of you, but sweetly stale now. It will become my familiar T-shirt as soon as life takes over, and this is a lesson on what is and isn't precious.

Often it's not what I do, but what happens in the in-between, in the shadows, that matters and frightens. I went to London with Gail – you met her twice, I'm glad, so I can talk incessantly about you. Well, this was a second trip to England's 'Big Apple'. The first being with Amy to see Vanessa Redgrave in the adaptation of Joan Didion's *The Year of Magical Thinking*. I hope, by the way, that when this book is made into a West End play it's better than the Vanessa Redgrave monologue and Kristin Scott Thomas will play me and Leonardo will play Neil, in a way there's a Titanic connection, or is that in bad taste and am I the only one allowed to make bad taste jokes? Maybe Emily Blunt can play Zoe and one of Anthony Minghella's puppets can be you, or Anne Hathaway. Anyway, the fact is, you have to get these adaptations accurate. *The Mel Gibson version of* The Passion *about your son was much better than the Robert Powell version I saw a million years ago.* Anyway, London, we did stuff, planned stuff, Rothko, Manon, Covent Garden, champagne, memories, lovely. I was obsessed about bumping into our Uncle Jason. I kept thinking that Friday night that I'd see him stomping out of a pub and then he'd wonder why I hadn't told him I was coming. But really I wanted to see if I could do it before there were family complications. Then guess what? There he was, totally surprisingly, in Trader Vic's. With a friend. I was stunned and overjoyed.

It's my birthday tomorrow. I'll be 45. I always thought you'd be nearly 17. I have a 17-year-old daughter, but I don't. I feel the rawness of that now, the hole within me opens up again and the crying at the back of my throat is about to come. I resent that.

It's Monday and I'm in Atlantic Village alone, writing and studying my Italian, thinking about the pointlessness of my existence. Oh and drinking crap coffee. Why don't they listen, double espresso with hot frothy milk on the side? I have here a small cappuccino, too much milk. It makes the whole experience poor. See crap and bollocks. I eat the chocolate from Getty's restaurant in my bag and it reminds me that the encounter with Jason was real. Oh, we went to lunch! Wow! There are so many people in my life, so why do I feel so alone? I have people to tell, but no one to tell. Maybe I should integrate more with those I have. I think about the school and about your cousins Bec and Imi. I received a present from them this morning.
I'm 45 today and no card from you. Complete sorrow. Will I ever get used to this living, pure hell? Also, of course, I'm pre-menstrual and tired. Cards adorn the kitchen table with lovely hand-picked flowers from the Morses. The ones from Grandma and George are hopeful for the year ahead. These could be cards for a teenager. For a daughter, but just a daughter, not a wife or a mother, no cards to testify to that.

Did they know you were His mother, down the line? Were you recognised? Did you wear the brow of the sorrowful? Did you enjoy wine with friends afterwards? Was it His wine? Did you overhear words spoken about the man who was crucified? Did some of your colleagues suggest you find a part-time job? Doesn't it sound ridiculous?

I'm so sick of the lectures about me finding voluntary work. I feel paralysed, unable to function in a way that's required, and yet considering what I've been through I challenge anyone to function this well. As Amy says, it's like being treated as a teenager whilst contending with a very adult deal.

Grandma wants to kill her doctor – metaphorically speaking, of course. I think it's because she expects more than she can have, and therefore feels failed. Whereas I expect less, and am overwhelmed. Yes, I'm overwhelmed, by people's kindness and their need to do things for me a lot of the time.

I feel like such a loser. I'm unable to do things. Maybe this is how it is. I smell your room as I go up the stairs and it terrifies me. I want Grandma but she's 85 and I'm no longer nine. It's six o'clock and I'm in bed. I remember when I went to bed early with you as a baby. Because you never slept, I often needed a head start. You were little then, I'm little now. I don't want to be in bed. It's too dark, it's too early and I am too awake. I'm scared without you and I don't want to go and sleep at six now.

It's punishment in the extreme. People talk about their daughters, and how they haven't seen them for a few weeks and how they miss them. They don't look at me in acknowledgement, can you believe it? They don't invite me to join in, and I wonder if I should, and as I wonder I get more and more worked up. Yes, I haven't seen Charlotte for 20 months, let me see now, is that over 80 weeks, yes, I think it is. Well, can't wait for the prom, she'll be back then from her round-the-world tour, or will she? … oo-er, incorrect answer, Charlotte won't be back, not soon, not ever, she's underneath the ground in Fremington cemetery and if I think of any more description I'll shudder.

Still no sign of you and I feel I have to work very hard at keeping you going, alone. And yet, didn't they make the best of you when you were here? It was Charlotte this, that and the other. They wanted you then, but now they've left, because there's nothing to have.

I feel I represent to some what is unpleasant. I seem to be a reminder of discomfort. They can't even spare that moment to enter into my world, the world that I carry so that they're spared, in this lottery life. They won't even do it for a moment, and they roll their eyeballs when they have to leave a pasty queue to say hello to me as if they're doing me a favour. I'm that necessary burden, or is it that grief is that necessary burden?

When you look down on me, what do you see? Are you very sad to see me suffer like this? Do you wish you could be closer to me? To look after me? It seems that somehow new life emerges, bit by bit as it would do if you were away studying, or in the Gaza Strip, reporting, or at Harvard studying law. But when I check myself, when I stop, and take stock, there you are, in your blazer, pockets crammed with cereal bar wrappers, walking towards me, expecting. I don't know what to do for you now. You see, I don't know how long to wait for you.

I wish I had one of your disciples to look after me. They are too young though, really. But we could share the love of you at least.

I really got wet today. I thought of you, there, with them, and I was sad. The wetter I allowed myself to get, the more I thought of you and cried inside.
And then I torment myself watching videos of you on my phone. Why? Is this the way, is there an alternative? When I see you in action, I can't believe what I've lost. You danced so beautifully, your trampolining was excellent and as for your gym, well, Grace is incredible like you now. Is there an alternative to the immense torture?

Was I supposed to bury you with one of your toys? If so, which one? The bear from Copenhagen, the magnet game I bought you for a quid that last Christmas.

It's the season of good will, upon us again. It's business as usual for most people as they can't possibly fathom out my predicament, and my God do they try. My daughter, that's you by the way, has died and my mother, that's Grandma, keeps asking me if I'm wearing a vest. And people are buying cheap wrapping paper, for cheaper presents.

The school sent me an envelope today, inviting me to the Christmas service. There was no mention of you, of my suffering or of anything relating to me, beyond being a parent, and I'm hardly that. It's so destructive. The way they seem to deal with this makes me very angry. Where's the humanity?

What happens when I'm old and have no daughter to bring me beautiful flowers in hospital?

I went to Burgh Island with my lover for my birthday, Charlotte. I decided that as I can die at any time I shall have a bit of fun first. Of course, Grandma mustn't know because she'd need to control it.

Christmas has appeared. It's December 2008. You know, the nothing is OK. When I am in it it's OK, when I know the parameters. But when I want something more, when I see that there's something else, that's when the unbearable begins. I feel I've lost my share and I'm begging for scraps from other people, which are not of the same calibre as what I had. Then, of course, I yearn for the second-rate because it's better than nothing.

I'll try Christmas out, if people will let me. Are you asking how they can make it different? Well, they just need to make it not so much like hard work. It's a look, of expecting misery. I'm supposed to be unhappy. But not so

116

much that I cause a problem. But I don't know where the line is, you see, I don't know where I'm supposed to sit so that others don't find me uncomfortable. It's everywhere. I have to join in if I'm living. The choices are limited and the struggle is the norm. I just don't want to be watched in it. It tires me.

I sit in The Plough, surrounded, of course, by Christmas cheer. Do you think I should get more of a life, Noods? You used to tell me that when you were here, can you imagine how it is now, without you? I'm at a table for four – deliberately, you remember the one for four? The times we met up with Grandma and you arranged the seating plan. It's different now Grandma doesn't come any more.

The Plough is contaminated by over-protective families. It's theirs, you know, the world of film, the world of dinners and lollipops. It belongs to them. And there's no concept of how the other four-fifths live. But for a certain sperm and egg, eh? Why are they so lost and out of touch, especially at Christmas?

I feel now that I'm in that 80 per cent of misery and I'm not allowed into the shiny zone. So, then, what of the spirit, what is it? Why don't they know this is not a time of luxury, of happiness? *Were you ushered away, Mary? Did they sanitise you? Were you given a cup of tea and told to shut up, that it'll be OK? Were you pathologised, discarded, not respected, and inconsequential?* There's no room for Christmas reality at The Plough, no room for Christmas reality in the West. Nobody must suffer, at any cost.

I'm in the bookshop. It's Saturday. I imagine you in your seat. I used to wonder what it would be like if you weren't there. If you'd got lost, died. Now you're not there, and I know. If I left and came back in, would you be sitting here reading? If I go to the chemist and I wish really hard, will you pretend to be here? Your bones are underneath the ground in Fremington cemetery. I swell up. A man says 'Excuse me.' I can't move. I can't talk. It's all detail again.

Am I wallowing? I want to tell the next invader to fuck off. They don't know, it's not their fault. In turmoil again.

It's 17 February 2009. A man in the pub last night asked me out. Sounds simple, doesn't it? Wait for it, he's your friend Katie's uncle. And worse, he has a daughter called Charlotte. She's your age.

Now, assume I date him, and we get on, things work. What do I do if I'm ever alone with Charlotte and then we bump into someone who doesn't know? How do I introduce her and what do I say? 'Not that Charlotte'? 'My Charlotte's dead, this is another Charlotte'? Then what if we bond, will I feel guilty? Will she feel second-best? What if her mother dies, will she be my Charlotte then? Do you see my problem? Oh God, is it always about you? Today I don't want that, I don't want to talk to people in car parks about my grief and if I'm working or not. I want to eat a lot of chocolate and see a film about a mouse.

We're at the Portrait Gallery and I'm trying, dark-haired girls not withstanding, to formulate new life. Yesterday I heard that Natasha Richardson died after a skiing accident. She was only on a nursery slope, but without a helmet. She was 45. Whose fault was it? I want to write to her mother, none other than Vanessa Redgrave. Liam, Natasha's husband, said that the family is cursed. I identify with that.

At the Portrait Gallery I look at Gerhard Richter's paintings of the Kennedys. I wonder, do some people who happen to love life seem more likely to die earlier than others, or get lost or hurt? *I immediately identify with the cursed and colour myself with that. What happened to our blessedness, Mary? What happened to us?*

Why have I left it so late to get to know you? I want to talk to you, find out about you, and understand you. Did I? Am I unrealistic? Do I just have more time now? Perhaps I'm distorting the past. I talk about you now where there's room, and even with the best there isn't often. You were so methodical, so studious, different-coloured pens for different bits of work. So much pleasure from your studies, what a waste, I look at some other children and I think, 'What a waste of space!' but who am I to say that, who are you to be such an example? And then I feel guilty for falling short of the person I've set out to be.

Did you realise who He was when He'd gone? Or did you always know? A carpenter, like His father, a boy, a man. Was He someone who never cleared up after Himself, who was so taken up in the task that He didn't stop to make you a cup of tea? Did you believe Him, in Him, in the Him you had? When He left, did you want to understand more? Was He suddenly so much bigger, so ephemeral?

I'm confused about a child dying before a parent. But maybe Charlotte's 15 years was it, the full term, the sentence. *Mary, where did they go?*

It's 26 March. I'm not doing it very well again, Charlotte. I've run out of something. I'm so tired, but can't rest. Agitated and tearful, but I can't find peace. I've been away and had an idyllic time, a semblance of new, but phoney.

My life is too huge for people to understand. They make me smaller, patronise me almost. Even the select few can't understand something they have never met and probably never will.

I keep dreaming about you and it's maddening me. Once again it's more torture. Andy Caros has suggested that litigation is possible, but Vanessa and Anna are at the school, so he can't lead the case – a conflict of interests. I'm foiled – stumped again. I feel alone in a fight now that's overwhelming. My life is turning into a bad American cop movie. In our society we let a good many things go because we haven't got the fight in us to oppose them. I fear being the enemy, the scapegoat, because I'm taking action now, but I have to do this, for you, for me and every child that's taken somewhere, without enough care or planning, and abandoned.

A week to Easter Sunday and the Friary can't take me. Jean is having a family meal. People everywhere are doing their thing. Gail's daughter is wondering what she's doing. They have eggs. They exchange Easter eggs. The eggs are individually sanctioned. No egg for me. No daughter, now no egg. I panic. I tie my dressing gown cord round my neck. Is this the way? I lie on the bedroom floor and Custard Cat comes.

There wasn't an egg for me. There's no comprehension of what Easter means – there were many eggs, all allocated. I was late. The simple sacrificial concept of giving one of the eggs to me, any egg, has escaped them. They seem not to be able to understand the bigger right. Why is this? What a waste of a good Western education, if love and sacrifice are not written into the curriculum. More treason from the vanilla classes, who seem to need it all, always. *They know not what they do.* They own the world or at least 80 per cent of it and they still 'know not what they do'.

As bed and breakfasts go, it was probably the worst. The view of St Ives bay from the upper window was beautiful, and the saving grace, but the food, oh my God! And the man didn't realise, you see, not self-aware. How do you do that to a tomato? And why make a smiley face for an adult using a luke-warm undercooked hash brown as a nose. Oh my God, Charlotte, I didn't finish it of course. I was called a fuss pot by my old work colleague, Lucy, who, by the way, is a small-portion-eating vegetarian. And actually small in stature. And she complained about her room! There, angry am I? I am with nearly every one, mainly at being misunderstood or undermined or forgotten. I have standards, and this cooking did not meet them.

Anyway, in search of joy or distraction I decide to indulge in a little new behaviour.

Have been a bit slapdash and somewhat intimate on the kitchen floor. To my surprise, in my teenage fusion, I looked into my garden and my neighbour was trimming the privet – my privet. So, locked in dance, we sidled past the table out of sight. Of course, I don't know what he saw or didn't see. And also, from now on, what any of his facial expressions might mean. But it's a story to tell the grandchildren, oh no, not in this case.

Amy reminds me that I've been dealt a bad hand, and the Morgans have a reasonable one. I play mine so well with an ace or two and allegedly a joker up my sleeve. The Morgans play theirs badly and seem to need much more help than I. They get angry when they don't receive it. Amy's advanced empathy can sometimes fuel me with an unmanageable amount of fury, as Morgan 1 and 2 seem unaware that when they whittle on about their difficulties, brought on by poor financial decisions, and put it heavily upon me, over and over again, it causes a reaction. They are in debt by a million and 600 thousand pounds because of their property overspends. That's a lot of penny chews, isn't it, Noods? They don't understand basic financial management which says that if you have more going out than you've got coming in, then you're in trouble. And yet they want my advice about their latest scheme, nearly called it scam. Well, can you imagine my reaction to the idea of the Morgans organising a home birthing pool for pregnant women in one of their two-up/two-down houses in Exeter? It's beyond belief, isn't it? Moyra fell off her chair laughing when I told her.

And, of course, the only problem I want to solve is you.

There's cleanness and purity to this suffering that rarefies its subject, me. It almost makes me a cut above, apart, better. It highlights what other people don't seem to be able to do. I'm a teacher now.

Sometimes I find solace in something unexpected. *Genova*, the film, was useful. Colin Firth played the dad of two sisters, the mum had died and they went to live in Genoa for a year. I wish immediately this was my life. I would then have escaped this pain, bit selfish eh? If we'd moved, far away, then you may not have died. Willa Howard played the older girl and could play you in the film about my book. I think of all the losses, the darkness and the emptiness that the film evokes. How can this mortal suffer so much? How do we survive falling apart when we shatter?

I seem to have a right/wrong radar. I immediately feel discomfort when something that's said doesn't fit.

Did you know that in 47 years on the Moor in the Ten Tors, this is the first fatality? Or should I say you, my Noods, are the first death. Oh well, that's all right then, why didn't you say that? *Hey, Mary, your boy was the first and only innocent man that was taken and pinned to a tree. Good, eh?* Well, as long as we're the first and only ones that suffer. It can only be acceptable.

More crap and detail and therefore pain, but only for me. We're doing the family in Italian. My daughter is dead, my beautiful daughter is dead. My husband is also dead. Yes, nine years before today. How do you say he hanged himself from the garage roof? It's pretty advanced vocabulary. And she died in a river. I actually know the word for rucksack now. Of course, while everyone else can talk about their family, there's no room for mine. I can't talk about them being dead or, in fact, alive because in an Italian class it burdens people, and God knows I don't want anyone to carry any weight like me.

I'm going through a new meaning of the word 'hell'. Litigation means proof, and proof means that even though you've died and my heart has been ripped out, I have to prove that I'm unable to concentrate and that I'm traumatised and don't function as well as I could. Did you know that you get more money if you watched your little girl die than if you were somewhere else? Or if it was immediate. Tell me how much you get for 12 hours of waiting by her bed, by her tubes, and for two months in a loony bin afterwards? Do I get an amount for the times every day that I see you in the dark-haired, olive- skinned beauties? There are two over there, right now. What about points for when I smell you when I sleep? Or in my nightmares, when you're running away and then found, and then my relief and then the reality, the despair? What about when I'm useless in violin practice, because I'm preoccupied or when I panic and freeze in the supermarket queue because I get overloaded when they ask me whether I want to pay by cash or card? Or when I stop at a junction in my car and am overwhelmed and a driver beeps behind me. What about the two years I've spent crying and the 50 more that I will cry. And the acupuncture, the pain of my own personal crucifixion: the feelings of despair that lead me to look over a cliff edge to see if it's high enough and then wonder how have I come to this? How much do you chalk up for that? I wonder. Articulate, but broken am I, Charlotte. It rains and I'm inside a tea shop. I'm 'happy' and satisfied, but any moment I can feel the torrent begin under my diaphragm and link with my throat and explode. I crave you. I long for you. I pine, I ache. I just want you to sit on the arm of the chair next to me so that I can smell you, feel you and dream of you. My sorrow is heartbreaking and I'm surprised that I'm alive again. Come back to me. I just want to hold you, my little girl.

Shebbear school children are off to *1646*, the Torrington exhibition. Do you remember when you dressed up in the garb and I dropped you off? We were late, but just this once. I did so well, was it too well? I see them going in from my car and my mind as always flashes back. I walk to The Plough.

Marc nods off in his junior Scrabble in The Plough. He rocks. In both senses of the word. I remember you rocking yourself and falling face down in your mashed potato. Were you always going to fall? You were a different person then, a little person, now you're big, but not near. It's funny that I get transported back to the various ages of you. I'd happily stick in any one time zone for things to be different.

I shouldn't have loved you so much, and then I wouldn't miss it. I went into your room. It's always for the first time. The cosiness of your bedtime, reading you stories: *Winnie the Pooh, Wind in the Willows, Alice, Aesop's*, they're all here, like me, pretending to be useful. Your CD player, Karvol, your water glass, the water has now long evaporated, lip marks still there, dust collecting, your silly putty pen in your stocking the last Christmas, your peacock feather earrings. Your longness, your beauty, your calmness, your smell. My longing, never goes, don't want it to go, agony.

Having you nowhere is hard, seeing you everywhere is necessary and takes every fibre of me.

I went to The Plough with Madeleine yesterday. Of course, foreign film night, Wednesday. Teenage girls were rehearsing in another room. Ponytails, dark hair, dance costumes, leotards, legs, dark colours, gum, shrill voices, laughing, running up and down. Are you there, I wait to see you, it's so familiar, you must be close. Where are you? Does Madeleine notice, does she know? I stare, I follow, and I'm on red alert. You are here, I know you're here. I'm getting closer, there, she's like you, and I can hear the sound, the rudeness, the high pitch, the pinkness, the seriousness of you. You're coming, I know you are. You're somewhere, I wait. I'm patient, they arrange tomorrow. They go. They return, they go again. Silence. Did I miss you? You are nowhere.

Having you nowhere is hard, searching for you everywhere is necessary.

This wall looked different before you died. Well, it's the same wall but my relationship with it is different. I feel distant from the wall. I'm not integrated with the wall. I look for you on the wall, maybe you touched it sometime.

Is this madness?

I remember when I hurt you. You smiled to win me over. A pure smile, I resisted. I'm so sorry, I regret, I hurt now, please forgive me. I see that smile, your innocence. How many hurt you. How many tried to slay you. *Mary, how many bore false witness. How many hurt after? Mary, what was it like after? Did they regret, feel remorse; come to you for absolution?*

I want to clone you. I could get your DNA from a used towel, or the car: your fingernails clicking, I remember what they looked like, the way you rubbed your nose, the way you were. I go to the bus stop, I catch the bus, the old familiar route. I just want something, anything, to be the same.

Seeing your name on a solicitor's letter with the words 'Ten Tor's death' or 'inquest' is really hard. What can you say to me to help me? I never thought when you were little and we were intact that this would be my life now. When you dressed with your long dark shiny hair, when you jumped about and darted, when you were vibrant, alive and shining, did I ever think of you under the ground in a place which is now covered in weeds and moss and broken flowers and letters, untended and a mess? I leak sorrow, but there's no way, or no one really, to mop it up, and I wonder what the point would be as it keeps seeping out anyway. Maybe just carrying it is enough, never mind the emotional incontinence. It is, after all, not me who can't cope with it. So I just go on.

Looks like I'm taking legal action against someone. I have a shit-hot solicitor, Charles, a good man who talks fast. He's very minimal and I wish he'd fill out his sentences. Now he's getting a shit-hot barrister and it looks like we're gonna kick ass and fight for you. There are so many legalities, so many bits and pieces to understand. It's so tiring on my own.

You know, you died before you had any secrets, or should I say, enough secrets. Although, of course, I don't really know that, because by their very nature secrets are, well, secret. I say this because right now I have a secret, I'm away from home. I'm at 'our hotel', our Flemings, just for a few hours, just to see.

It's surreal. I'm paying the price already. Oh God, I see you, especially here. It's you. You're coming towards me. Not you, useless hope.

Unbelievable: I've been propositioned. Now, if I told you this Noods, I know what you'd say: 'You think every one fancies you." Well I do, because in the main they do. So there. I wish we could go on talking like this. Anyway, I was having a gin and tonic at the bar, when I got chatting to a man. After telling him my story and our agreeing on the virtues of family – he has a wife and five children somewhere – he paid for my drink, which I believe was some 10 pounds, and promptly said, 'I hope you don't think me rude but would you like to come upstairs with me?' To which I replied, 'I hope you don't think me rude, but no!' Now there are so many factors to consider here. The first is, I went to 'our special hotel' in the first place because I wanted to be where we were together last, but that involved naively having and paying for my own gin and tonic. Secondly, isn't it wonderful to have a story to relate that I was in fact chatted up, by what was a rather charming young man. Thirdly, I found myself thinking that I'm so naive. How could I not know he was chatting me up? Do you think that if he'd bought me dinner, I might have joined

126

him – 'in our special place' – no, surely not. I'd never knowingly sleep with a married man. Not there or anywhere. How virtuous is that?!

Mary, were you propositioned after Jesus died. You must have been a beautiful, highly gifted and therefore sought-after Jewish woman. So, did sex, if encountered before, stop for you? Did you lose your libido? Did you wish for physical comfort with someone close to you? Did someone hold you? Two thousand years on, can we ever know what you, probably the most famous woman in the history of the world, did in the privacy of her own home, in the days and weeks after the agony. There was so much scandal involving you performing miracles and going to the tomb, and so much fear about your presence. Was there room at the time to add on what might have been thought of and still is, as sexual depravity, because most people think that when someone of the nature of Jesus or Charlotte dies, then the mother should weep and physical closeness and touch, something badly necessary as a release and a comfort and in fact distraction, are judged by the unknowing as bad. The middle classes need everything to be 'just so'.

Leaving *Mamma Mia!* I feel happy and sad, at the same time. Happy to be here but sad that you're not by my side, sharing. I recall how we left *Footloose*, all that time ago. I crave for the times when my feet could touch the ground, when I existed, when we were both alive and laughed, walking together.

On the underground I see a woman like Grandma, but she's black, and this is London. For a moment I'm confused as to who is dead, I miss Grandma, yet she's alive, albeit confused and in Devon, currently, but the times when she travelled on the Underground eating crisps are over. So that must be what I'm mourning. And also I'm no longer 14 and doing the same. Yet we're still here, she and I alive. It's as if the middle part of my life, the 20 years that I had you and

Johnny, never existed. That's the problem and the consequent head fuck. Again it's all in the detail.

No sooner am I back from London than I'm back there again with a friend to indulge in Patti Smith and a very casual moment encountering Jude Law in *Hamlet*. My life is anything but dull. *Is it the equivalent of all your surreality, Mary? Is this the speed at which people like us now have to operate? Do we sometimes have to get lost in the continuous overdosing of drug-like experiences to numb our reality?*

It's 21 June, Father's Day. Should I care? Do I give George something? You have no father. But you're not here, not having a father, so I don't have to be careful of your feelings. So it's one me and one father and nothing else.

I sit and prepare a strategy for our case against well them, whoever 'them' will be, and a time line. I'm giving this my best shot. I'm neat. I use a ruler. I take pride in my sheet of paper. And then Gail notices the incongruity. I'm working so hard for a reason that's gone. I live with so much paradox, detail and torture. It's like being so hungry and being given by your captors a meal you love covered in flies. If I wasn't somewhat ruthless, then I wouldn't go through this. If I wasn't capable of cutting off a dead person's thigh, so that I could eat it if I was starving, then I couldn't survive. Strict vegetarians are beginning to get on my nerves. Sorry.

I'm explosive. I've received the advanced disclosure documents from the coroner. I've discovered that my grace need not only cope with lack of ropes, bad practice, risk assessment not properly carried out, poor crisis management. A new fact has emerged. This is shocking, shocking, shocking, but I won't mention it, I don't want to have to handle a libel case on top of everything else.

Well, it all seems to be kicking off now. It's so stressful and I'm sure that you wouldn't wish for me to be suffering like this. And yet in a way I fear it all being over and having no it and no you.

Sometimes I feel like it's my duty and the right thing morally to bring in that teacher to account for himself, even if I have to drop the case. I feel like showing him how to face the music. But I don't. He is and was then an adult with responsibility.

I'm sick of re-inventing myself. The inquest has been postponed to probably December. That teacher is on holiday for three months. Also, there's not enough time to organise certain witnesses.

Your Yasmin is worried about being called as a witness. *Disciples fled and felt bad, Mary?* Your friends, Noods, are dispersed now and broken. She thinks that she'll be in trouble. I'm sad about this. Never has the responsibility left them. Some people surely have to face things now. They should have looked after you all better. I think Yasmin's testimony will show her that she's important for the first time. The most devastating changes in life have such an important role in our growth. I think I'd prefer to be small again, though.

I've closed your bank account, with the help of a good man, another solicitor. And this is how it begins. Sometimes life takes on its own course and you have to follow how things evolve whilst steering well. *Like Him in the garden, Mary, could this be a defining moment? He stood, didn't He, beckoning them, allowing it to happen. Not defending, not accusing.* The solicitor on the case wants me to know that I can take a charge, as he puts it, against the school and possibly the teachers. Well, how do I decide what to do? The moral and practical issues begin. It sounds complicated. I don't want to break them, but I feel reparation must in part, in some way, occur. The loss of you disables me so much – I can't find the motivation to work, or even to get up when I feel I want to. Justice and knowledge are so important in this sea of storms. Would some money also be handy?

What if I got lots of money and bought a brand-new car and drove it to the supermarket and bumped into the teachers with my acquisition, how would that be? Would I feel bad, guilty? This isn't about them or me, is it? What was your school isn't there. This is about the walk, a trip that went wrong, and you and me and a few other people. There's nothing personal here. I've decided on a middle course of reparation, not breakage.

My barrister is a proper person, imposing, generous and so, so sharp. He even has a great name, Michael Powers. Look him up, Noods. At last we have a team working for you. I'm relieved. It's as if I've waited, remained, worked, and I deserve this shot. It amazes me to feel like this. It's so pure and yet at times I can get carried away. You'll never guess who this is? He's the media commentator at the inquests into the deaths of Diana, Princess of Wales, and Dr David Kelly. I'm so unexpectedly excited, at the opportunity of meeting him – and, with him, Charles, who did the Napoli insurance claim. My word, such fitting guns, for the likes of you, Noods. I wish they could meet you and you them. Finally we're mixing with brains, compassion and ruthlessness, my favourite combination.

I want to say that, unabashed, Guy barges into my life, with unashamed vitality, like the traumatised guy said in *Fugitive Pieces*, and he does. So I'll say it. It's almost knowingly disrespectful and insensitive. It's not that I want people's lives to close down, but I want them to be aware of and take certain responsibility for the differences between us. It's an acknowledgement that probably requires a certain effort, a touch of the arm. I should know that he's thinking about my inner world at least some of the time. I carry the pain for you and you carry the responsibility for me, simple when you know how, isn't it? I really don't want his expectation thrust upon me, and then my failure to reach the dizzy heights of vacuous happiness noted. I want sorrow and difference to be OK. I want pain to be what we seek to share, because it has to be, and joy hereafter. No, my goodness, I've just worked it out. It's about shame. He's making me feel ashamed of my loss. My loss is dirty. He is society's representative of 'pseudo-perfection'. And yet my vulnerability is necessary. It's a good thing.

There are no short cuts to that thing you seek that's missing, illumination, my friend. And this is probably why there's such jealousy towards me. I'm doing the work, to transfigure the darkness, I've found what's missing, and I'm beginning to embrace it with a kind of freedom and grace. I am the suffering that makes happiness contemptible. And then there's the guilt.

But paradoxically there's a part of me that loves that any irresponsible, transparent vitality, because it reminds me of you, and it's you I seek. With all his faults, Guy's vibrancy is pure and childlike and he shows a sense of hope that I never thought I'd experience again, a joy of discovery. Sometimes I see little boys on scooters racing as if for the first time and I'm excited. The swimming pool in the park is clearer, the sun warmer and my raspberry ice lolly tastes like heaven. He's like you without being like you, and I revel in the qualities which propel me from being face-down in the dust which I taste at the back of my tongue and makes me reach, as my nose pours over the stench, to the light, the glorious light. He lives life to the full. He enjoys to the full and wants everything and works hard to keep it and to give well too. For all these reasons he must not be barred, but he must, like you, my sweet girl, be celebrated, for to be all things is a rarity, an art form. To pass it on without losing it yourself is a wonder.

Is my task now to live well? And to begin the process of recovery, which includes stopping blaming others for not knowing my pain, not feeling it and not seeing it, enough?

However, it's so tricky, for I no longer have a firm answer to the question, 'Do you have a daughter?'

Oh look, I've met another expert. Another person who doesn't get the hang of the fact that I'm more than I was, not less, for I'm navigating a serious crisis, a rescue if you like, a big job, and I have to be super-big to do it. Got it, good, so what were you going to say?

Oh God, Mary, did they say 'poor Mary', or 'fucking amazing ponderous Mary'? Hey, that's apparently an oxymoron, 'cause to amaze is the opposite of to ponder, according to one bloke on the radio. I digress, see how easily distracted I am? Well, anyway I met this expert, Helia. She welcomed me into her home with my friend Jean and then got power-hungry or rescue-conscious. Then we were all invited to a party, or to be precise a third anniversary of a civil partnership of two women, two lovely women, it was just one of the guests who was crap: Helia. However, I was trying to be separate from you, the incident, just for a bit, you know, lead a bit of a parallel life. So I pressed on and tried to ignore her. Well, she began: 'You must hate people for having live children' – oh! – 'when yours is dead! ... You must be so angry.' And then, just in case it isn't clear to me: 'Because we each have two live children, whilst you have a dead one.' Then, having highlighted my disease, she then began her advice on recovery. 'Little steps, little steps,' Jean agreed. All it needs is for an idiot to say something idiotic and then for a second, more respected idiot to agree. Jean didn't defend or comfort me. I'm appalled at the comparative reference to the live children and the lack of compassion, Charlotte. Although I discovered when I met Helia's entire family that I'd rather have a dead one of you than ten alive ones of hers. What's that about? Well, are her children are visibly hating her? What a shame, little steps, I'm so glad that my dead child loved me. How low can I go, eh?

Oh, as for little steps, quite right. Now comes the one-upmanship, the how- more-is-she-and-how-less-am-I moment that I've been waiting for. Helia again: 'My daughter Ruth nearly died, you know, but I'm good in a crisis, some of us are just better in a crisis than others.' Now let's unravel this megalomania, shall we? Just in case I've got it all wrong. Let's for a moment ignore my instincts of injustice, and work out if there can be any possibility of taking this well. No!

I think, well, my hypothesis is that she's so overwhelmed by this that she has to talk herself through it, but loudly. She immediately comes to the bit she can't cope with, and distorts it, making sure that it's known that I can't cope either. She then does the only thing that makes her feel good, which is a rescue attempt, which she believes is successful.

Keep graceful, keep graceful.

Mary, did you investigate the trial at all? Was there any means of retribution? Did you want to fight after the dust had settled? Were you so traumatised and confused? Was there anyone on your side? Like I have Michael and Charles and Mark, a junior. They've fallen from the skies, how about that then, eh?

Was the injustice of the lack of a hearing and so little officialdom so deep-rooted that complaint was futile, if not impossible? The Jewish people, His own, the Sanhedrin, the high priest and Pilate himself went along with one of the greatest miscarriages of justice in legal history. What could one woman do? The curiosity for me is in what lies beyond this, Mary, what only you seemed to know. If you knew that He had to die, was it then acceptable? Was the prophecy of history and dream fulfilled, His still body in your arms, part of your growing place in a story that was written. As for the baying crowd and the corruption, were these things catalysts, like the rucksack, the stone, the swollen river and the oh-so-freezing cold?

Jesus said to his friends: 'We are going up to Jerusalem, and the Son of Man will be betrayed to the chief priests and the teachers of the law. They will condemn Him to death and will turn Him over to the Gentiles to be mocked and flogged and crucified.' (Matthew 20.18–19)

Charlotte said to her friends: 'How would you prefer to die, by fire or by water?'

And it all seemed to happen in a frenzy. One minute they were eating, then the question Pilate would sanction, and then let's arrest Jesus quickly to avert delay. No one knew the charge. They seemed to work from the desire for death backwards.

Children were alone, freezing, soaking, hypothermic, with blue fingers, and they couldn't see their way through, and one died, my one. She died because she was the strongest. She died for the others, so that they might be saved.

I'm now het up in anticipation. And what's happening now is that I'm finding things very difficult, and when people even slightly annoy me I react badly, especially when I put them centre-stage and expect more from them. The trouble with feeling explosive is then they condemn and punish me, and the cycle continues. There's little unconditional love here. I'm tortured and then tortured again whilst this is happening. People are cross with me for having this, the best and biggest crisis. They can't do it, wouldn't be able to do it, so they are jealous of me, of my capacity and indeed the way in which I'm trying to spin straw into gold.

Look, I'm creating my own genre of widows with dead only children, and the extraordinary grief and detail that go with that. There's a woman in Scotland, Mary and me so far. Grand. *And, Mary, you are disputable because it's thought in some circles that you may have had other children after Jesus. Well, Trevor thinks this, and we know how much of an authority he is at times.*

I'm on the beach surfing – well, lying on a long flat thing intermittently. I brought little Marc back to the car. He wouldn't have made it if I hadn't been there. It would have been too hard, and he too tired, but I jollied him along, distracting him out of his exhaustion. That's what you should have had, you, Yaz, Zoe and the rest, as my barrister says: biscuit sharing and egging on to the next post.

By the way, I borrowed your wet suit – it fits me like a glove – and your sports bag and your lunch box. Is that OK? I understand why you bought the wet suit now, but the legs could have been longer. My little white legs were cold. You looked better in it than me. After the swim I walked around the Ho! Where we used to go. Yaz was working at the bakery. She's coming round tomorrow. How brave is she? I tidied your room so that she could go in there.

Yaz parks her car, she's a grown up girl now. I greet her outside so that it's easy. She looks tired, like the world is upon her shoulders. Her smile is with a cry. She's doing it, she's here – she's come to us, Charlie. We have some tea and cake, or it might have been juice, it's funny but I so wanted it to be good for her that I can't remember the little details. We sit in the kitchen. She goes to your room. I leave her there for a bit. I wonder. When I go in, she cries. She asks what everyone asks. 'How do you do it?' Just 'How do you do it?' A single tear falls, it seems hot, and I want to hold her forever to make her pain go. She looks at things, and more things. She's afraid of touching, like it's a church, she says she doesn't want to take anything from me. I give her your toy and a sports top and she holds them tight, as tight as she'd hold you if you were here now.

I bought new jeans. The first ones since you left. These jeans won't walk by you. They won't be seen by your eyes.

'Oh Jenny, it's your choice, you can think about something else, no one forces you to think about this all the time, why don't you get a job, or do some voluntary work, take your mind off it?' What a good idea, and then at the end of the day, more work, get drunk, reclining on a park bench or perhaps I shall come round to your house and eat ... no, didn't think so.

'Well, if I were you ...'

'You know what, I'll help you be me. I'll come round to yours, hang your husband in the garage, drown your children and then you can tell me what you'll do tomorrow. OK? Until then, shut ... fucking ... up!'

'Jenny, why do you have to be so dramatic?'

I'm angry. I want everyone to know my pain. I want all to be humbled by it. I want everyone who's close to me to sacrifice a lot, to be as close to me as they can be. Don't get me wrong, I don't want them to be Abraham and sacrifice their children, I'm not nuts. I just want them to risk a lesser or actually what I think is a richer experience, perhaps less sanitised, perfect and Western, to include what's difficult for them, me.

It seems that everyone has at least one daughter more than me. Everyone in the country has a daughter, daughter, daughter, and daughter.

I'm angry with that teacher for having breakfast with the rest of them, whilst Yasmin's hands were turning blue and freezing. Oh Charlotte, why are you still not back, please talk to me, advise me, you were so sensible.

George has macular degeneration disorder on top of prostate cancer and emphysema. Does this mean that the people who never run out of cling film or light bulbs are leaving?

As things stabilise, I have time to think. I worry about the conclusion of the inquest for us all and I worry about the

136

journey towards it. Will we forget the details? Will the things people say be reliable?

Two women were talking about you in the supermarket, they didn't know me, they were looking at your picture in the paper, and it was so surreal.

Oh Mary, did you hear them talk about Him after it had happened. Did you overhear talk of the man on the cross, the bloke that was crucified. 'Jesus something, he was from Nazareth, wasn't he?'

When they were talking about her, you know, they called her 'the girl who died on Dartmoor'. You know I'm trying to make the best of it. I have it, so I use it: it's the lemons, lemonade story. And yet when I tell certain people that I'm going to give talks on grief, interviews and so on, they say that I'll be tied to the grief forever. A funny feeling of nauseating irritation comes over me then and I have to be careful not to rant and rave. How stupid and narrow-minded. Do these people think that if I decide to do something else, then Charlotte won't have died, in fact she will have returned as if by magic and my life will automatically be grief-free? I cannot choose not to have this. I do have it. But I can choose a life parallel to it and in spite of it. This is, after all, not a state of mind. It's real.

Please don't condemn me, everyone, for doing it at all and doing it my way, when you aren't an expert and are so far away from having to make such a choice. Maybe you're angry that I'm more than you, again, people.

If I want to hug you, Noods, I'll have to dig and I can't imagine what that would be like, it sickens and terrifies me. Sometimes the urge to hold you makes me want to find anyone who looks like you, and yet I know this is futile. Even now I cry underneath my diaphragm. The searching and the longing continue, day in, day out.

Are you Ophelia? I think you must be. You lay in the cold water and just let it take you. I'm wrong to romanticise that, but if I think too carefully, then I see you as not fighting, not able to fight, exhausted, maybe with hypothermia, and losing the life you had. That hurts. I can't do that.

When people let themselves rudely into my world, I really feel I want to reciprocate. 'How does it feel when your husband is inside you? Are you sure? Or maybe you're in denial or you need me to come and have a look at your positioning, and the fact that there's no room whatsoever for improvement. Because you know that there's the very likelihood of you doing it wrong, oh and by the way … are you sure that you orgasm? Maybe it's something else! Perhaps you're confusing it with a twitch.'

There seem to be two ways of living with this, or three if you combine the other two. One is sitting in the nothing; the other is having something to look forward to more than I've lost. Now, that's a funny one, I don't mean that there can be anything more than you, or that anything at all can outweigh the tormenting pain and sorrow, but there can be temporary solace.

This apparently is called 'moving on', I say 'apparently', because the people who largely use the phrase with a hint of pseudo-emotional intelligence never seem to know what it means when interrogated, and why should I agree with them, Charlotte, you wouldn't have, *and Mary you fought the priests, didn't you?* They measure, they don't know, but they can judge, and advise, it's amazing, on this basis I'm going to advise a crew of the next round-the-world yacht race how to sail even though I haven't even got a day skipper certificate, and I've hardly been out on a boat, but why on Earth should that stop me? I can tell them what to do with masts and sails and how to eat carbohydrates. I know everything.

Sometimes I feel I have to put so much effort to get people to like and trust me, it perpetuates my assumption that I'm 'less rather than more'. And I have to prove myself. I feel I represent, half the time, what's amazing to them, because I've survived this far, but the other half the time they can't believe it's possible, so it can't be real, so they don't trust it, or me and it, and I become unsafe. So I cannot come to the ball. And ironically I don't want to go anyway, because their ball won't interest me. But it still hurts. Why can't they see? Is it because if they acknowledge me as more, they are automatically less ... oh my goodness, that's it, they will be less, so it's only the 'more thans' already who can cope with me. It makes me angry. I feel so superior and I want to say, 'Look, take a risk and let me in, you fool, don't be without this amazing person in your life, if you're too afraid and untrusting, let me explain it to you.' There are so many middle-class vanillas who fear the crisis that's already happened. You know, Charlotte, I have to prove myself to take part in lesser activities with lesser, quite emotionally retarded people, when all I want is you. *After being mum to the Son of God, did you, Mary, have to put up with pseudo-emotional intelligence?* Why are you people not significantly humbled by it and me, why are you such arrogant experts?

Amy calls it 'hygienic hardship', the way in which those not in touch sanitise my grief. It's all in the way they say 'ah.' As if I need a plaster for a cut finger.

Huge step, Noods, an invitation to go shopping with Helen, your Grace and one other, you won't guess, you never met, but she feels that she knows you, how great and how adult is that? Now you're wondering if I'm the arrogant one who has to have attention, but I'm not, I just want my dues, I just want recognition of you and your existence. It's hard without it, you know.

Well, here's a lesson, sometimes the hardest thing to anticipate can offer us the most. I was terrified to go with

139

another girl taking your place so close to Grace and having fun. I couldn't foresee making this right. But it was so right. Firstly, Millie is so like you and she referred to you immediately. She's unafraid. I was overawed. She seemed humbled by me and it, and I loved her for it. We stopped for coffee and cake, of course, pretty immediately. And within moments we had that conversation, everyone except me cried. It felt like you were there within us all, but you were there specifically in Millie, she was you and you her, not in a bad way, but in a positive good way.

Father, forgive them for they know not ... Did you Mary, did you as mother forgive, mothers have to forgive, yes, we have to be soft, yes, bending, acquiescing.

I knew it would be upsetting. I saw Hagrid first, Robbie Coltrane, he was at the station, and then I felt you beside me and the lump came in my throat. Gen, the tall one, was sitting on the left of me and was you for a moment. Then Hermione Granger came onto the screen and Ron, and Harry is grown up, and Ginny reminds me of you, her hair especially, and now there's the familiar music and you are here, and now I'm crying completely and sobbing, and sobbing a lot. Tall Gen notices. We drink our wine and she eats carrot cake, no popcorn or slush puppy today. She smells different from you anyway. And once again the moment goes. I even grieve for the moment.

Even now they come with tickets, the first-class avoidance, second-class morbid curiosity and their sledgehammer presence. I have to hear them say their piece and it's boring to me, repetitive and boring, because they don't know, but feel they do, and I'm too intelligent for it all and have little time now.

You know, pain is my friend. Don't worry about it or try to understand. Please don't expect me to explain and then put me right. Now, that would be a real put- down.

It's September 2009 and your last year at school begins. But here I am, I haven't even got up in time for assembly. I'm disappointed and angry and abandoned. In the end I feel betrayed by everyone. *Once again, Mary, how did you feel after the event about Judas and Peter? Did you see them afterwards, bump into them? Perhaps Judas killed himself too soon for that, but Peter, what of him? Did you see him? Did he look away in shame? Did he hide? Did you adopt safety behaviour, like me? Because I scan places before I enter, in case I encounter representatives of pain. Of course sometimes I don't enter at all.*

To be holy is to go forward without significance, stained, suspect and without reputation or explanation. I come to you. Do we go forward quietly?

Did Jesus mind dying? Was it necessary, on the basis of no alternative? Is it the case that sometimes choices are made, not based on what we want, but on what we definitely can't accept? A sort of what-else-is-there? Do some of us begin upon a road that must be travelled?

Was there just no place for you, Charlotte? Were you extraordinary? Did you have to be quiet or die? *Do you think that Jesus wanted crucifixion? Did He want to be somewhere else?* Did you, Charlotte? Do I? Do we sometimes want to pass over to what we consider another place? Do we all become extraordinary when we have to? Or do only some of us rise to the challenge? And then what? Now I'm a saint, is this how it's going to be for another 10 years, me at night in my chair with a cat and chamomile tea, still waiting. If I think enough, I could sink into all the 'isn'ts', like I never got to see you become a beautiful woman and enjoying it, and now it's over. And truthfully I have nothing, and no amount of money, or chocolate (because that's what money buys), will do. No wonder the only way forward for people like me is to produce something extraordinary for people who might otherwise not take part.

I never knew with you, Noods, that I was once in the presence of something great. *Did you, Mary? Did you know who He was, did you have any idea who the baby you carried was going to be, did you foresee at your tender age that this would be Christianity today?* Mind you, people never can see things until it's too late. Did I know that you'd become a bronze statue in the grounds of the school for all to see? A reminder of what's good? A permanent reminder of what is transient: youth, beauty, life, connection.

It's huge news to me that I'll never see you again. I thought that after the inquest you'd be back. I had a sense, you see, that if I put in such effort I'd be rewarded, by your return. But no, there'll be nothing, the same nothing. Should I just go and die quietly? No, you wouldn't want that for me. 'What would Charlotte want, Jenny?' Who cares, really, who cares? Why do I always have to do stuff for other people? Why can't I set everyone up and go somewhere quiet when they've forgotten. They won't forget, will they? That's the thing. I'll know your people for the rest of my life.

A lover might say that they can't live without the loved one. And yet they know they're alive. They can glimpse them over there at a film, or passing in their car. I don't have that. I'm poles apart from them. I'd give anything just to see you for half an hour, from behind a curtain. Even without you knowing me or seeing me, just once, I'm begging, just let me see what's like, just let me have it once, please. You know, sometimes I think I'm going to break, to snap in half, or shatter. I've reinvented myself so many times now that there's no substance left with which to work. I'm nothing, I fear and embrace that. Yet I know that to have you back means that you'd have to die all over again. It would be selfish to even think about this happening to you, and what if it was within my lifetime all over again. If I'm careful and don't get too close to you, then I can do it. Or I can pretend that you're just over there, and I'm separate from you for a bit longer. But then you come back, your face is familiar but I can't find you. I don't know you any more.

I saw a film that echoed my little world and its complexities. *I've Loved You So Long,* it was called. Kristin Scott Thomas played the lead. She was ethereal, knowing and patronised, just like me. Nobody can see the continuous fight. 'But Jenny, you don't have to have this, it's all about choice.' 'Fuck off, idiot.'

I'm under it again, buying wholemeal rolls when I know you like white. Should I get you a gingerbread man? What colour buttons? Must hurry. You'll be back soon. No, nothing for Charlotte, not today and not tomorrow. I don't need to feed Charlotte any more.

Custard is so big now, do you remember when she was such a little kitten? You told me she has a small mouth and I must chop her food into smaller pieces. She still has that small mouth, and she isn't a big cat, but she seems to come across as a bruiser, all feisty and fluffy and a bit ginger. I want you to see her. I want to show you how well I've looked after these cats. I want you to look at me and feel proud.

When the school calls me, I get anxious and hopeful. I think I'm going to find you there. You're not here, so you must be there, right? All the uniforms, the friends, the stomping ground, and then of course there's the emptiness, obviously. Am I stupid, looking for you, constantly looking? And you, you're somewhere, not found. But there, you're there. Then what do I wear to be at another expectation of you. Will I be on time? In fact, will I score more points if I go early, in a nice outfit, and how many points do I need to get you back? Perhaps you're not coming. When I really get emotional, I feel that Julie is right, Johnny has stolen you back and maybe in eight years I'll be allowed to see you again. Because, you see, I think maybe we can each have you for eight years at a time. And I've had mine. You'll be 22, that'll be OK. Won't have missed much. Oh God, what am I contracting to. Is it second-best? Wouldn't it be a hope? It isn't going to happen. I'm never ever going to see you again. That's the reality.

I'm so up against it. Even the people I know and like get it wrong. 'I went to the unveiling of Charlotte's memorial statue today.' 'It was painful,' I say. 'Why did you go? You shouldn't have gone, if you knew that it would be painful.' 'Would it have been less so if I hadn't?', I reply.

Charlotte's not in her room, Crumble, she's dead. *'Hey Mary, how's ya boy, still preaching that funny stuff?' 'No, they crucified him last week.' 'Oh shit, I've put my foot in it. Oh well, no words. I'll call you. You still in the same shack? Good. Working? No, oh well, you've got young John. I'll call you. We'll have bitter mint tea at the café soon.'*

I find new things. In your school bag is a silky rose-coloured bag of sanitary towels. Very organised. There are spare knickers and, here, a used towel. I'm tempted to unwrap it. People would find that strange and dirty. But if I could feel your skin and hair next to me now, smell you, know that you move about me, I wouldn't be contemplating this. I cry. I cry for who I am now. I hear the neighbours laughing next door and I cry more. I put the towel back. It can still be there, dirty tomorrow, next week, and still after that. Your room is bright and full of your bounce. But it begins to feel out of time. You're starting to be too old for this colourful place now. Do I face a big change? You're a big girl now, do you still need the games and stick-on tattoos and counters and soft toys? Should I let them go? Should I let you go too, then? If so, what's left for me to hold?

I bumped into the Graham twins in Atlantic Village. One is happy to see me. The other isn't. Her face falls. She looks almost irritated at the intrusion of this sense of death and memory of life into her world. She puts up with it, it's not my fault, she knows that. She looks angrier now at having complicated thoughts. I suddenly feel a sense of bitterness. We make pleasant conversation. I've no idea why we bothered. I roll the dice so many times, still no you, never you.

I had a dream last night, you looked straight at me. I asked if you knew me and you said that you belonged to me once. I want you, this is crucifying me. I feel like I hang in slow pain. Unable to speed it up, unable to undo it. *It's a humiliating death, Mary. Do you want to know that? People look at me. They can see it, but they're not sure what they see.* They smell strength and fear and it confuses them, for they don't know yet that you can show both. I'm a spectacle and yet I'm perfect. I'm death and the personification of life, because of death. And all that's good. I'm discomfort.

I lit the fire and Johnny was in the other room and you were little. I felt secure and excited.

I made some soup. Is it me or you who's ill? Do you want some tomato soup? The soup is yours, the bowl is yours. The closeness comforts. I read nonsense. Did you know that for three pounds a month you could adopt a polar bear, remove a cataract, or have two coffees in Atlantic Village? I flit, I'm distracted. I'm mad.

Well, I've just been out for a very bad dinner: the food and the company both. And a very 'religious, loud ladette tried to tell me that what I'm doing is unhealthy. Of course, she'd know. She says that keeping your friends in the loop and associating with them is wrong. What an expert! My internal heating system is on 'explode', and I shift about in my seat. Why don't I just say, 'Oh, you're an expert, are you?' How is it that people can wound me with such misunderstanding, and yet I'm unable to retort, for fear of upsetting them and putting them in their place?

Susan is hosting a New Year's party. I dread it. Lots of professionals are there. The middle classes, with their own rules, out for the night. They lack emotional intelligence and are guilty of doing everything right, for the wrong reasons. Don't some call that treason? I'm the one everyone wants to see. I'm that minor celebrity in their world. The woman who has lost, who lives the nightmare they can't even begin to fathom. I'm the Victorian plaything, amusement for all. I'm the virtual life they can tap into, the CD-ROM of sorrow, to play when they want that fix. I'm popular. They all want to be seen as my friend, even the ones who never gave me the time of day before, they want that accolade. It's set to get worse.

Put the Indian between your feet, Charlotte. Hold it upright, Charlotte, or it will leak. Oh no, no you. Just food: meal for one. It's not leaking: it's steady in a bag on the floor, no legs, and no legs to keep it steady, no body, where are your legs and where is the body of Charlotte? There's no passenger today, or tomorrow, only a bag on the floor. I like Indian food.

I saw you on Johnny's shoulders. I stared.

It's 16 Jan, 22 months and a bit. I'm going for a walk round the village. I'm on my own, What's new? I want to clear my head. I pass the man and the little girl. I go up the road to where your bus comes. It's nearly bus time. I drift back. I meet you, I carry your bag. Life is different. All the other people didn't exist then, just you and me and cats and the world. You talk. You're lively. You're alive. I can feel your grace, the breeze in your hair, the rain falls. I want to go to a neighbour for a cup of tea. But the sympathy will be useless, it will help me through a moment, when I'm not sure I want to take away that pain, and afterwards nothing will change. So I save time. I go home because that's where I'll end up anyway. So, lesson learnt. Then I want to lie on the side of the road or stand in the middle of the darkness.

I feel deranged – too much talk by the Morgans about the impending inquest. And whether I should take legal action against the school. It will cost. It will cost grace and something else. I can't work it out. I put it aside. The inquest will come, things will work out. I mustn't get caught up in the media, money, projects and limelight, just the fight for justice for you.

Was crucifixion the right punishment for truth, Mary? Once again, Mary, did you want to fight? Did you want to fight? Whatever that means.

I will just write and coffee – that should be a verb. I coffee, you coffee, we all coffee.

Relationship a bit vacant as well, so I feel lost and apart. Oh Charlotte, please hold me. I need your sense to get me through. I'm always alone even with other people, especially with other people. I'm on my way back from the theatre with Eileen and Richard now, Peter couldn't go. I look out at the black night.

It's February now and Crumble is in the snow for the first time ever. He regards it with gentle suspicion. The sweetness of the scene makes me look back.

You said when Johnny died that you'd give everything up just to spend a week with him. Would I do that now to have you back and then have to let you go forever? What an interesting question, and yet one that isn't really viable, and therefore I shouldn't torment myself.

What really happened on that trip, Charlotte? The newspapers have printed some incorrect nonsense, hearsay, not accurate. You didn't drop your kit in the water. You dropped Yasmin's. The question is, why were you carrying it, and yours, and who told you to do that? And how did you get in that position?

Why didn't He run far away, why didn't He deny who He was? Do you wonder, Mary? Do you blame Him for your suffering, even a tiny bit? Do I blame you at all, for not thinking of me? No, not this time. I don't blame you, not one bit.

I look back two years and I remember what you were doing then. You were ill. It's 12 February tomorrow and two years ago you came back from a school trip to Madrid and you were ill. I look back now to what you were doing then. Where are you now and why didn't you take your precious stuff with you?

Is it true you predicted your own death in the tent, the night before? Yaz said you brought up the choice of dying by fire or water. You know, your friends gave video evidence to the police about your last moments and the rest of the trip. They must be like the gospels. They're the telling the story.

It's a week away from two years. Sophie hurts. She rang me. I hurt. I wait, still. The inquest is coming, overriding next week. I'm terrified. I tell myself there'll be nothing new. But there'll be a certain amount of end and I don't know if I want end, because then I have to have to find new, and like it, and like it without you, and people won't see, and they'll call me 'misery', and I won't think that's fair. I need the door to be open. I feel depressed. I can't go back and I can't go forward. I want you. I feel alone and untethered, unwanted, discarded. Where are you, beautiful Charlotte? The pain never changes. Sophie said it. It never goes away. When will it go? Either come back or go, for God's sake. No, I don't want you to go. Don't ever leave me.

You wrote a diary for me. You got these cats for me. You told me not to worry. You said once that if other mothers lose their children, their pain will be the same as mine. Do you remember when I was worried about you in Madrid?

But I feel like I'm the only one in this pain. And I'm worried.

The inquest will take place within the next few months. It seems like it's going to be massive. Many days, a jury.

Sometimes it's very hard to keep my huge anger in check. I feel it's going to explode inappropriately. Your death has been undermined in the newspapers, in the reports of the Ten Tors, this year. Neither the reporter nor the reported speak of you. You do not exist. And yet you do. You are in the mention of the few accidents this year. You are in the reference to the weather changing. You are in the word 'heroes' that describes the participants. You are in the pleasure it was, for the Brigadier Stephen Hodder to organise. You are in that article for me. You scream out. You are the word that now cannot be spoken for fear of reprisal. You are the past that broke, not the pseudo-successful present. And yet we all sleep with the taste of this in our mouth. We all must share in the hardship of this loss. There is no other. We all have lost. We are all grief-stricken. In the same way that we are all beggars because somebody is.

Why did I bother with all those wishes? Candles and eyelashes, the same wish over and over, it hasn't happened. I'm not living happily ever after with you. Maybe the wish should have been smaller or not repetitive.

They've got it wrong again. Or have they? I try to look at it from both sides. I'm invited to the annual gym prize giving to give out the prizes. It's funny, I always have the discipline to arrive on time, pace my day, eat well before, but them, well, they begin late, there's no explanation as to what's going to happen. Nothing to put me at my ease. And then the worst, I'm introduced as Jenny Shaw, a long-time supporter of the club. Is that really why I'm there? Nothing to do with the fact that I'm your mother. The mother of the recently deceased Charlotte Shaw who was the best dancer and one of the best gymnasts. I am she.

The other way of looking at it is, of course, that they 'ummed and ahed' about how they'd introduce me. And really everyone who knows, knows the circumstances, and everyone who doesn't will ask, or not care that they don't know. But still, why didn't they ask me?

I saw the video of you and it hits me. I long and long for you, until I feel the pain ripping me to shreds. I can almost taste the blood from my broken body. It's so untimely to cry all the time. It gets in the way and I'm sure if I keep presenting this, people will say 'Oh, what now?'

Well, you are famous. Everyone's heard of you and I looked you up on the internet, nearly two years on. There is George Bernard's 'Charlotte' and there's you, the 'shining light'. Hey, you're like the Light of the World, wow, or is that me now? It's well, good. There are tributes galore to you. Finally, in the freezing cold –and let's not underestimate the shock value – I managed to face a tiny bit of the many tributes to you, by people I've never heard of, most of whom think that you had two parents and also are unsure about what happened on the Moor and are therefore a little inaccurate – more detail which means everything to me.

You know my friend Morse? Well, she and Chris are still going strong. Well, not so strong at the mo', 'cause the bottom has fallen out of the holiday let market and they've stretched themselves too thin, so they're in dire straits. I took them out for coffee this morning, on my way back from a tryst south of the river. I can see that you're more interested in the tryst then the Morses. However, Morse, still a large woman, has decided on meeting two chaps from Pakistan, who may buy the business. Now she wants a change of career and is going to become a hostage negotiator. She'll call herself 008 and a half, on account of her largeness. She jests and recalls her connections to MI5, when Chris went missing two years ago. And speaks of her 'man on the ground'! I told her to have some of the pumpkin cake. She said it was too fattening and then ate three-quarters of it. She commented on the fact that I never put on weight even though I eat the same as her and proceeded with her extra large cappuccino, double froth, with a smile. Chris saw the irony, whilst I had my little espresso in what, comparatively, looked like a doll's tea cup. They are lovely, and have been so supportive, with so little, but is anybody realistic?

I need you to share a loaf of white bread with me. It's too much for one. I never realised how many things we liked that other people in my world now don't care for. I'm shopping at supermarket again. I go on Mondays at about two o'clock to miss anyone who might know me. It takes 25 minutes. Of course, I saw one person, but only when I was returning the trolley. It was D.L. Now, on our last two encounters she'd seemed to look at me with irritation, which I fantasised was because of my intrusion into school functions like a dirty smell making them confront what they chose to forget. It made me angrier with the school, which was responsible for you in the first place. And made me almost want to acknowledge this. But today she was pleasant and free, as we spoke in the car park about the merger of the schools, and potential job losses. Oh you don't know, do you? Your school and the Grenville school people, including some not so kind like Harry, are merging, what bad luck for someone. Oh and Harry might be pregnant. Well, for now. According to a gossip. She lives in London with her boyfriend. Let's hope she doesn't call the baby Charlotte. And if she does, that she treats it better than she treated you. So many changes, eh?

I forgot, I saw Yaz and Rebecca A yesterday too. They were shopping in Morrison's. As I said, I only go at two in the afternoon on a Monday because I feel least likely then to bump into relevant persons. But there they were. And guess what, only a small amount of discomfort. They actually wanted to talk to me. They needed me. For 45 minutes they talked about the trip and that teacher and the scout and your last moments, and how when you drifted away you didn't protest at all. You know who you remind me of, him on the cross again, not protesting, not one bit. All this was yet more highly emotive news for me.

Of course, the following night I dreamt about you. In an orange swimming costume you were in the swimming pool. But I wasn't paying enough attention to you. Instead upon my lap was a smaller child who was taking up all of my energy. The previous night I dreamt of you also. This time you were younger, about six or seven. You were missing. People were hunting for you. I was uncomfortable. Finally, two police, one of whom was a woman, came to say that they'd found you sleeping rough, in the front of an old wreck of a car near the station. I was so relieved and ran and ran until I got close to you. But then I awoke and the shock of reality pierced me. This kind of dream has happened a lot since you left. And now I blame it on Amy's sleep eye pillow. In a way I'm now addicted to this world of dreams and processing, because although entirely painful, it's a world that allows me to be near you at least for a while. Who wouldn't be?

I seem to be really wallowing at the moment. Desperate to find news of you, I looked you up on the Internet again. There are many listings and many reports, most incorrect. Some journalists don't seem to bear in mind what it's like to read something wrong about such a fragile matter. But I have to find you in anything, anywhere. If I can just see your name, it's sometimes enough.

Jean says she won't blame me if it becomes too difficult and I decide to end my life. This is yet another gift I'm not sure how to deal with. Is she absolving me, is she God? Has she had enough, does she even know what she means? And she's amongst the best of them, you see, like you wrote about a few of your class mates. I too have class mates in my form who sometimes get it wrong, because it isn't right. But at least I have them, have her. Where would I be without such care?

I'm violating your room. What would you say to see me looking at your stuff, meddling, searching, taking things out, and wearing your clothes? How can doing something so wrong be so right? All I know is that if I leave your stuff alone and you alone there's no movement and that doesn't work either.

I used to sing to you. I'd forgotten I did that. And just now I sang to Crumble and it's midnight, and I feel such sorrow. I smell your pyjamas. After two years I smell them and give them to Crumble to smell. He went to your door and cried. Am I imagining this or does he make associations. Those pyjamas would have been washed 100 times since then, if you were alive, but I'm scared for your smell to go, so I keep them as they are. I'm so scared of losing you. And yet I have. And then again, I haven't.

I'm certainly in a kind of madness.

The vanilla people, as I shall now call them, keep using the word 'cathartic'. I assume this is how they pass exams, loads of expensive books full of theory, but no emotional understanding. If they start asking emotive questions, the shortness of time make them inappropriate and then there's a pause during which I presume they tick the box for effort. Now that they see themselves as 'empathetic', a word that vanilla people have coined, they then move on, bypassing successfully their own emotional shortcomings, to talk about my practical issues, you know, same house, working, filling the day, friends, and so on, with what I shall now term a 'pseudo-emotional intelligence of the underqualified'. The continued arrogance of the middle classes and their 'expertise' never ceases to baffle. It is, however, turning from irritation to predictable amusement.

So dangerous to remember on a Sunday night. All those 10.20s in my life, when I was 14, when you were14 and now. *Oh, Mary, what was it like when Jesus was 14? What did you do on a Sunday night when the light faded? Of course, for you it wasn't the Sabbath. It was not a day set apart.*

It's April 2009. Have I made it?

Your death has come and gone. Johnny's death has come and gone. I'm here, though, still here, pondering, waiting. It's the most difficult thing to do, wait, remain, ponder, be unamazing, and have sustainability. It's the silence that's tricky, and the keeping. It's very spiritual and almost holy. You see, I'm the only one who knows. So I go and come, knowing but not sharing. I hide my reputation and am without status. Something is shining within me.
I wish someone would come and share your room. I want to rough it up a bit, sort it out a bit. Is that all you are now, a few boxes?

Happy 17th birthday, Charlotte. It isn't happy. I don't go into your room or need to do anything different for a Monday. Italian lunch with my pals, my Italian lesson, not fencing though, because Moyra is having me over for dinner. Have had a leisurely shower and breakfast. Do I miss you? Well, I miss being intact, OK, without pain and discomfort. I miss hope.

Why don't you pick up the towels from the bathroom floor? Sorry, they are my towels, not yours. I knew that, I was just pretending, maybe hoping, maybe longing, wallowing, again. How can they be your towels? You're dead, did you know? It's shocking to say this truth, but you are dead. You have no need for towels, no need to dry yourself any more. I know where you are. I go to that place. I can't bear it. It's something I can hardly face, the state you, my beautiful girl, must be in physically. I don't know what you would look like right now. I wish I'd had you cremated. The thought of you deteriorating and being temptingly close, but untouchable, stabs me and the blade goes through me. I heard your name on the radio, Charlotte, a word so sweet, now so sorrowful, when will the joy come?

I pass the cemetery, it's 4 August 2009, and I can't understand why you're in there and not beside me. My beautiful Noods, dead, 'killed'. I feel that I've left you here, and I don't know what to do. I'm helpless. You're gone from me. I'm to use up all my strength to 'Count My Blessings', and 'Dare to be a Daniel' and 'Dream the Impossible Dream'. Ironically, these three were my first school songs. We sang them a trillion times. Never knowing what they truly meant. And now? Now they come in handy.

When He was buried, left, did you go back for one more look? Did you smell Him, touch Him, and feel His heavy, hard, lifeless body. Not the flesh you knew. Did you feel that aching sorrow, did you cry? Oh, Mary, tell me what to do, I'm lost.

Why was it so easy for you to die? It would be so hard to kill Custard or to fall and bang my head, or hurt someone so significantly. How come it happened to you?

I lie on the floor. I've lain like this before. Before I knew you, before I could see your face. Then it was just a floor and just me lying, just me peacefully lying and over there a fire. Now it's you, and about you. The floor is you, the lying on the floor is you, and the fire is you, the space between is you. The air is you and the dust is you. Maybe, chillingly, the dust really is you. Does anyone with a beautiful alive daughter know what I feel about the dust? It's OK, you're all entitled to your lives, I don't wish it to be anything else for you. Just think about me, just a moment let yourself into the abyss. Please, just so that I'm not alone.

They come in pairs, the tormentors. I see a girl who might be a friend of yours, but isn't, maybe a little Zoe five years ago, and then you tall and dark and serious but breaking into that luminous smile. For a moment it's you, I make it you. I know it isn't and I hang onto it like an ice lolly bite melting in my mouth. I suck and the fruitiness is all but gone. Nothing again, but more longing and the knowledge that soon, unexpectedly, there'll be more of the same, and then more still. And then again, and then still, and then some more. The never-ending magic porridge pot of grief. In a way, I'm glad I've got loads of friends and associates, because this takes it out of people. It's just too much for a single one. Sometimes I fantasise that a lot of them put me on hold because they can't do it today. And so I go to the next and then the next until I'm accommodated. And that's how I get through. On the other hand, there are mainstay people who are there for me no matter what. They know that to be in my world none of us has a choice with this, at all.

I don't know how old you are now. I get so confused. One minute I see a girl of 14 and see you. Then I pass two 18-year-olds as I did in Claytons wine bar the other evening and I talk to them. They wonder what I'm asking, then it becomes clear, I want to know if you touched their lives. I want something new about you, something different, refreshing. One of them played netball with you, the other, short hair, incredibly dark red lipstick, knew of you. Is it enough? No, it isn't, they failed. I risked an association and they haven't given me enough payback. But you aren't 18 and will never be, in fact younger children than you will one day be older.

Some of these little people look like a younger version of you already, and soon they'll probably be the older version of you as well. How odd! They look as if they are about seven, the time after Johnny's death, the time of interesting facial expressions and tongue movements, you made them, possibly to masquerade your own agony at the time. I wonder, did you feel it more than me? – he was, after all, your flesh and blood. *Did Joseph die before Jesus, Mary?*

Did you talk about him, did Jesus talk about His own conception, the angel, and did you have conversations like that around your kitchen table?

God knows what he was planning before he died. I found a wig and a pair of spectacles hidden in the garage when I sold the Land Rover shortly afterwards. I never knew what he was doing. Just his history.

I blamed myself for his death and at times poor little you even blamed yourself, but goodness knows what he was contriving. He was a lovely, intriguing gentleman but, you know, I don't think I ever really knew him. Questions remain unanswered. And are probably best left that way. My life was full of hurdles around how I'd eventually explain things to you and I'm glad now that we're both saved from this. You would have had to share it with a friend and where might that have led? – some girls of 14 were unkind to you without that. Weren't they? *But every great individual has a couple of betrayers, don't they, Mary?*

Check this out, Mary. Three women are accompanying me to the inquest. Jayne, one whose mission it seems to be, is like my cherished companion, who has come to me every Sunday since this began, with food. She'll look after me and take me back to her house when required and probably even hold my hand and wash my feet – it's serious, this business isn't it? The other two, Helen and Moyra, are the most trusted of good friends, and of course Helen is Grace's mother and is linked to Charlotte. And Moyra has given everything she possibly can. It's the nature of women that they need to witness and sacrifice and want to give readily of their services.

I wonder, in 2,000 years might they look back and make these assumptions: that it's the nature of such an occasion and of women particularly, that you could say that as Jennifer's parents were in their 80's they most certainly would have remained at home, whilst Jayne would have gone to the inquest for the entire time to support her good friend. And other two women, if not more, judging by how I spend my time, would be there as well, in case Jayne was ill or tired, or if extra driving or support were required. You could also make a wild assumption that Jennifer's mother, although 86, may have wished to come for a day, in which case some ad hoc transport and support might have been necessary. With all this in mind, as fact meets fiction or assumption, it's easy to see that there were four women attending you and your boy on the Sabbath after His death – that they would have done this on your behalf, Mary. They may very well have looked after you beyond the crucifixion, to ensure that all your basic needs were met. And indeed they would be hugely worried about how they would move the stone blocking the entrance to the tomb. Then, hey presto! No need.

What did the cross taste like, Mary? And what of its smell? I'm at the Friary again, sipping tea, by a plinth with a beam on the top, the entrance to the dining area. I imagine it's the cross. I'm drawn to it. If Charlotte was up there, how could I sit by it? And what if it was she'd wanted, how then? How did you do it, Mary? What a remarkable woman you were to allow Him to choose such a path and not try to stop it. As we know, the bravery is in the sitting and witnessing, not in the trying to change things. The bravery is in the suffering and in facing yourself as I do daily. Have we ever thought of this before? Were you right or wrong? Do we as parents allow our children to choose something that's going to incorporate such a degree of suffering and terror? What if there's no choice but to allow it to continue, perhaps because you know that it will happen anyway.

If I'd seen her drowning I'd have jumped without question, immediately, no thought to my safety, no question of consequences. I'd have tried to change things, perhaps to no avail. The only one who could was me, her mother. So I'd have tried, tried to save her. Even though it may have happened again. But Mary, you couldn't. It was different for you. He wanted it this way. Imagine your choice? What else could you have done? There was nowhere to go, so you had to stay where you were, right? You were stricken, broken, acquiescent. Did you want to be up there as well, Mary, was that denied to you? Did you want to feel the pain of the nails in your flesh? Did you want to hang alongside Him? Did you feel cheated of the physical pain and the proximity? Did you feel angry that He chose it and angry that they carried it through? Did you want to cut Him down when the pain got too much for you both to bear, did you want to hold Him? Were you scared of that Pietà? It's my one regret, Mary, that I didn't get the staff at the hospital to remove the tubes so I could hold my Noods.

I wanted to be in the water. I was drawn to the icy water, like a need for extraordinary self-harm. To lay my head in icy current, to beautifully hurt myself, I wanted that.

'Spinning gold from straw', that's what I call it – Brother John likes that. I tell him that I'm privileged to have such grief, and he calls me generous. He says I've given him lots to ponder on. Did you get that, Mary? Did they credit you with the necessary wisdom? Did you deserve it? You can cross-reference the Gospels, even though John could have been written many years after the death of your boy, but Noods, it seems like you have your own 'Gospels', about events unfolding. The books of Neil and Yasmin, for example, were written a few days after you died, and the two can be cross-referenced. In fact, my solicitor and I have done so.

Here we go again, I'm sitting opposite two what can loosely be called 'prats', and worse, they're prats with power. They know stuff but are seemingly stupid in terms of their experience. They are quoting someone on how to get over the death of a child. 'It's understood that...' Fuck off please! It isn't understood, *you* don't understand, *I* understand. Because, idiot, I do it. I *am* 'it'. It's strange to me that people who have a little power and status really want to show that they're on top of experiencing someone's pain. In fact, it takes a really big individual to say that they don't know and to be humbled by this. Just because you're called a priest, it doesn't mean that you know my pain or can translate it. Because you offer solace, it doesn't mean that it can always be well received. And there's another – would you believe it, Noods? A person who now thinks that from seven seconds of my life she has got me and my situation figured out. I speak to her, not crying but actually laughing. That's the first quandary for this naive one, and she already senses that something is wrong. She wants to offer an opinion and help. For all of 36 hours of knowing me, she wants to change the way in which I deal with death. 'Well, I hope you can cry, otherwise it's not healthy." Bring on the explanation! Which one shall it be today? 'One swallow doesn't make a summer'? Or maybe it's the moment for 'Even in times of war, there are football games.' I wonder, does she want me to perform for her? Does she really want to witness my misery at the Friary on this day? Does she want to say that she saw, and that I'm oh, really sorrowful, or not coping, that's good, not coping, then she could say that she helped, great. Does she want to see the football game or the war? Is she only important if she can see the war, if she's allowed to see the war and be permitted into the inner sanctum? Can these people not just be still and let it happen, witness and wait, without status?

I want to see people humbled by this, and me, not because I have an ego that needs massaging, but because it's fitting and right. This is a circumstance that, although horrific, could happen to anyone. It's happened to me. The way I navigate and manage it is state-of-the-art, so give me the humanitarian respect I deserve, or don't enter. This is big, I'm bigger. If it's too big for you, and it may be, don't attempt to make it and me smaller, for it won't work and I shall walk away.

The dark is pitch, but known, and for that the light is more precious and sweeter. When you see the joy within me therefore, don't mistake it for something else. It doesn't mask the pain, it's born of it. So, join in it with me, and bear witness.

I'm not sure. Is it worse to be bad or to see bad in action and look away? To condone what's wrong? I know there's a famous quote about it. About how evil prospers when good men do nothing – well, they aren't good men then, are they?

So, Mary, over to you once more, what distressed you most, the Roman whip or the whipper? Or was it the otherwise 'good' individual who wiped our Lord's piss and blood from an expensive Roman garment, as the spray got out of hand? Tell me, oh blessed of women, did they avert their gaze? Did people you'd passed in the streets for years, and said good morning to, and laughed with their children, avert their gaze? Did you feel blessed or wretched when they looked away embarrassed by the wrong they shared? As they wiped your good boy's warm juices from the stony ground? Was it rage, disgust or sorrow you felt? Or did you have the capacity for all three?

As I watched what I thought were good people turning bad at the inquest into your death, I felt sad and cold and alone. With every averted gaze, every once-warm embrace, closed down to me, I shuddered with how the fear of the week can be so easily bought. And I see clearly how, as these privileged people, one by one, sell their souls, we cannot begin to stop atrocity in more corrupt places, where so much more is at stake. What examples the vanilla people make once again!

They didn't talk to me, Charlotte. The deputy head, a governor, a teacher, and two parents, they didn't talk. They silently sealed off the seating area to accommodate only them, and they no longer made eye contact with me, a woman whose little girl most of them knew since you were three, they used to called you Charlie. They played with you, worked with you and saw you at your best and your worst. How could they stop seeing that I was there? Even worse, they'd walk towards me with force and promise and then physically fold away, giving me nothing. Am I suddenly the bad one here?

Oh my sweet Noods, they weren't worthy of you.

But you know this only too well, don't you, Mary?

The priests, the ones who colluded with His death, after your such extensive suffering, they didn't allow you to go in peace, did they? Instead, they stopped you from going to the tomb. Didn't they try to beat you up, to finish you off and then to burn down your house?

Oh Mary, my roof, although small, is also one of reed and straw, and susceptible am I to the rage of the 'guilty'.

Let's see. I have a question. On another note, was it a warm day in September, if we stick to the well-known December date, although He may well have been born in June, anyway a warm day, perhaps in September, a beautiful teenage girl fetches water from the well, she not having emotionally yet reached womanhood, knowing little, sweet and sheltered as the only child of older parents is likely to be kept. She fetches the water. She rests in the shade out of the hot midday sun. Now, what if she was startled by a figure, a male figure? We know that only occasional visitors and Roman soldiers came by. Suppose this was such an occasion. The figure blocks the sun. He towers over her, and she only sees the silhouette: the plumed helmet, the winged cape, the silver gleam of wing or armoured vest. She asks his name, the reply a softly spoken word, 'Gabriel'. How similar to an angel a Roman soldier looks. Wouldn't it be so easy to mistake the two? And isn't it more likely that you'd have the visitation of a virile, young, aggressive soldier in such times than an angel? Was it a

Roman soldier that came to the virgin teenager that day in Nazareth in the hot sunshine? Did he talk about your virginity, did he dupe you with your beautiful spirituality into succumbing to his favour, and did anyone in Nazareth see all this that day? In fact, could he have said that he was an angel and lied to the innocent, wide-eyed teenager, who surely would have been more naive than today's girls of the same ranking?

Is the dream that Joseph had more about him coming to terms with something so unusual rather than a message from God?

Can you imagine anything more threatening at the time than a young woman betrothed and with another man's child?

I put it to you, Mary, that in your first acquiescence you allowed a soldier to enter you, thinking and believing him to be, as he may have said, an angel of God. Allowing this to happen would indeed remove the trauma of what today we call 'underage sex'. Both types of individuals were messengers from elsewhere. In fact, angel means that very thing, and a Roman soldier would indeed would have been a government herald. What could be the difference to you, there, then?

So, were you really that special, Mary? Fourteen, maybe, underage, pregnant, against your will, possibly, with child, ashamed, definitely terrified, knowing that you may be stoned? Passed off to someone who thought he was doing you a favour. Did you look after Joseph's existing children? Did he get the measure of you, then, at all, ever? Were you the archetypal woman who carried all the responsibility, the curse, the drudge and majesty that are womanhood? And when you came into your own, did anyone notice? As you suffered so quietly, did you want them to notice? Did anyone know you?

Mary, did you keep a piece of Him with you? Did you drag along a soft toy belonging to the greatest man of all time? Was it something He made for you, maybe from wood, a pendant perhaps? Could you wear it without longing? Could you wear it without feeling the piercing of your heart? Could you wear it without fear of reprisal of a double violation? Would someone have seen it and torn it away from you?

Mary, this is a hard question to ask you, but did you ever feel that you were entered maybe by the same force that ultimately stole Him from you? Roman force?

If I hadn't married Jonathan, who'd had dealings with the law, would you, his child, have been torn away from me, so violently? Is it some kind of payback? Am I paying for the misdemeanours of another? Are things so linked?

Were you contaminated by Jonathan's problems in the same way that Jesus may have carried the genetic make-up of the man who may have violated his young mother? Is this what sealed your fate and his? Do we two mothers then have to put up and shut up and accept what is our life and death? Is everything connected?

It's astounding to me that because people have met me, they think they know me. They know not my education, my mind, my grief, my secrets, my loves or my fears. I'm a complex book, which they don't have the patience to peruse. So I seem colourless.

Like you, Mary, were colourless. Neither of us seems to have anything to say. Why do you think that is? Is it because we already know that what we'll do is beyond human experience? That it's all too much for people to comprehend? So we have to keep it concealed, and then because we say nothing we're construed as without colour. Which then brings about a lack of interest? How did you become the world's most well-known woman when no one was interested in you at all?

If I ask them now what they know about Mary, they say, 'Mary who?' For God's sake, is it that you have to be obviously loud and immediate and jump up and down to be noticed, or indeed interesting? You have to be the right kind of good or the right kind of bad. You had to be acceptable and you weren't. Were you bad? Were you free from sin with all that virginity and Immaculate Conception? What's good and what's bad anyway? If you were raped, were you bad? If you'd experienced sexual pleasure, were you bad? If you held yourself comically above other women, were you good? If you said that your child was special, were you bad or good? If you knew that He was going to die, were you bad? Was your goodness too boring or was your badness too hidden?

Am I bad?

Your blue hot water bottle reminds. I wish it didn't. I tire of the continuous bore of repetitive reminder. It's like being in a prison with no bars, and yet no escape. I bought you the blue and me the green when Jonathan died to keep us warm, sometime in 2002 when you were ten. I remember that it was Christmas and Exeter and Boots, the chemist. I gave you the blue bottle because it was fluffy. It has your smell on it. I never washed it. It was brought to me at the hospital when I got sent there after you'd gone. And I held it close to me. It warmed me. Now I take it when I go to cold houses, as I like you to be there too. If I feel warm, then you're sort of alive.

Were you addicted to pain, Mary? Could it be said that if you could have had Him back, you wouldn't have wanted it, because you'd gone so far down this path of loss and potential martyrdom that it became a journey you relished in a way, a sort of self-flogging of a spiritual nature. Could it be that to have had Him back would only have been temporary, only to set more grief in motion? Neither you nor I, Mary, would have wanted to go through this thing twice for the sake of a reprieve. Would we? How would we know?

Is there a point when you like even what you have when it's so bad, because you get used to it, like small shoes? I have to say, I wonder what will happen next on this startling journey. Is that right?

It snows. I miss you. Whenever it does anything, I miss you. You are it and me and the missing and the fibre of everything. You are what is there and what isn't. I anticipate the cosy and there's a void already, before cosy isn't there. I'm stuck and terrified.

Stupidly, I'm half way up a hill in a blizzard. I shouldn't have come this way, wrong decision. I'm reminded of their wrong decision to leave you stranded on the Moor and then the panic that lead to your death. Panic and more panic.

They panicked, didn't they, Mary, when they thought He was bad, they panicked and this lead a chain of events to hunt Him down and eliminate Him as soon as possible. And then He was gone, hanging, no turning back.

When you fell, my Noods, there was no turning back of time. It was the beginning of the end for you.

So I'm in the snow on a slope feather-breaking backwards in my car, wondering why I'm alone, asking myself if I'm going to get home tonight. I have shopping in the back and I'm scared. There's no one who can rescue me. If I get home, I'll be good forever. If you survived and got even to intensive care, I'd be good forever. I said it then, I remember. I'm good now forever, anyway, even though I didn't get my prize. I'm good. People helped me to be good. People helped me on to the road away from the slippery patch. People are good to me, I'm proud to call them 'Christian'. So there I am in the blizzard driving home, wanting desperately to get home, and as usual having a parallel thought of *What's the point?*, when I believe that I'm going to get there and I do. But when I do, you're not there and I'm sad. Little girl next door has made four snow people, representatives of her family, which serve to remind me that I'm alone, a single snow person, and also that you're too old to make snow people and even if I coaxed you into being silly enough to make snow people with me, you are just not there. You're in an unmarked grave with your daddy in Fremington cemetery, cold. Maybe today you're so cold you *are* a snow person.

I'm a widow who has lost a child. I'm going to invent a word for it, maybe 'mothmorn', the mother of a dead only child. Do you dig it, Noods?

Do you dig the snow, Charlie? If you were on top of the snow rather than underneath it, would you make me two snow people?

Sometimes we have to let ourselves metaphorically die, in order to restore ourselves in any way.

I'm sick of living a half-life, crumbs off other people's table with my nose pressed against the window of their lives. I feel like a nothing. I'm closing down again.

I just realised I don't go into your room any more. It's shut to me as you are shut to me.

There are now different accounts of what happened that day on the Moor, as there are indeed different gospels, some of which cross over.

I must be the most stupid person alive to think I can make things different for you. To think even now as your body turns to fragments in a place I never visit, that I can make a change, make your life better. Do you know what I've been thinking, Noods? If I arrange your room, and put all your leotards neatly on your shelves and sports wear near by so that things are less random and more accessible, you'll be more organised and have more time. I get lost in that. How dangerous can I make things for myself, eh? Going along this path not only makes for you being alive, it also gives a future that doesn't exist, a possibility that torments. Why do I let myself have such hope? Is it worth the drop, this single moment of joyful possibility? Is it the ultimate fantasy to will your dead child alive for just a little while?

Is it different when you lose an older child? Did you acquiesce more because you had got Him to a state of being fully grown or did you still get locked into the fantasy of what might have been? Did you sometimes pretend John was Jesus? You must have given someone His clothes, but who? Where did His possessions go, Mary? Where did it all go?

I'm still loath to give your stuff away in quantity, in case I lose you completely. And yet I'm aware that those who should have it are growing slowly beyond it. But I just can't let you go, not just yet, maybe not ever.
When I ask people where you went, Charlotte, they cry.

You cared about people, Noods. Did you care for me, do you look upon me now with huge sorrow in your eyes. You said to me once that every child has a mother who'd be sorry if he or she died. Do you remember when I told you not to be the first one by the door, in the beds, in the hostel in Madrid, on the bad trip before the bad trip? You said that it isn't only me who has a child. You seemed quite callous in your disregard for my anxiety, and now it seems like it was fitting.

Do you remember the poster you made about Jesus, did you identify with Him? As I do with Mary?

I have to say, probably a little disrespectfully, that both you and Jesus shared a sort of ruthless compassion, almost a cruel-to-be-kind approach. I can see this in the way you both spoke to your mothers – sometimes.

It was as if we were both lucky to have you and therefore didn't count in the receiving stakes.

I think Jesus would have liked me. Apparently He had a strong affinity for widows, after all His mother was one and He must have seen her struggle. Maybe if time hadn't separated us, then we could have made a four and shared takeaways and cooking in Bideford or Nazareth. What do you think they'd have made of the complex way in which we live, Noods? The chicken is the same, the sauce and packaging different. How do you think Jesus, Mary, you and I would have gone down in The Sagor? I know, I can see you looking at me again as if I've lost the plot. Well, you try living with this, Noods, no, better not, don't you try this, you stay where you are – don't come back for another round. I'll try and get used to it, I'll be all right, I promise. Only another 45 years max to go. Yes, it does sound mad, doesn't it, and it is, very mad and uncomfortable.

Do you ever say, 'What if?', Mary? What if I'd stopped Him from going to the temple? What if I'd been with Him at Gethsemane? What if I'd steered Him towards something else? What if I'd ignored the prophesy, told Him He was ordinary, punished Him when He got lost in the temple at Jerusalem, grounded Him for a month. Then I wouldn't have this agony, day in, day out – sometimes alone, sometimes without a single soul-bearing witness.

What if I'd encouraged you to do the child protection course that weekend, or the gym competition? You could have done that. What if I'd said no to Ten Tors completely, what if I couldn't have bought the equipment, sent you to a different school, told you that you couldn't go out at weekends or evenings, what if I'd said no and no and no again. What if?

Shall I tell you what if? Well, we wouldn't have had a name for, or the underpinning of what sane and moral people do, Christianity and Grandma wouldn't have lost the plot so soon, and I wouldn't be wondering what to do in between crying.

One thing I've learnt is to try to steer a true and straight course, undeviated by the actions or words of others. This can be tricky. You see, we live in a world of connection and response, whereby if you put your tongue out at me, I necessarily do it back – but not so for me now. To do what you'd do anyway, in spite of anything else, is to be grace, is to be true, is to know that you follow the path you intended. Sounds great, doesn't it? I must tell you, though, that the animal in me wants to take certain people round the back and beat the shit out of them. But I shall refrain.

To raise your head high and behave impeccably is like cutting through butter with a hot blade. It has its own satisfaction and purity. It can become a habit and be quite addictive in its own right. This grace is unique, and it's the only non-reactionary force I know.

However, sometimes, whilst I aim to be a cut above the rest, others will try to provoke a violent response, and indeed sometimes I appear again colourless as a result of my lack of force, just like you, Mary, dull and unresponsive. This behaviour doesn't mean in any way that I can't describe in detail the wrongs of others, or how angry I am, or disappointed. It merely means that I behave in an unharmful way, moving towards a graceful and emotionally economical conclusion. I am, if nothing else, true.

What did you do with His clothes? What am I supposed to do with her *clothes?*

Clothes are so personal, and every garment tends to tell a story, has a history: the orange suit that you bought from Mexico when we went on the cruise, your knickers with pictures that I put in your nearly adult stocking that last Christmas; all your trainer socks that remain unpaired; your long stripy socks with individual toes; the dress that has been handed down through the generations and that now only you could wear. And, of course, the leotards. The ones you bought yourself, saved up for, the one Grandma bought for you with the matching scrunchie, it was called Electra – oh God, why were you so special?

It just came to me. Were you already caught between two worlds, maybe pulled between there and here? I thought you were brilliant, but maybe even slightly autistic, but now I see that you were lost and found at the same time, familiar and strange, here we go again, maybe 'holy' in fact.

Change anticipates her return, Mary, so many changes. Change makes possibility, and then I can't help but feel that she must be on her way to me. I want her. Sometimes as a reward, I want her back.

Isn't it so, Mary, that people look at me, Jenny, they see what they think they know and yet I represent a new unfamiliar landscape of searing loss and survival? I'm not who they come to see, I too stand now between two worlds and with a foot in each, I represent the link. I'm the 'who' they have to be, the sacrifice they have to make to get their ticket on the ride to the greatest journey of all. I'm untouchable and apart, different. It makes them angry. They just don't want to pay the price.

It gets worse. I sit and yet I'm not seen by those who sometimes pass me by. Cleo at The Plough just walked right through me. Am I invisible or am I just not recognisable? This happens a lot.

At first I thought I was wearing Harry Potter's invisibility cloak and they really couldn't see me, then recently I realised it's something else. I change. I am changed. I'm a chameleon, always different, often strange and yet familiar.

It seems that this defines 'holy', I'm desperate, aren't I, Charlotte, to be great without effort, I can see you rolling your eyes at me. It is so much effort.

Anyway, at first you could say this makes me the perfect spy, but it isn't about subterfuge, although this is often tempting, especially the jet set lifestyle of a Bond, with gadgets and girls and fencing and good wine. This is about something different.

It's about who I am, and who you were, Mary. It's really about being on the border of two worlds. Being familiar and strange at the same time, or rather how the strange comes out of what's familiar. It's like magic. It certainly feels magical. It's like I'm human and transcending at the same time. Does this come from insurmountable suffering that the human psyche cannot hold and the transfiguration of that into a spiritual joy, the ecstasy of which causes an ascendance, a movement upwards, beyond human experience, a glow? Free. Untouchable. As if I'm preparing for heaven.

Gen said she saw it in me, the 'glow', when we were having illicit chocolate cake at Atlantic Village, she saw it. She said I looked young and was going to be on the front of *Tatler* as a hot woman transcending grief, a guru. I got excited, but then worried, in case my ego gets carried away. *No media in your time, Mary, no ego formatting, only since, so you couldn't get carried away, with the material offers of sainthood on the cover of a glossy magazine: 'Mary, sexy icon, woman of our time.' What would you say to it now? Your continuous two-dimensionality, your stylisation? Were you ever a woman, with breasts and a vagina? Did you feel a sexual hunger, a need to wear cloth that matched your eyes and hair, and skin colour?*

I do, however, want to sell myself, I'm aware of this. I'm caught in the prospect of fame, the tastes, the colour, the massage, the compensations, the vacuous excitements. But I can't have both. If I do, then I don't go forwards, without status and reputation, different yet familiar, and therefore cannot assume the title of 'holy'. I need. *How much of the trappings did you need, how much security?*

There's so much more wrapping today, so much more comparison, so much more stuff and ego rubbing and requirement and publicity. *When you went home at night, were you quiet, restored, ecstatic, familiar, strange?*
Looks like I'm caught between two worlds, in more ways than one.

Charlotte, you're always with me in my journey, surging towards the light. In my flight I become you, the 'you' that I fostered. Sometimes I can't feel the pain that I've endured for so long, and I know that to break from it is necessary and good. I become you – there's no distinction between us. We are one. I'm alive again. My life has adventure and possibility.

Mary, did you use His death as an excuse? 'I am Jesus's mother, please let me off my parking fines. Donkey has only been by the well for three water trips.' I'm sorry that I'm speeding, officer, sometimes my mind isn't quite on the job. You see, I'm the mother of the girl who died on the Ten Tors practice? How long before I see myself as others see me? Someone who has just parked for too long and deserves a fine.

The trouble with spouting this claptrap is that it's often beyond the realms of others' experience and they may become frightened. After all, what people don't understand often makes them afraid. They can't possibly see a connection to anything else, because they can't see 'it' in the first place.
Usually if I say anything that gets tangled up in this grief, it's met with a blank look, or the thought that grief excuses my behaviour. Or, you know what, they compete. Beware: you can't educate people in something so far removed from

themselves that they can't see it. To appreciate the complexities of grief you have to have vision. It must be the most creative and destructive force, and is therefore the ultimate paradox. The tables are then turned. I imagine I shall be labelled as mad, perhaps having gone mad as a result of the incident – that's your death by the way, Noods – or worse, turned religious, yes I think to be known for that can only be worse. 'She has found religion,' they may incorrectly say, rolling their eyes upwards to the heavens. I run the risk of isolating myself, which is far worse than just accepting my people, who are trying hard but not getting it. I really ought to do something else, and I'm boring myself with all the self-pity, the wallowing, the dislike of everyone.

Did they say that about you, Mary, that you'd found God? I mean, there must have been a period of time in between what we shall call the incident and modernity which allows you just to be His mother. Was there a period when you were labelled as off your trolley, two slices short of a loaf – after all it wasn't a very long time after you and before me that they banged widows up for wailing and thrashing over grief. Bedlam wasn't it, related to Bethlehem?

There were three sightings of you in 15 minutes this evening. I can't believe it. I'm so glad you're not missing, it would be agony. I think I'd spend my entire time following people. But it's getting more predictable. The thing about repetition is that it desensitises. I really am getting used to you being almost around, well sometimes. But I still don't know whether it's a source of pain or comfort.

I switch on a TV programme and see a 17-year-old girl ice skating. She argues with her mother about entering a competition. I remember. I'm back there with you, frustrated. You're separate from me. For a moment, I don't understand you. We argue. You're unreasonable. I'm angry. We're caught in a kind of battle. But you died. It's unjust. I'm confused once again.

I want to know if the cake I had in Madeira when I was pregnant with you in 1991 was holy. It seemed familiar but also it was strange. It looked like a Swiss roll – you know, the chocolate type with vanilla crème filling. Can you taste it, Noods? Well, it tasted like wallpaper complete with paste. The worst thing about it was that it was bland – definitely a holy cake then. Not what it seemed. On the border of two worlds, wallpaper and food; bland and therefore going forward without delicious cake-like status and reputation.

Madness?

I don't have you and I don't remember the detail of you. But then I do. I stare. I look in a magazine and see your head in a hair article. It's your parting, and your wet head, and then your shoulder. I can nearly see part of your face and I feel that it's your grace and stillness I'll see if I walk round the other side of the page. I remember all those haircuts. All those times, when I didn't quite know the individual who was next to me.

Did you know Him, Mary? What was He like? Was He clever at His studies? Was He athletic, did He tell stories? Did you kiss Him before bed? Were you actually wise enough, as young as you were, to give Him appropriate counsel? Was it easier because He was an adult and responsible for His own choices in the end, or is any death of a child before its mother the pits?

Even with seemingly secure friendships, there's a honing-down process with conditions attached, and only the best survive. In my world people who've been amazing sometimes fail me or they can't change with me and can't be open to my ultimate journey. Also, they assume they know. They get jealous of what I've found to motivate me, and they put me down. They assume things. It's quite anger-making and dirty.

Funnily enough, it's the ragged ones who come through, the free spirits, the unconventional, and the ones outside, the ones who've been shunned. Not necessarily the ones who have enough discipline to see me with regularity.

So was it Mary Magdalene, the erstwhile possible whore – well, she had seven demons, anyway, maybe she was sick, so a sick whore; in fact, as she thinks she saw Him resurrected (maybe she wanted to so desperately, I know that feeling), we will comically, for the record, call her the sick whore who founded Christianity, something all followers in their vanilla-ness should immediately heed – anyway, was she the chosen confidante, the equal to you in depth of spirit and pathos? Did Joanna patronise? Was it the same with Salome? I cannot think that a woman who was an important member of Herod's household and a woman who wanted the Baptist's head on a plate for her mother could have warranted such close affection and proximity. I feel it was another Salome, for sure, although Joanna may have been more than one thing to many people. What were they like, these women who were there with you until the end. Spill, Mary, spill.

Do we just use who we've got at the time, after such shock and confusion? We let anyone in at first, don't we? Anybody will do at first.

I look at women with little girls, beautiful women, and beautiful girls. The men look proud. I liked that pride in Johnny, all those years ago. I felt like a woman then, all woman, beautiful he said. 'You have a beautiful mouth.' He told you to take heed of your mother when eating: 'Look at her,' he'd say, 'look at how beautiful she is, eat like her.' He never waited to see you become so enchanting, so perfect. You're even more perfect now than I remember you – easier to grieve for you, if you're perfect, I think. I was all things then: I was all motherhood, all women, now I struggle with identity. I break, I lose, I nothing. Am I an icon, a representative of more, but just two-dimensional?

I'm back to not knowing quite what's happened. It's that confusion again at who's lost, and the connections that are lost, and the relationships that are lost.

I assume, Mary, that by the time your only boy had gone, Joseph and your mother and father had died as well and you were alone.

I sadly slamdunked a woman today for believing herself incorrectly to have the monopoly on grief in the bookshop. She picked the wrong person to meddle with. I was talking to Grandma – I don't call her that by the way – telling her something trivial, perhaps complaining, when a plain individual cut across and said, 'You shouldn't be so sensitive about something so small, if I can give you this advice: sometimes problems can be so much bigger for some people.' I felt my verbal rocket launching. 'Can I give you some advice?' I replied after a long pause. 'Don't give advice, especially not to me, especially not in a bookshop. I know, you're suffering, let me take a wild guess, you've had loss, or huge suffering, and you think you've have got a monopoly on it. You see me, a woman younger than yourself, talking about trivia, with seemingly the whole world ahead of her, and you make an assumption: this is the sum-total of my suffering. What have you lost, a child, a husband, a dog, a crate full of people?' My taunting built to a climax. 'I lost my son, boo hoo boo hoo,' she said. 'He hanged himself, seven years ago. He was 25. My husband was a horrible man, and although I have a daughter, she doesn't talk to me.'

'I win,' I shouted. The entire bookshop, especially round the paperback, popular, latest-stuff-in section had come to a standstill. We had an audience. I was eloquent. I played with them. 'Oh dear, you've lost a son, he's died, my heart pumps custard.' My audience was temporarily lost, and then the big reveal: 'I too have lost a child, my 14-year-old daughter died on Dartmoor only two and a bit, never forget the bit, years ago, and the inquest goes on. My husband's also dead, he killed himself, I found him hanging in our garage.' Always create a build-up, never give all the information too soon. 'My life is broken beyond repair. I've no other children. So please excuse me for not welcoming your intolerable intrusion into my conversation and the words "Don't be so sensitive" do, funnily enough, irritate me. The lesson you've surely learnt today is engage brain before opening gob.' I know our audience would have applauded if they were foreign and passionate, but they looked surprised and embarrassed, so I assume they were entirely English. They just displayed the British equivalent of passion as always, a look of bemused justice.

How would you like to spend your 18th birthday, in May, my Noods? It just about coincides with the 50th anniversary of the Ten Tors and we'll see which gets precedence, although I feel one need no longer rule out the other, although the army, the schools and all future Moor participants are here, but you are not. You aren't here, once again, to open your presents. Well, it's just as well I don't have a thing for you then, isn't it? What would I have chosen to surprise you? Well, what you would have wanted, I wonder? Perhaps you'd have liked any money sent to Haiti to assist those who are clearly, gravely without. Yes, I think then that's what I'll do, from Charlotte with love to the people of Haiti, some pounds, maybe to help someone, somewhere, with something.

Charlotte died so that you won't, not today. The odds are against it happening. Lady Luck is on your side, little girl in Haiti, pulled from the rubble. Lady Luck is on your side and there are some pounds coming to you instead of my Noods' birthday present, because that's what she would have wanted and I knew her. I knew her soul. I saw it become a soul, I saw it emerge.

I still wonder if it's ever going to hurt any more than this, and, actually, if it *can* hurt any more than this, but then certain things remind me of you, constantly. And whatever anyone says, there are times without choice, when you pervade my thoughts and senses, now strangely. I can't help but wonder if this is people's experience of God. I let you in and you play, as Grandma used to say, 'merry hell' with my psyche, and my memory, and my heart. You're in the fridge, it's Saturday morning, and you can make anything for breakfast. You chose yoghurt, cereal, chocolate, lollipops, I come down and see the evidence. Not any more. Where are the wrappers of your world now, where's the proof that you eat and move and laugh? Where's the sun that used to stream through the half-closed curtains? There is none. You used to watch *Friends*. I woke up to the theme song most Saturdays, ironically. It began, 'So no one told you life was gonna be this way...' They didn't.

In an hour and three quarters you'll be 18. This is the worst day of my life: next to the first worst day of the same life. There's just one thing that stops me from smashing up all the cars that are in the way of me parking outside my house, and that is reason. Well, two things, reason and the terrible muscular pain one gets when one bashes things in an untidy and forceful manner. Also, I can't bear the thought of a prison cell for the night, and that would be inevitable for causing a disturbance and damage. The trouble with behaving well is, it has to continue once a precedent's been set. So once again, I don't act with passion, but my head rules and you'd think I have something to lose. You did what you felt; so, I gather, did Jesus. When is it right, productive, I wonder, not to calculate, to be all of yourself and think later? Why can't I smash up, let go, cause a scene? But then again, neither you nor Jesus would have behaved like that, would you? Your hearts may have led. But your behaviours were always the embodiment of grace.

I saw Grace earlier. I love her. She has an exam tomorrow and needed me. I'm honoured, if sad. We talked about exploding when you're so alone in your grief in a packed place. She's moved schools, where nobody knows of her connection to you and her searing loss. Where life goes on around you, how frightening it can be, and when you try to contain the grief, it has to have somewhere to go and then ... bang! The explosion. Crying is a bit like bloodletting, it does what it says on the tin. It lets, allows, gives. It's good. I made Grace cry. I took her a bag of tricks from your room. Your letter to Angel was with them, I feel it was meant for her. She took the red and gold leotard out of the bag and smelt it. A silent tear fell onto her cheek. Her skin is so lovely. Helen and I cried too. We miss you. When will it go away? And yet it mustn't. I made Grace cry because I knew she had to, and it would help her and she'd know it was OK and then she could do it again in the future, and then again.

Hello, Susan, sorry I haven't got back to you, but it's Charlotte's 18th birthday and I'm having a busy time. Is that healthy? Sorry, is what healthy? The fact that it's her birthday, the fact that I'm busy, or before you even can say 'pathology' I'm doing the wrong thing again. Think pathology, dimwits, where is C.S. Lewis when you need him?

Noods, I called her. Did you call Him something similar, Mary? Maybe 'Jesie' or 'Jes' or 'my boy'. You know, you could sue. If I were you, I'd sue Caiaphas and probably Pilate or maybe the Sanhedrin – like me you could have a first and second defendant. You know you could summon up the 12 or now 11 chaps who liked your boy and take legal action. Or maybe you could find Nicodemus or Joseph of Arimathea, whoever he was. Think what you could get for services, apparently it's a category. The services that the deceased would have provided, that you've now lost. In your case, Mary, probably not gardening duties or cups of tea, but a remarkable amount of story telling and prayer. You never know, that might have been the case with Noods too. Oh sorry, I've overlooked the fact that no amount of money could bring Jesie back or eradicate the trauma. Your post-traumatic stress disorder must have gone through the roof. But nor have I had any thought that a saint in the making doesn't give a rat's arse for dosh. Shit, am I wrong again? Mary, you just won't take advice, will you?

I'm in such an interesting position. I have this legal team that's state-of-the-art working for me. I'm able to influence them as well. But whilst this is all tenuous and my dreams are now less about Charlotte and more about my unwanted fame and people whispering about me, I feel more and more isolated.

Of course, feeling ill and pre-menstrual doesn't help. I've returned from London with a cold and a cough and I feel wretched, which of course exacerbates my aloneness and makes me desire some sort of fix of a futuristic nature. There is none. Future doesn't happen like this. So I resort to the cup of tea, and the handkerchief. And I am.

Having returned from yet another tryst of a shallow nature, I feel pressurised. He wants to move in with me. I find it very irritating and odd that he just doesn't read the signs or look at the bigger picture, but only seems to address his own needs. Or is it that I just don't love him? Or is it that I'm cold and not capable of love? Or is that just what people say when there's just no reciprocation?

I called it off for three months. Then I bumped into him, which coincided with my loneliness, and we were intimate again. I took him to this lovely party. He wasn't particularly discreet, an annoying quality for me. I felt ill afterwards, we went back to his place. His wife, in name only, as usual has returned to their central core. I feel the inequality. And I don't feel enough, currently, to wish for him to change anything.

I find it astonishing that he expects so much from someone who's lost such a lot. He is lacking, and is therefore unsuitable. Worse still, he compensates, which I find boring and predictable, leaving me with an overwhelming sense of guilt, which as you know I could very much do without.

So, now I'll have many headaches again.

When and if I get my cheque, I'm going to put it on your pillow, and wake it up in the morning for breakfast.

I'll see if it will be the same as being with you, Noods.

Sadly, I've figured out that the only way I seem to separate from people is by death. Johnny couldn't divorce me. Instead, because I was so bad, he angrily hanged himself in our garage, presumably for me to find. *I bet Joseph's departure wasn't so dramatic, was it, woman of God? I daren't refer to you as Mary at the moment because Amy has just told me that I'm comparing myself to you and therefore have delusions of grandeur – well, she said 'grandiosity' actually – and, of course, she knows best. Sorry, am I suddenly lacking grace? I bet you said the equivalent of 'fuck' sometimes, didn't you, Mary, Mary, quite contrary, I wish I'd known you. So sue me, Catholic Church, for defamation by historical proxy. I've got the hot Powers QC. You never know, he might kick your ass.*

Anyway, separation, yes, I'd never have allowed you, Noods, to leave home, so of course you had to die to get away from me. And I'll inevitably never separate from my mother, or indeed any other members of my tricky family, wait for it, unless by death.

Oh, I don't know, I'm tired and a little drunk and fed up. I'm running out again. The best people in my life are taking the piss out of this book idea and I'm feeling that I'm growing out of my friends and too much ahead of them. Of course, in my most vulnerable moments I wonder if I'm lying to myself and they're right.

I'm going to create a talent competition, called 'Nearly Charlotte'. Contenders have to look like you, walk like you, be brilliant, sporting, amazing and compassionate, have a sense of humour and also smell like you. The closest lookalike etc wins. The prize is that I get to stare at them all day and be a bit happy. Oh dear, does that sound pathological to your radar, everyone? This is what I call 'moving on', oh dear, have I got it wrong again?

So change turns out to be a funny thing. It's not so much that I need to work out how I turn away from one thing as how I go towards another incorporating you. I feel free. And freedom is very confining if I don't know how to use it well. It can be a burden. The freedom of being at the top of the death slide and wondering what will happen if I allow myself to fall – like the freedom of cancelling routine and going to an station or an airport, the freedom from life and of life. So what is it I chose? It's all over now. The past, it's over and I want more than anything to tear myself away and begin again. But I don't know yet, what I want to leave or take. So maybe the best way is to go and do and find first and then put away what was. What's the worst thing that could happen? Whatever I do, I could change my mind five minutes in.

How did you move on, Mary? How did you put aside your unbearable grief and embrace anything new, without losing control? Tell me, Mary.

And what is this grief that I feel so privileged to have these days, this connection with a world that's hidden from us? This pure hell which by its lack of dilution becomes synthesised into something heavenly and therefore by some conjuring trick gives way to joy. Perhaps – and I can only think this must be so – because when you emerge from the pitch black, any light is sought, chased and mesmerising.

This 'chiaroscuro' of my soul brings about feelings of two extremes in such proximity. To feel pain of this calibre is to lie down with arms outstretched and allow a long, thin, sharp knife to run through me again and again and again and again. So much so that when I'm not doing it, I am anticipating it, and when I'm not anticipating it, I'm anticipating the anticipation, the doing and the shadow of both, and the joy that's felt when the blade is removed.

Life and grief are interwoven. As they should be.

Life is not a pleasure, we're wrong to expect such a shallow time of it. Life is hard, hard for us all, and if it isn't we must make it harder and feel privileged in doing so because only by these means do they, over there, suffer less. Carry what you can. I'll carry this for you. It remains as always my pleasure and my pain.

And yet bizarrely I'd rather be me now making this exceptional journey, with these interesting people that I've made privy to the ride, than any one else alive. I'm excited, at times fiercely excited.

I saw a girl in 62 The Bank in black and white. She's 15. I cried. I thought of you waitressing. Now I can see you. I know your mannerisms, you aren't looking at me, you're doing your work, your job, I annoy you, and you want to be apart. I feel the tension, I long to touch you, to hold you and to smell your neck. These are not mine to have, to take, you are not mine. The pain rips, I cry out. Grandma sees. She knows why the tears are hot on my face. She shakes her head. She purses her lips tightly to stop the sound. It travels down her body. We change the subject. We have to talk about something else. We *can* talk about something else. We laugh, and for a while forget. For a long while we laugh, we forget.

Broken, I am broken. And I'm frightened. What if I don't repair and nobody sees. I will just be dying. I feel bloodied and battered.

Walla Brook and Watern Tor, over and over and over again. Charlotte fell, Charlotte fell into a river, and Charlotte fell into a swollen river. Charlotte got swollen in the river with water. Charlotte Shaw drowned. I didn't know. Before the inquest I didn't know that Charlotte Shaw died at all, I just knew that she wasn't here. And I was waiting for her to come back. Now the bloodied arrows of hell have made sure that I properly understand what happened that day, and I do.

I've been there watching. I can see you exhausted, looking for a place to cross. Alone, feeling the responsibility of your peers. I can see you soaking wet, straps of your redundant rucksack cutting into your finally broken frame. I can see you trying to lead your miserable, wretched friends, in the freezing wind and mist.

There you go alive now, available to save. Last chance to save Charlotte Shaw. I can't, I wasn't there. The teachers couldn't, they were two or so hours away, couldn't get to you in time, separated anyway, by dangerous water in too many places, I hear now, not only Walla Brook but also a flooded ford near observation point 15. Oh yes, Charlotte, I've taken it all in. I've been respectful. I've dressed the part, and eaten, and put on my make-up, and washed, and smelt nice, and got good sleep, and drunk water, just so that I could hear, again and again and again once more how you died. From everyone's angle, and from many parts of the Moor and the river, from friends and strangers there's an account of how you fell. 'The last moments of Charlotte Shaw,' the Coroner called it the other day, that brought a refreshing new kind of sorrow, I hadn't heard it called that before.

It's come to me so many times now that I'm hardened, switched off, numb, fragmented. I'm emotionally shot and shot again, and beaten on top and kicked. I've heard it. When Charlotte Shaw fell, when Charlotte Shaw slipped into the river. When in Walla Brook, near Watern Tor, o

the way to Hangingstone Hill on Dartmoor, on Sunday 4 March 2007. These are bad words now, blasphemies. They affect me. They don't seem to affect the other people in the court. Nobody looks at me any more. Charlotte Shaw slipping is how they earn money today. 'Pockets, a Brief', their barrister, is earning money because you slipped and so he benefits. It just doesn't make sense.

I'm on guard against the rain of blows. I can defend myself now against 'swollen river' and 'Charlotte fell'. Can also manage 'children crying' and 'soaking wet' and 'wet through' and 'freezing cold' and 'we thought we were going to die'. But can't manage 'face down', or 'her leg was out of the water'. You see, I knew your face when it wasn't down and I knew your leg when it wasn't in or out of the water, but warm in our house. And that's what I cry for.

It's time for the Coroner to sum up. It's been over seven weeks' worth of evidence, although there was a nine-month gap after the children's accounts last December. And I've sat through it all.

Day in, day out I've found a way to confront my worst fear, that you suffered even for a while.

Oh Mary, was I right? Is it worse for you and me? Reliving the beating, the falling, the bloodied body, the over and over again, and then some more. Was I right that for Charlotte and Him it was only once, but for you and me it's over and over, daily, even in our sleep.

It finds me, the grief, the violent grief, it finds me, Mary, like a bully around a corner. It lurks, seeks and pounces. It has left me for dead.

I can taste the blood, I stammer, I'm virtually colour-blind, not great at traffic lights, because of the disassociation. My

brain's overloaded and yet there's nothing there. I'm mad and yet terminally sane.

Over and over and over again I can see you, my little Noods, wanting to prove yourself, walking upright, and wet, tired, and carrying that huge bag. The jury saw it, the rucksack. I saw it, pictures first. In a police booklet, a blue police-evidence, crime-scene, worst-nightmare booklet. That was a bad day. I didn't know what I was looking at, at first, and then I realised that it was your wooden spoon, your New Look top, dirty now. Your father's socks and the brand-new walking socks I bought for 10 pounds in the Mountain shop. A police booklet with photos of your stuff. The contents of your rucksack, the one I bought that day from the nice man in Millets in the High Street. My little Noods' little bits – clothing, wrappers, the cereal bar wrappers, I bought those, I recognise them, I remember their journey. Oh, the emotion over a piece of paper, just paper and material, a torn tea towel, such history in a tea towel. It's killing me and killing me some more. I yelped in the court, people saw, I yelped like a dog that had something sharp run over its foot. That's it, the difference, when you're hit with a sharp thing rather than a blunt thing.

A nail rather than a hammer. It causes a severe, not a dull sound. The sound of anguish, death, end, broken beyond, no hope of getting back. The compensation that I hope to get, Mary, is supposed to restore me, to where I was before, can you conceive such a possibility?

Can I feel anywhere close to what it was like with Charlotte, could you with Him? Could I undo the breakage, the time it's taken, and will take, the civil case they believe is going all the way to court? And then me at 50 maybe, what will be left, what can be salvaged, what undone? Miracles, helping, meditation, like you? Or park benches and drink, like every one else?

By the way, did you have nightmares about His nails? The ones that were driven in, without hope of undoing. Did you feel them in your flesh, one twice, always? Did you see it, make yourself look, four times as they were banged in, four times, in places severe, did you look, Mary? I dream of a scrunched-up, unidentifiable body in sodden waterproofs that have taken on the billowing murkiness of the water. They display always just enough characteristics of the human form to show that somewhere there is my little Noods, my Charlotte, Charlotte Shaw, C. Shaw, in the water. But not by the seashore having fun with sand castles and flags in the hot sun, with ice cream and laughing. Cold and dying and alone. Nails not for joining wood, banging into a hard, meant-to-be place, creating, excited, next project, but punishment for bad Jesus, young sweet-smelling boy, smiling at his mother through the pain.

There are too many unwanted images now. Too many tastes of blood. And too much cold and wet. I shiver and sneeze such a lot. I ask why the school always made you do five hours too much. They made you walk five hours from Rough Tor, when you needed to be home with me in your dressing gown with a hot bath and soup. I mustn't think about that because then I'm doing that for you and it's dangerous, because I want it so much. And then if I can't get you to be with me, the only choice is to be with you where you are, and that's another story.

One of the teachers must have really lost the plot. My psychological friend Amy says that he's removed himself from this, and has developed an alternative narrative, which he now believes.

You know, if I win the case and get money, at any one time, all it will buy me is coffee – a cup of coffee in exchange for you. I'm petrified by this outcome, and yet it remains one that I haven't chosen. I can only have a cup of coffee in exchange for you now.

So I've finally almost got through the inquest. It's been seven weeks of hell, including last December, and I'm changed.

I've heard things that have upset me beyond belief, and other things that have made imagery very sharp. I've felt helpless that I wasn't there and guilty because I should have protected you, and not left you with people who were going to discharge their duty towards you so easily. I've had to curb my rage and turn it into compassion and behave with grace.

I hate the teachers and the representatives of the school. I hate them for, as I may irrationally feel at times, 'killing' you. That's the bottom line, and then I rationalise. But before the rational, it's important to say that, more than for their behaviour which led to your death, I hate them for hiding the truth so inhospitably that we've had to dig so deeply to find it. I hate them for misleading me, sending me to Coventry and creating 'sides', and then calling the process 'adversarial'. I hate them for not caring whether or not I die now. And yet the hate is not quite that, it's more a deep sadness, a disappointment, the shame of a misguided trust, that once was there.

The only thing I could say to the press was that the school hasn't even said 'sorry', and that's spread about like wildfire, and I'm glad. This lack of apology is inverse to the amazing compassionate thing that you were, and that's something that needs to be said. I think Charles wanted me to rant and rave, and I'm doing that internally. But with my disposition it may not stop there if I begin.

Sadly, the inquest was limited, it can't bring about anything more than it has. A narrative that's bland. It's unable within its brief to slamdunk, and consequently I feel that we, collectively, have distilled for years, using amazing, polished, state-of-the-art machines, a single drop of quite murky, not even pure liquid in terms of this result. And that drop has struggled out of the tube.

I told someone from Launa Windows, someone who cold-called me out of the blue, I told her, a stranger, what the findings of the inquest were. And what was known to be true – sometimes I get the two mixed up. Sometimes, if some of the facts are left out, the rest falls short.

So what were the facts?

Like the other story, there are so many versions it's been hard to know what's what. But there's a thread running through that's indisputable and therefore enough. In a sense, when you know these facts, nothing more is necessary. He died on the cross. He was put there. His only crime was freedom of speech. And trying to encourage better life. We all know this. All of us are familiar with the story. Facts are facts, and the facts are friendly.

So you died by falling into a swollen cold river. You died from a word beginning with 'h' which gave you heart failure and caused you to drown. I believe and I hope that you were unconscious. I know that you hit your head and had another word beginning with 'h', which is to do with blood and a great knock. I always knew that you'd die in water. I know that most of your friends saw it happen and that they and you were extremely cold and that you were very likely to have hypothermia – see, another word beginning with 'h', I could almost start collecting them. You and they must have been terrified. And that, more than anything, gives me nightmares. You see, again I say it, I wasn't there to protect you, and that was always supposed to be my job.

I have a feeling you had hypothermia, because you didn't fight when you fell. You let it take you. This is what your friends said, and I wondered about it for a very long while. I romanticised that you didn't want them to feel bad because you knew there was nothing anyone could do, so you just gave in. I felt it was like Him in a way, you knew it was your time, or even that you were at peace, but there was a much more simple explanation. You were so, so cold. I feel that coldness now. I feel the coldness to the very inner core of my being. I am you.

The instruction, long before that point, should have been to get in your survival bags and wait for helicopter evacuation. The helicopter was called a little too late.

I gaze at your photo and wonder how you came to be in water. But really there was no choice, was there? It was raining. But not just rain, the kind that's relentless, and wind, practically gales, which made the rain horizontal and presumably blinding. This then makes communication difficult because hoods, though useful if you're falling into bogs over and over again, have to be pulled up tight and then you can't hear your friend. This would have made people isolated and miserable. The cold would have made everyone exhausted, not to mention the fact that, by the time of the incident you'd been in these atrocious conditions for seven hours, of which over five were unaccompanied.

Is this the new version of flogging in a public school, I wonder. As Michael Powers said, when he was cross examining that teacher, 'they learned their lesson, didn't they?' The teacher, of course, didn't get the irony about the situation he left you in. As I see it, this might have well been a punishment regime at Guantanamo Bay. You will go onto a moor with minimal access to kit and you will find your way out of it. You will be cold, hungry, wet and frightened in the extreme. You will be in winds, driving rain, with poor visibility. Go! Not much has changed since Tom Brown's school days after all. But at least my Noods took care of the one who was struggling. I'll come on to Yasmin in a minute.

It's always the one who survives who feels. The dead are gone. Feeling is heavy, very heavy, and Yasmin is bigger physically than she was three plus years ago – in many ways. It feels heavy for her.

He told you to look after Yasmin. And you did. When she was wet, you helped her on, when she was frightened you said it will be all right. When the foaming white water terrified her and Zoe, you said you'd look after them. I don't need evidence for this. And when Yasmin's hands turned blue and swollen, you said 'Enough'. You took her rucksack, you gave her the courage to cross the raging torrent and you tried to throw her huge bag on top of carrying your own across the river. You fell. You fell to your death and she saw. And now she's heavy and tired, always. Can you help her again, my Noods? I need you to help her again.

She is alive and carries an overwhelming burden of guilt.

Can you help in the way that Mary's boy helps some people on – by example? Can you do that for Yasmin, just once more?

I'm finding it so hard to rationalise the effort put into the inquest with what has been returned by the jury. Not so much the choice of words or phrases used, but the energy of it, the blandness, the lack of bite. Is 'blame' the word I'm looking for? No, it's 'truth'.

There were more barristers at the inquest than I've seen in my life. Of course, like attracts like, excuse my cynicism, Charlotte and Mary. But my team were top-dollar. The school's and the teachers', on the other hand, to me, were not. Their skills included misleading and fudging, perhaps that makes them first-rate in something.

Sometimes it seemed like a spoof of reality.

Back at 'the ranch' life goes on and there's a chasm between life as it is now and where I've been.

Crumble the gentle has been attacked by Grey Paws, I don't think you met him. He's beautiful and nasty. Maybe there isn't such a chasm then between here and there.

He had obviously established territory before we got Crumble in 2006, and that territory is the entire world. So Crumble slinks low around the decking when he's around, and looks pitiful.

If I don't look back... If I don't see you on the sofa in your white dressing gown... If I don't see the orange juice you've put down on the floor, I don't worry about it being knocked over. And I'm not drawn into your world, or the world I shared with you. Then I am all right. I'm outside. I'm not with you. I don't need then to long, or tear myself away. I don't watch you stuff your noodles into pitta bread. I don't watch you gaze at the TV, engrossed, concentrating. If I don't think about you at all, then I'm OK.

But then you're twice dead. You're twice dead and I have no feelings and there's a nothing, depression. Better to be alive as much as memory and desire allow you to be. Better a painful feeling than none at all.

Two more have died. My life is like war. Always a casualty, here, there and here again. Today, tomorrow, yesterday and then again. Always death, more death and then some more. Eat it, shovel it in, get to know every part of it, Jennifer, death will be your friend, your companion in your cell. Know her.

On the morning of my birthday, our very good friend Trevor died. Remember him? And with him, 19 years of friendship. Was that a present? Maybe so. He may be with you now. That's good for me. What else is good is that so much death of such important, well, significant people in my world means that the flow between life and death is much faster, the passage is closer, it becomes normal, commonplace and then acceptable. It's almost easy and then OK. Life becomes shorter and therefore more precious. And we then must work hard to make every day count. Because we're lucky to have it. Yes, that's another aspect of it, the fact that it takes nothing short of a miracle to conceive or, *in your case Mary, apparently a miracle,* but in most peoples' lives the concept of producing an embryo is quite remote. And therefore can only be precious, and must be guarded. My life is important. I must preserve it. OK. I hear what you're saying, 'Another U-turn.'

Were you alive when Mica changed her name to Katie? Well, check this out, I'm having a 'mother, behold thy son' – well, in this case 'daughter' – moment.

Do you remember Deana, Mica's mother? She taught you in the kindergarten. She always looked a little sad, which could well be because she was so 'religious' – well, that's another story that needs globally looking into. Well, of course, she has died. When will I ever mention anyone, except in connection with their death? She had a battle with cancer. She's had it on and off for a while, I think. Anyway, she's gone as well, maybe you know this. Maybe you, Trevor and she are playing cards in the holding Zone right now. Maybe there are all these makeshift families there that do so well. And you know each other – what a bonus. And like each other, even better. Is this what they might call pathological? By the way, when does 'boxing' and feeling content about something become creepy and mad to the non-expert experts?
Anyway, I drift. Mica is without her mother, as indeed I'm without you, my daughter. Daughter, behold thy mother. Mother, behold thy daughter.

Mother, behold thy son. Well, you know, why not?

Oh don't worry, I'm not going to dress her up like you, like I dressed Peta pussy cat as a baby when I was five. It really is just something to do. There's a space, a vacancy. So fill it. We can be useful to each other. Me more to her, I suspect. But she seems to be doing just fine. She's left the family home, told lies, met up with her 25-year-old boyfriend, gone to live with same and shut the door on her auntie's hand. I'd say she was bang on track, wouldn't you? *Sorry, Mary, but it's 'our Good Lord this and our Good Lord that', with some of her family's friends.* There's something very uncomfortable about that for me. Maybe it was just too much for her. It feels like words without real meaning. I forgot to ask you if it's all right to take Katie on. You have to say yes, don't you? Or you might hurt my feelings. Guilt? Even for the dead?

Day after day, I wonder what I'm supposed to be doing. Life does not and cannot continue for me in the way it was. You were it and now there's nothing. I wonder if this is what it's like to die.

I'm worried about two things: the aloneness, and having no money whilst being alone. There's no compensation here. At least not yet. I seem to have nothing and no one, and as things get worse for other people in today's world, this becomes more prevalent for me.

I wonder, am I going to starve, maybe starve to death? I'm eating less now, feeding your cats less and making things last in more compromising ways then I could ever imagine. Sharing food in my house now with anyone with any principles is not an option. First, snacks went and weren't replaced, and now wine. Chocolate has become a luxury item. And I portion off bread and freeze it and measure it out. Promise not to tell where I've come to, my Noods. I'm beginning not to socialise now, because I can't keep up. So there could be adverse effects for my mental health. I may become isolated. The worse thing, though, is witnessing other people being worried about having less. And here I mean less than 200 per cent. No wonder there's a third world. People are reluctant to give up anything.

I'm getting bored with waiting for a conclusion to the case, money, justice, and wonder if I should begin drastic measures, those used by my predecessors to get what they wanted from rigid institutions. Should I chain myself to the railings outside Whitehall until the school admits liability, apologises and pays up? Are there railings outside Whitehall? Or maybe take the protest around the school itself.

I'm now so worried about money. I work it out all the time. How long could I last, and I wonder what happens after that. When I have none left as I become overdrawn and bank charges escalate and go through the roof, I wonder what will happen to my emotional equilibrium – maybe I just won't be able to take it. The Neuropsychiatrist did say that I should be sure to get any payment due to me, because at least then financial pressures will be lessened, but once again the wheels have not only ground to a halt but the seeming resistance of these people to repair is frightening. I wonder if any other school and its representatives would behave in this way. And I'm reminded that this part anyway is not personal, that it's litigation and it's customary to fight.

No grandchildren for Jennifer. Such grief in that. People talk about the experience, what it's like, and it saddens me in advance, and I'm sad for Grandma when she must hear people talk about it cruelly over and over again. I say cruelly because it *is* cruel. They must do it deliberately. And no, I'm not paranoid. I'm going to start being a little less polite. You wouldn't talk to someone who's lost their legs about the joys of playing football, would you? So why do Steven and Phoebe talk to each other in front of me at length about their four a piece, yes four, not even one, children and their endless pursuits, successes and failures? Cruelty, that's why, lack of empathy, insensitivity, competitiveness, who cares, it boils down to cruelty. Steven then went on to tell Ian that he didn't want to talk about the soaps on TV, because it upset him. Conversation was then ironically changed. Of course, I won't be dating Steven, despite his ongoing pursuit. The fact that he keeps correcting people on their grammar, seems to know everything and is so difficult therefore to teach are also not the main reasons. It's just that he's not interested. And therefore, he's not interesting. Plus, he's trying to be young. And has a very floppy hair style. He seems to be resisting what is. Therefore he's stuck in the wrong time, and that makes for unhappiness. I know this. I no longer resist. I acquiesce.

Vegetarians (the Western variety), I hate them, have I told you? Steven and Phoebe are both vegetarian. See how it all fits? Loads of unreality.

Not seeking, but knowing. Is that the way? Is that the way towards holy? If I go to a far-flung corner of the world and know who I am and I give all of that, without any need to say, without the need to carry with me all of the past pain and, worse still, to present it. Will I be holy then? I want to follow in your footsteps. I want to do the unthinkable. I want to find the thing we seek. I want to bear the pain in every sinew of my flesh without pomp. Indeed, is to seek holiness unholy? The wanting must surely go against the grain?

It's a big deal to talk to people I don't see very often now. It's a risk. It's not so much that they might steal from me, but that they may try to change me, fix me. People can be very naive. They storm in. They don't look before they enter. This is so true of the people on the periphery of my pain. The ones who weren't at the inquest, who haven't known you, who don't have children, and cannot see. They always seem to ask a question that sets in motion a judgement. What do you do with your day? Answer, 'Nothing.' Answer to answer, 'Is that wise?', or a derivative of the same.

Driving back home, I realise that I can't see Trevor. That I won't see Trevor any more, ever again. I begin to fixate upon him. An image comes to mind. He opens his front door. I can hear his voice encouraging that crazy dog to stop bounding. I want that now. I want to have that again, now. I'm sad that I'll no longer sit with him and have lovely cups of Darjeeling tea and any chocolate torte he could rustle up. I used to envy his many copies of *National Geographic,* under his coffee table. I'm sure I could have them if I asked. I won't.

It's Trevor's funeral tomorrow and I'm in a dilemma. I don't know whether to go. I've been enticed in a rather disparaging way by Susan. I always seem to cause controversy. I seem to offend middle-class politeness of what's right, the sense of OK. Her question is, are they actually going to see me there to say goodbye to an old friend? It sort of sounds like she's asking whether I'm going to bother. This immediately makes my not going wrong and impertinent. The fact that I've already said goodbye to Trevor in my own way and don't want to watch the boring people do the same in a vacuous, virtual way, sanitising again, is seemingly beyond her. If she'd asked me if I was going because she wanted to go with me, then it would have been a different matter. I'm not going, because I know I won't respect anyone there. I have, as I've mentioned, said goodbye, in fact by text in the end because he was too weak to come to the phone, and his children, who will all be consumed by grief, won't know until long after that I wasn't there. That's when they'll actually need me, when no one else is available, because that's how it works in Vanilla Ville.

We'll see. Watch this space.

Well, I didn't go to the funeral. For once I made a personal choice. And felt suitably guilty for letting a friend down. That's the one who's died, not any who are alive. I then realised that it's the done thing to go to a funeral to show respect. Crap. Actually, crap. I've shown Trevor much care over the years and huge love and interest during his short illness, so for him I don't need to go. Besides, the thought of coming home alone, sad and confused is not for me today. So I pondered my choices. What do I do while everyone is hypocritically at church? Now, I know I seem to be labouring the point, but there's method here, as you'll see, Noods.

No one could see me at the required time for coffee. No one could offer solace. This got me thinking that perhaps I just need too much. The crisis is, after all, over. You're long gone and I must expect to get through
ordinary lonely moments alone. So I hatched a plan. I would play the battered violin, go for coffee in Atlantic Village and then bring a Chinese home and watch a film. Stunning. Inevitably I thought about it too much, time moved on. I was too late to realistically coffee at the Village, so I changed location. I went to The Plough in Torrington. It's always open, needs the money and by 5 p.m. on a Saturday all the little ballerinas and busy people have gone to their 'in between places'.

For some reason I procured a small coffee, even though I had plenty of time, and I hovered around the booking desk, where, I have to say, I spend quite a lot of my life.

Then the magic happened. A man was spreading CDs across a table. I asked Claire who they were for. She pointed to the poster. The three-quarters pose of Midge Ure stared back at me. As I pieced it together, she said three magic words, 'One ticket left.' What? 'It's tonight, Midge Ure, he's here now, he's a really nice bloke. He's back there setting up, A5, we have A5, just one ticket left. It's a once-in-a-lifetime opportunity. Just him and his guitar.' It's 14 pounds.

In my purse there was a tenner and four pound coins. It was meant to be. I handed over the cash.

Trevor and I used to listen to those very CDs.

Things do happen in threes. On this day of the unattended funeral, on the news I saw a graceful, beautiful woman walk away from captivity, Aung San Suu Kyi, but looking at her I'd say that she was always free. And I also received another letter from a national newspaper to put our story in their Sunday supplement.

Life is exciting, after all. In a surreal kind of way.

All in all, it was one of the best weekends I've had in a long time, despite untimely death – sorry to all the people who for this one minute are taking death seriously, whilst I'm not. And things work so well in threes. On Sunday I visited Amy, well for 10 hours actually, more of a holiday. She went to see her dad whilst I had a coffee and window-shopped. This mirrors my life. I seem to like window-shopping too when it comes to that.

I have a mince tartlet, which begins my own personal festivities. I begin to wonder if some magic will happen then too. At Christmas, I mean.

Wandering about Exeter, I saw a shivering, homeless girl selling *The Big Issue* and drew out 20 notes but she'd gone by the time I returned. When I say magic, I mean the unexpected gifts that are borne from openness to experience. And indeed waiting.

Amy and I saw a Mike Leigh film, *Another Year*. It got poor reviews from the *Sunday Times*, so on that basis I felt it would have a great deal to offer. And it did. Imelda Staunton opened and wasn't seen again but linked two of the next characters. We wouldn't have noticed her lack of reappearance if she wasn't so famous. The film was about the panic of being left out of society's game, and the making of family history, and witnessing the good times that we're all supposed to enjoy. I identified with that desperate Mary too, the one in the film, who seemed always to be on the outside looking in – remember the 'crumbs off the table' scenarios? Then off to Amy's for her beef in stout with a berry infusion. This was the day when I'm happy not being vegetarian. I didn't have to lie when I said it was the best beef dish I've tasted in my life. I think what made it was that it was slow-cooked and the beef once had a name. On this occasion I was happy to go along with the pomposity of choice that we have in this hemisphere. I'm truly get too tired to fight, sometimes. And realistically, if I'm willing to go along with flea-infested rice and the last piece of worm-ridden pork that they serve up in the poorest parts of the globe, I should equally, if given with the same grace, embrace the best parts of a beast, slow-cooked to perfection, of a once blissfully happy cow called Daisy infused before me now. The wine was good too: 2008, not a bad year, apparently, for either beast or grape.

The low point of the evening was a major discovery. Amy, whom I've known now for some 20 years, practically, has an alphabetically arranged spice rack. Jesus Christ, what you don't know about people! No wonder people have discovered that their brother is really their father. Things really shock, don't they? That spice rack is going to cause me huge psychological issues now, for sure. Already I've blocked out the one beginning with 'a', it may have been aniseed.

I seem to have a mixture of magic and misery. There's stuff in between, but it's unrecognisable, because it can't be categorised into dark or light. I wonder if I turn the grey into black out of fear. Or maybe I just need, and am extreme.

Sitting near two teenage girls and an adult woman who doesn't seem to be the mother, I fantasise. One of them could be you. I stare at the girl. I want her to see me. I want to talk to her, hold her, smell her, breathe her in, get my fill of her, pretend she's you and make her you. 'Bad, bad, very, very bad and possibly pathological.' I get carried away. I want to talk, find a way in – I'm searching, slyly foraging for ways to catch their gaze. I know I'm doing wrong and I know I could avoid this. I don't. I'm already feeling too sorry for myself that I'm stooping so low. You'd be so ashamed of me, I can see the look. But you, Noods, are only dead, not dead while being alive, like me. My heart beats, it beats until my teeth chatter so hard that they almost lacerate my tongue. A single tear falls, another and another to join that, and then more. I'm invisible. They get up, all laughing – they don't notice I'm there at all. Serves me right. Even I think that. This is a complete waste of grief, self-pity and a fantastic tantrum. I stop. I've been here before. I can recover. I do recover. I read the paper. I sit.

And I am alright. The worry is only whether I'm pretending. But isn't this what most people do all the time? Everyone pretends, that's why they use the phrase, 'I'm fine.'

I watch the coverage of the release of Aung San Suu Kyi and I wonder what her regrets are. I focus as usual on what price she's had to pay with her family for what she's chosen. I find myself myself asking, *Was it worth it?* In what circumstances could it be worth such a big sacrifice? Did she put her cause, albeit one so much bigger than mine, before her dying husband? Did she want to rail against any harshness of treatment and would she do so with grace? Is she all she wants to be? Is being democratic difficult for her, and when does democracy become lies? I want answers to my questions because I want to know how to behave.

O Mary, teach me the wonder that is you.

Regrets, although futile, can meddle with my status quo. They cause me anxiety and then I begin to go over and over and over things until I'm defeated and I make them right, whether they are or not.

When I look back, I do wish I'd appreciated things more. I wish I'd had concentrated more on what I was doing, taken it in, and in a sense been mindful. Like I am now. I own my space these days and I could have owned it then if I'd known what it was. I could have enjoyed every minute, and I regret that now. Or am I clutching at straws? I could have just done Charlotte, that's you, and I regret that now; I could have been more cohesive with family, and more proactive, and I regret that now. I mourn for what we could have had, for the efforts I should have put in and didn't, and that I'm now attempting to achieve, perhaps a little too late and against the odds.

Lessons, eh, they all come at a price. What rubbish! I did my best, tired as I was.

Talking of lessons, once again I come up against others' need for easy growth and significance. No one seems to want to lose in order to gain. Nobody wants to sacrifice. Everyone has a picture of how practical daily life should be, and there's no desire to challenge an experience for the greater spiritual good or any openness leading to the same. They are afraid of contaminating life and opening themselves to suffering, but they want a short cut to spiritual growth. They want the diamond but don't want to do the hard grind. I have no choice.

Some people by excluding the dirt want to have the perfect time. They don't want to risk including anything which makes the picture imperfect. I am that imperfection. I am the archetypal old maid aunt now who is like coleslaw, missable, on the side, only a little necessary and then only if you like coleslaw.

When they are seeing their daughters, they won't share. They will have it all, now and next time. They need it and will not dilute the experience in favour of a person that has lost more than they could ever conceive.

As we travel towards yet another Christmas, without you, I find myself filled with the joy and expectation that it could bring. This I cannot understand. I'm excited – why? It's as if the warm feelings are still there, a sensory reaction to lights, smell maybe, but so redundant. I must be miserable. Surely, I have to be miserable. I'm nervous because the feelings are inappropriate, because I know the reality will be with me eventually. In this way it's like torture. Sort of like seeing a Christmas tree with many presents under it, which turn out, one by one, to be empty. Torture, pure and simple. And yet I feel that it's acceptable, OK. It's as if the anticipation is enough. I don't, we don't, need, and there probably isn't any anyway, reality. And after all, you never know what's around the corner. Grandma said '*Dum spiro spero*' – 'While I breathe, I hope.' She's clever at times. Let me not underestimate this.

There is, of course, something about this season which favours rebirth, renewal, family and cosiness. And I imagine myself beginning again somehow. There are 60 million people in this country alone: someone must want me, and me them. And yet I worry about what kind of disadvantage a child, if there'll ever be another, in any capacity, would have to live with, coming after you.

I wonder anyway, if I could have you back, what I would do. What would it be like? Would we, even at your age, now go straight back to our arguments and difficulties? Has being away from me for four years nearly taught you such measures of independence that you wouldn't wish to relinquish them? How silly I am to follow yet another path of non-existent hope and impossibility.

Better, I suppose then, the pathological fantasy plan I had yesterday, of following nappies in the back of a car in the hope it would lead me to the infant who was wearing them. Don't worry, I didn't, I wouldn't, I know what's right and wrong, I'm not mad, and you don't need to lecture me. It was just a passing fantasy, not even a thought, more of an if-I-was-imbalanced-that's- what-I'd-do kind of thing.

I'm truly getting a bit sick of repeating our story. Especially to the press. I'm fed up of waking up three feet from your room. I'm wondering when this is going to stop. Of course, the good and the great have wondered for some time when I'll move on – no trust, you see. But I do feel that I need a new plan. It's OK to write about the grief, but I think I need to look now for new experiences, and my line should be, that I wake up three inches from a 6-foot tousled-haired American. Yes, that does sound amusing. You see, you can get sick even of this. In 20 years will I be telling people I've lost my daughter? And how will I say it? I will always have lost you. But will I have a new daughter, ever? And then what if I lose her too? Of which daughter will I be speaking? Am I now willing the same fate to be repeated over and over again? Can I not conceive a single chance of happiness?

The thing is, the reality is, there's no plan for starting again. There's no step. It just occurs. There's no 'line', no 'next', no 'moving on', there's just now. What am I doing now? And this leads to the next now, which becomes then, and then another now ... if you follow me.

It's new life and commitment I need, not experiences. I'm now on the line that separates past from future. I have to take a leap, a leap of faith. So I've contradicted myself, haven't I? There seems to be concerted choice and movement involved if I want something to happen, and that is so hard. But maybe it begins with putting one foot proverbially in front of the other.

It really is better to move forward than stick in the past. Life is really all about choices. And how we use our energies. I have a choice right now of how to use my rage. I could stand outside the school and pass out leaflets telling parents what kind of place they've signed up to, but it could hurt me more than them. I foresee that I'd be outside the place you loved and supported for so long with different feelings. I can feel the sadness and confusion already. And what if I was marched off the premises, what then, and what is it I want to achieve? Better that my energies are used to make a life better, not mine or anyone else's worse. So my goal will now be, by concerted effort, to create a space to begin helping women like me come to terms with grief and its accessories. If you lose a child it's only right that you try and live as well as you can, and help others with your experience.

I don't believe you have to have a lot of money or resources to begin something. I think if I just do it, then it will fall into place.

And so life goes on most of the time, and depending on what I think, I feel down or up.

At the moment my solicitor is gathering children's evidence once again, this time for the negligence claim, and I can't help worrying about the time that's passed, and the children who'll be asked this time who were not before.

It's all about a defence point that has become quite big: whether or not they were told to cross the river. I don't even need to name this now. My feeling, and that of my team, is that whether or not they were told to cross is immaterial to the situation, as they were as a group in rag order, freezing cold, soaking wet, tired in the extreme. They also had no, and I repeat no, other choice. If they'd walked around the head, they would have come across another obstacle, and so on. Oh, I forgot, it was you as well. *You* crossed the river. Oh the confusion! It was you as well, that's why I'm doing this.

I'm depressed, and my guess is, this is the fight. And people will be dirty, because that's apparently the nature of litigation, and the nature of some people also. I must be there to look into the Judge's eyes to make the difference. I can remain decent, I know I can. My God, I see why sometimes people are driven to take matters into their own hands. And indeed how they could wait to do so. Charlotte, would you like to know about the crazy fantasies this Scorpio is having about futuristic revenge? I won't do it, don't worry.

Don't give me the look. I can see you. It's always accompanied by that displacement licking of the lip. When I do that, I feel that physically it must be to keep one's mouth in check and indeed to stop oneself talking. I wonder what you would have wanted to say to me if you could. I miss the mixture of behaviour and your father's genes that was you. There was really nobody like you in the world, was there? Have people forgotten that I wonder?
And so I go on and try to reframe and look at what is good.

Not many people I know are mixing daily with such a high-calibre legal team like Michael Powers and Charles, witnessing such interesting expertise and being able to call them friends. And having now an inroad to phenomenal reporting, like *The Telegraph*, *The Sunday Times* and John Paul (famous) Flintoff, as well as, I feel, in time, linking with *Woman's Hour* on Radio Four, then I could really reach women in need. I've also made friends with Catherine, although I already know two saints by the same name. She's a *You* magazine reporter who thinks I'm the most incredible and real person she's ever met. I don't know that I've ever received such an accolade.

The writing goes on and on.

Soon – I mean in the next decade – I may begin to help women severely traumatised by grief. Once I'm on social media – and I'm being set up next week – who knows? It really is all a bit exciting in a way.

And don't forget, Noods, my endless practising – and I'm never sure how my neighbours feel about it – of 'the violin'. Now that's a rap. As well as seeing friends now and again, stroking cats and drinking fine wine, what else is there anyway apart from memory? I do believe then, based on this definition, that my life must chalk up amongst the best. Did I mention that in five weeks I'll run out of money? Fine wines finish then, I reckon.

I'm terribly sick of vacuity. This disease praises speed and immediateness and calls things amazing, when we should notice and ponder that wonderful things only happen slowly, not as a one-hit wonderness. I'm also saddened by the fact that no one else seems to have this view. I'm the most interesting thing I know. Oh yes, Noods, I can see the face in passing. And for those reading, I'm not a megalomaniac, but there must be an incredible depth to a woman who, alone, has survived this – I'm pointing to a double dose of death – and still is fun and is motivated and has passions. I attribute my long-term success now as survivor to having passions which motivate, something that most people, I notice, lack. And actually, ironically, are beginning to be jealous of in me. They have nothing to fill their time, apart from distraction, and therefore only dribble from day to day. There's no one as unhappy as an individual who doesn't strive for something, and I don't mean in terms of acquisition, I mean growth and knowledge.

What's happening now? Am I destined forever not to concentrate? I nearly went in front of a truck. I saw the truck. It was there. I was concentrating. I just didn't connect it as a truck. It wasn't something that could harm me. My associations, my connections move really slowly. The concept of this being a truck that could wipe me out if I crossed its path was only known to me as I nearly walked in front of it, and that has scared me. The fact that therefore maybe I'm not in control of my own safety is a problem.

Sometimes I'm scared of more death, and then more. And I wonder when it will come. Sometimes I'm even scared to think about it in case I bring it on, like a period, or a cold when you stand in the rain for too long. And yet I know it will come. All I know is that one day all those who are part of now will be gone. It's fair to say that in 50 years the people who were part of our parent's generation will be lost and forgotten. This continues to teach me that we must be with what is now and spend our resources on trying to minimise misery and not mourn too much for what isn't.

Oh God, it's all happening again, the unhappiness. And then I eat chocolate. If I said that out loud, I know people would say, 'What could you possibly have to make you unhappy, look at you so young and healthy and well dressed.' Yes, look at me, look at me and weep for what's inside. I hold myself together. I try hard. I work at it and it cannot be seen. I eat chocolate, not because I've broken a nail, but because it provides me with calories that I sometimes don't get when I eat too small a portion, because I've forgotten how to swallow. Because I need to do anything sometimes that makes it look like movement is happening. And even then I eat a small portion of that. Also for the iron. I'm worried at the moment that I'm one of the following: stressed and ill, beginning the menopause or pregnant. I've missed a period, for the first time in my life. Am I dying? I can't be pregnant because *I haven't had sex, wait a minute, no, let's not go there, Mary, I've just replayed my thoughts, they'd lock me up if I began to question that 'immaculate' notion as well, and yet for you, many do. Not to mention, if I lost this child too. Oh no, we're not going down that road.* It must be stress, because there are no symptoms of anything else. If I did have a baby, it would be a sister for Charlotte, oh no, can't have a sister for you, you're dead. So another only child of a single parent, protected and yet hopelessly vulnerable. No!

One minute I'm happy, the next heartbroken, one minute I'm coping, the next anxious about sailing through a red light because my disassociation means that colours don't mean the same any more, have I said that already? To be a parent you at least have to know the differences between the colours. I really have gone back to the beginning.

Life is moving on. Prince William is getting married. She seems like just a girl, but of course she's a woman really, Kate Middleton. As I watch them posing for the cameras, I'm reminded curiously of you and Neil. Some of his mannerisms, a sort of resignation and holding of pain, are Neil, and her gentle charisma and naivety, but also her steely preparedness, are you. Unlike your life, though, let's hope theirs is not spoilt by her death and his family having issues about the legalities. Better say no more, else may end up in the Tower. On another note, it's funny, because the press have uncovered a school play that the teenage Middleton was in. In it there was a proposal for her from a prince, whose name was William – life mirrors art once again. In my school play I was Old Gobbo, Lancelot's father in *The Merchant of Venice*, a nutty, older, what seemed like transgender figure, I played him as a woman, a comic character, but even with a small part that no one else would have wanted I seized opportunity and took the place by storm. Life and art come to mind again.

It's easy to forget sometimes that people are dead. I turn to you, Noods, 19 years of age, vibrant, clever and beautiful, and you are not there. I want to tell you so much and you are not there. Sometimes I want to tell you about you, and you are not there. I call to Custard, and sometimes when in what seems to be a full house, with energy and memories and hope, I call her Charlotte, and I'm reminded once again that I'm stuck in the past, and you, Charlotte Shaw, may very well have been a figment of my imagination. You are, after all, not there.

Am I stuck? This is such an awkward time for death to prevail. To begin to look back is the beginning of old age, and it's too early for me. I wonder if I can make for new life, if I can adventure, or if I want to adventure again.

I think about people. I fantasise about whom I'd like to share life and intimacy with. I need a mate and I need the extensions that brings. Family, I want and yearn for family. I want to witness someone's life, build memories and buy presents. I want to mean something to someone, who notices when I'm not there. Should I just go headlong in without thinking? I mean, just get pregnant, ignore past, present voices in my head. Maybe I should just find a partner and start from there, but then I'd be 50 before I'd conceive and that would be 10 years after my mother had me, and she was tired. Maybe I'll join a family that already exists, a widower with two small children, no, that's getting far too prescriptive. So back to where I always get to after the panic, carry on doing what I do, the rest will fall into place. I must remember not to do anything for the wrong reasons. If I do, then things could be worse. It's not a good idea, just to tick a couple of society's larger boxes and because people want to see me 'settled', to marry a man to whom I'm not attracted and have a child who may be challenging at best or have a physical abnormality at worst. Charlotte, you were after all perfect and I loved your father deeply. If my life had run its course and you were away at university, and I mean far away, and he'd left me, in fact geographically things would be the same and yet I wouldn't so strongly be craving repair. I have, after all, had the experience, even if it fails to continue.

And yet still I see a little girl in the bank, she runs up to me with expectation. She hands me something, I don't know what, and I wish so dearly to take her home, cook for her and put her to bed with a story. I've grown so tired of waiting for you, Charlotte.

Helen's baguette is bigger than mine. I make it mean something. Helen has Gordon, and he's a man who eats lots of baguette, Grace will be eating baguette too, as will the friends she'll invite whilst eating baguette. Helen, of course, having bought baguette, will be only too happy to eat the same. Now, if we do the equation and give all these people baguette shares compared to mine, it goes something like this: Gordon 3, Grace 2, Graces' baguette-eating friend 2, Helen 1. This then explains why Helen's baguette is nearly nine times the size of mine. See, inequalities even with Helen, in the baguette-eating challenge.

I have too much time on my hands. I know. I can see the silent stare. And the whooshing sound of despair you often used to make.

You think I make too much of every little thing.

There might not even be a tomorrow. So really I have to do the best I can today. I have what I have now and that's what I need to remember, not regret, not wish back. Easier said than done. I must be responsive to my parents and enjoy them. Enjoy, before I can't and then it's wishful thinking and regret. And looking back again at something else.

Grandma wants to stay the night in the hotel next to 62 The Bank. Which is quite good really, isn't it? It means she's branching out. It's only in Barnstaple, and she's still pre-contemplative, but we'll get there. Seize the day, isn't that what we said? I'm thinking that she hasn't wanted to do too much since you left, but as soon as she has an idea it's good to act upon it. Unless, of course, it's unsuitable. Do you remember the time she got into the Cage at Butlins? I tried to warn her, but she liked the idea. When she came off, she felt that all her internal organs had been rearranged. And she thinks she can advise me, what a joke. I stuck to the Merry-Go-Round, the tamer the better.

The dreams are constant now. Or rather they're nightmares. It seems I'm under attack. First there was you tied up and being dowsed with water by your friends. You look cold and sorrowful and I'm nowhere near. Then Crumble comes in. As he turns around, I notice his leg is missing. It's a bloody stump. He struggles with balance. I'm sad to see the two most important, most significant lives in torment. It seems to be all about your suffering, my loss and the inevitable helplessness that follows.

Did you dream, Mary? Your subconscious must have needed to process. Did you wake up with the feeling that you were bolted to wood? That your wrists and legs were attached by small pieces of wooden pin to further wood and if you moved that your body would rip apart? Did you feel your body rip apart? Was there body left? Was there anything left?

Did you control yourself to move slowly as you woke so that you didn't disturb the nails that attached you to your bed? In the same way, night after night, I navigate my way now under a dark boat, through water, seeking the light beyond to respond and come up for air. I long for the day when I can control myself and not panic and wake up with an explosion of breath above the water, covered in the sweat of my juices, and occasionally, pitifully, a trace of my own urine. I long for the day when I don't wake up thinking that I'm drowning, feeling my throat scraping against brine, rasping, smelling of bilge, seeing her in all kinds of green and blue and brown and squelch and dirt, and confusion with a crime drama seen on TV the night before, and the words 'drowning, drowning' over and over in my head.

I have your baby teeth. I stole them from the fairies. I got them out just now, and lined them up. I was hoping to make your smile. I cannot. I smell them, a couple were extracted and have blood on them. I press my nose so close, but no smell comes. I want to lick them, but don't want to take anything away, so I don't. I'm crying. I look at your photograph, and badly want to touch you, to see if you're as I remember. I am so, so sad once again that I feel only death could ease this pain. I feel sorry for myself and that's even worse, because I think of all the things I could be now rather than this. But then I recall what Trisha said in The Plough yesterday, when I was coffeeing. She said I should have this forever because it's a bond, and it's a strong marvellous love between two people – you, Noods, and me.

Mary, I can't understand a world without photography when you're mourning the loss of a child. How did you remember what He looked like? Did you go over and over the curves of His face until you were unsure whether they ever really existed? Unsure of whether He ever really existed. Did you only see in your mind's eye the bloodied and battered, swollen-lipped and -eyed shell of the boy you loved so dearly? Was that the image now etched with permanence on your mind? Could you go back in time and recall the boy, the infant? Without photography, could you remember? Did you see Him in detail? Today so many memories we have are by proxy. We rely on photographic witness.

It takes a picture to jog the memory of you, in the garden when we had a picnic when you were four. I can remember the moment, but wouldn't remember who you were then, unless I had you on photographic paper to remind me. You wore a funny hat, your face was covered in ice cream, you were laughing, a trickster in a cardigan, with little shoes and socks, and colourful.

I wake up once again with images in my mind of you, just a hope away. The worst agony a mother can experience. Once again I'm committed to looking at you behind a glass screen in a dream. You're always over there, down there, behind a window or in a line of children. The agony of you being so close torments. I can feel even in sleep the hope in the rise of a heartbeat, the joy, the movement within me, the surge, and the energy as I prepare to move forwards, to take. I want to take. I want to go forwards and take this moment, to take you and have you as close to me as I physically can, and I want it now. I scream inside and I wake up with an overwhelming sickness and loss as you fade. You've deliberately taken yourself away. I hate you, I just hate you. No sorry, Noods, no sorry, come back, sorry, I won't do it again, please, Charlotte, come back, tomorrow night, come back, don't leave me. I will put up with the pain, I will, I can do it, you'll see, I'll be OK. Give me a second chance. Please Charlotte, Noods, please.

I'll be good.

Please, Noods.

Don't leave me. Not again. Let me have this, even this.

Did you just have a handful of nothing? I can see you, Mary, uncompensated, bending, searching, dust and status slipping through your fingers, one tear only mixing the dry remains of a great life, to make solid that which belonged to everyone, that you made, that you loved, that you and only you lost. I can see the dry earth on cheek, the stress making dry tongue in mouth, the precious one tear, rationed to fall.

It snows. It's a year or so since we last had such a shared crisis. I want to help. I think of my parents and whether they've done their shopping and of Sybil Shepherd next door. I think of saving them all from the weather. I didn't save you. A what's-the-point? feeling comes over me. But then this is what is now, and there's always point. As wise people say.

You know, I was sometimes a bit resentful of you, I am loath and ashamed to say so. But I know that as we're complex creatures, we're never one thing only. I often wonder if you felt let down by us all. And felt it was you against the world, including me.

There was a conflict in my love for you. I wanted you to achieve all your goals, and I wanted to watch you fly, but often I needed gratitude, or at least a little politeness, and I was resentful when you didn't display it. After all, it was hard for me as a single parent to give you such a lot, and psychologically, when growing up, I feel that less was thrown my way. So there were times when I compared, and was irritated and showed it, and then I felt guilty. But then I was just human, and I'd err.

I never knew how close to be to you. I could never fully understand separation. But you took it, whereas in my teenage life I don't think I did. And I wonder if I still can't. To be sure, I'd have to know what it actually means and also get the hang of the east-west differences. But then again I'm completely self-contained in this journey and don't really need my parents seemingly as they need me. So maybe I *have* separated. And if they haven't, so be it. And really, does it matter?

Oh God, sometimes I awake with a feeling of foreboding and I have to go through things in my head to understand which distressing piece is top today.
The most damming thing for me is when people don't listen or when their threshold for difficulty is so small that I have to keep humouring them. I just want people to take on a small part of this, a little of the unspeakable detail. Please someone take it.

I saw Jane. Zoe's home for Christmas. Jane supported me at the inquest. She wrote a statement. I'm surprised at her guts and pleased. You'd be pleased with her too, Noods. Do you think there could be a superhero called The Noods? I want you to come home for Christmas. 'Ah. you expected that, didn't you?' Yes, I'm so competitive. What Jane has, I want. 'Well, Jenny, just because someone else has an alive daughter who's coming home, it doesn't mean you can have it as well. You can't have everything you want in life, you know?' Ah, a nice helping of self-indulgent self pity to start the day.

You know, in a way I'm glad the inquest was so long after your death, because life had a chance to be clean, before the fighting, media frenzy, barristers and litigation took hold and then it became dirty. The fight began, the mess began, and the money began, this is phase two.

People don't understand me. They really don't see who I am. And I've nothing to say. I'm quiet, colourless once again. That isn't strictly true, is it? I have much to say when I have a receptive, risk-taking, open audience who delight in the truth.

But I see it now. Mary, you were like a white translucent light. There's apparently no colour, nothing there, vacant, and yet all colours must fuse to make it. So much behind what seems to be so little. And yet it isn't little. It's the silence that descends when all the work has been done, such power to seem like one thing when you're so much more. To be an integration of everything, simply manifested as clear, all that you are, camouflaged or invisible, waiting for the knowing, the believing to see. Of course, you may also be like black paint, all colours when mixed make that too. But most people are unable to see. They only know what's on the surface, the colourless light or the black mess.

The fact is, people respond to noise, and if you're quiet they think you've nothing to say. They also respond to action and status, and if you deny both, you'll be unimpressive. So who could you have possibly been to these, the masses, a mother whose son had been killed in front of her publicly, and a woman who was responsible for this man, who produced Him from her womb? And it was decided on that day by those people that he was bad and wrong and illegal, and you had to contain your pain. You were a vessel for the scapegoat of the wrongs of the world. And all its wrong decisions. You alone knew and you alone bore Him.

So what are you really about? Integration, knowing, without need to shout. It is still about the pondering, the wait, the holding, and the holiness. Frank said yesterday that my mind was elastic and incredible, as I described this to him. That felt good. I love the recognition. I must be shallow. I bet you didn't need praise, did you?

Of course, in many ways you and I have integrated darkness and light to form a calm presence. We are everything to those who wish to see. We have had to become everything, otherwise there's only death.

Hell is only hell until you know hell, and then it's only hell until you know more or different hell. We all think that our experiences are as bad as any can get. 'The worst thing has happened,' we say, because for us it's the very worst, but only so far. By the nature of our understanding of difficulty, things will invariably get worse, if they're already hard.

So what am I saying? If the hell stops here, that I can live it? If I know now or knew then that this is it, I could contain it?

But surely the hell is as much in the anticipation as it is in the reality?

I sit and no one comes, or seems to care. Is this the truth or my own self-pity? Whom do I care about? To whom do I go? I have to strengthen my good relationships. I feel everyone is against me. Is this to be expected? Is this what the law does: splits people into sides? Not everyone but some that I've known for too long. Some relationships have to mean nothing now. I need to get my head around this failure. They don't want to help me in giving evidence. They disagree with the litigation. But they are intact. They don't want to do it any more. I can't help but feel that people are turning, but there's no evidence to substantiate this notion. Parents, two, stupid cowardly parents, are just trying to protect their child, mine, that's you, has died, but it's OK as long as they're not put to any inconvenience.

I'm trying to put myself in their position. But I can't be so useless with so few values.

I question whether I'm doing the right thing in pursuing this litigation. I need someone to talk it over with.

I feel like saying goodbye to everyone and taking my leave. I'll thank the ones who deserve such an accolade and blame the ones who don't, in the form of a list.

Oh for God's sake, Mary, don't judge me. People must have added insult to your injury. Crossed pathways, not made eye contact, spat. Those who didn't think He was king of the Jews, did they spit at you? Did you feel like crumbling under the stress of it? Is that why you left to live in Ephesus? I think that's why John took you away, for that so-called 'fresh start', and yet you may have only lived for about 20 years more. It's suggested that you were about 64 when you died. And then it would have been a ripe old age, unlike today's need to live to be 100 for some bizarre, useless reason.

When it gets dark, I'm afraid. It's dark now. I try something else. It's nearly midnight. I imagine I'm returning to you and Johnny from our pizza shop 14 years ago. I drive along. Now I'm at the village sign and I can see lights on in our house from the back. You're in bed, Johnny is having a beer. I get the flavour, the feeling of it, of me, of us, of us three, then. I want to know what the formula is for that. I want to make that. Can it be scientific enough to manufacture? Or can I pretend? Is that what I'm asking?

Does it really matter that you're gone? What's the equation? If I can artificially produce this, does it matter? Maybe I can pretend, and then arrive home to find that you're conveniently out.

How am I doing this? Do I look at what's possible? I think it's like being in any prison. You have to work within the confines. Then you make good. Don't rail against it. It doesn't mean you can't fight some battles.

Did I want to be on my own in this house? Is that what I was looking forward to? Well, I have it now. I've got rid of Johnny and now you. Everyone has gone and I'm completely free. Don't all women want time to themselves, though? I cannot have wished for your death. I'm broken by it, and that alone tells me that it was not wanted.

I'm feeling very suicidal. I think, and I'm still not sure, that I'd do it if there was an easy way. What makes this more necessary now? I'm let down, and isolated. I'm angry and misunderstood. I'm paranoid that everyone is turning against me because I'm bringing down a school. Although I'm not. I'm merely seeking justice. I feel that my status and reputation are being destroyed by the concept of money, almost more now than that teacher's status is lessening. It isn't about money, this is the only way a lesson can be enforced. I feel people are now focusing on the litigation rather than on your death, and seeing me as grabbing rather than sorrowful. This is made real by the comments of two parents about their not agreeing with the litigation, but it's not their child, of course. And others' heads bowing, or crossing the road, to avoid me. This is again a symptom of middle-class uselessness. If you don't agree or you disagree, quietly cross the road. By the time you get to the other side, the problem will have gone away.

Who travels the furthest in betrayal? Who is the most disappointing? Is it the ones whom you trust the most and who undo the trust enough? Or is it the ones whom you trust the least and then who are most against you. I think it's in fact the former? The unexpected betrayal of those who appear closest to you. Keep your friends closer than your enemies, I think. Sometimes they're the one's to be watched. People are only as good as it suits them to be, particularly if they have something to lose. And in this world of plenty, when we all want significantly more, we watch and wait. We have to wheel and deal with goodness. It seems that it's a commodity that can't be given freely. They can't be totally 'true'. It's a shame. They are shame.

They are shame incarnate. It looks like they feel it too, the shame. But it doesn't matter. They're used to it.

That's why He died, wasn't it? To shame them, the greedy, the wrong, the misled. He tried and tried to make things different, and in the end He had to commit a kind of suicide, an 'I'll show you', a 'Watch this, you have become so rotten that I have to do this to make you see.' A sort of angry death really, a self-sacrifice, verging on a suicide by proxy. Selling His body and soul for the highest price, truth. Nothing has changed, you see, Mary, and He should have seen that. Despite this thing called Christianity, nothing changes. People are still dirty, and don't give or believe freely. They're still ashamed and predominantly guilty. They're afraid. Afraid of being outside of the circle, no matter what that circle represents. They bully and cheat their way through everything and then absolve themselves with holy wine, the rosary and justification. These animals we call humans show now the worst of themselves, just as they did over 2,000 years ago. We're right to think that nothing has changed.

Michael Powers said of your death and Dartmoor, there are so many ways to die and some are quite ugly, like a road accident on a busy, dirty street. We all have to die, somehow and somewhere, how better and where better than here in this way? On beautiful Dartmoor, doing what you love. Yes! Immaculate re-framing, only by such a person.

Ho ho ho, it's Christmas time again. And as we celebrate the birth of a special child, we're reminded of how he was betrayed, from the beginning, and encouraged to die at the end. And let's look at the beginning, and by whom he was betrayed the most. Yes, that's right, the ones who told Herod, the ones who blabbed, who couldn't contain what they knew, the ones who told Herod, so that all boys under two were slaughtered. The ones who then left quickly after most of the damage was done, because they wanted to keep

221

the prophecy to themselves, the opulent, possibly scheming, well- educated, wealthy, middle-class Magi, that's who!

So, Mary, you've been through it, haven't you? Your own seven sorrows? First, being told that He was special and that a sword would pierce your side. I think that the most painful sorrow must have been seeing Him on the way to Golgotha. Passing Him by as if you were a stranger. And Him addressing you as part of the collective of women. My sorrow is always in the fear of seeing her somewhere and her not recognising me. Or worse, me seeing her and her not seeing me.

Before I had you, I used to dream that I would stand in front of two barely marked graves, but they weren't those of my parents. I was sad as I looked, I now know them to be those of you and Johnny.

And so they betrayed, and betrayed some more. I wonder if there was any need to think of any good consequences. But you remain in a domain then, don't you? The domain of lack, of non-growth.

Were you afraid, Mary, from the outset? Did you never know whom to trust? Must have been like living in a bad cop movie. They called you 'woman' as if you were one of many. Like, I am the family of Charlotte. It depersonalises us. It lessens their concept of our pain if we're diluted. And yet we're the single bearers, the single witnesses, to the sorrow of life and death.

I notice that when things are bad, it's hard to prevent them from escalating. Soon, if I'm not careful, the world could be sealed off against me. Me bad, world good, me loser, world winner. Me dirty, world clean. I am the Third World. I am the dirt on the shoe of the West. I am the secret that they want to hide. I am the guilt and the shame and the rage. It's me. I am the thing that cannot be ignored. At least the Third World can be kept over there, but I can't. I keep turning up like a balloon that insists upon bulging through a keyhole. I burst as balloons do. The explosion won't be kept at bay, will it? Even the best often wish me to keep in a box, to take out during moments of plenty, when they can spare a penny, Mrs. Oh, how lovely! Is that what you support, oh the widows' charity, those who have lost children, you've given a tenner again, well that means you don't have to go round there for a cuppa this month. Oh, I hear she died. When will it shake you up? Starving babies don't do it, mothers with a deadly virus won't do it either, so why should a pretty Westerner who has her own house, why on Earth would you have time for her? Mary, I assume you had your own house. You know, Mary, I'm getting so paranoid that if someone I know is just having a bad time or preoccupied and don't give me the time of day, I assume they've been influenced by gossip about the litigation and are uncomfortable about me or disagree with me, without knowing the full story, of course. I must find a way of seeing it as other people's problem and not as my own. Maybe I should move to the East and be with my own kind, whoever they are. Maybe I could find a way of increasing their capacity so that the West becomes the poorer and more grateful. Isn't that what they call war? 'Big job, Jenna, big job.' The truth is that in taking on litigation I'm no longer chaste. It is, after all, black and white with the middle classes.

I've sort of confronted my fantasy lately. This means if I suspect someone of being 'different' towards me, I deliberately engage them in conversation. The trouble with the British, though, is you'll never know if they don't like you, they'll be polite until the bomb's within an inch of them. Anyway, I confront them and see whether the body language is different. I even hide after I've spoken to them, if they're with someone else, just to check whether or not they say something about me that makes the situation clearer. Oh yes, I've had that. That's the woman who's suing the school. Oh, I thought I was the woman who's in agony after losing her precious little girl. Didn't you know if you can take legal action, then your agony disappears? Just like that.

Perhaps in some cases none of this is true. A lot of people aren't actually aware that I'm taking a case at all. After all, most don't know what day of the week it is in others' lives. They don't even stop and think one way or another.

I think I need help. I need to live with another. I feel like I'm showing the symptoms of madness as I have no one to bat ideas off, and no frame of immediate reference. It feels necessary now to look at what's possible in the way of making changes. But it does seem like I'm reluctant to share my space or move. Which makes me assume it can't all be bad?

Crumble, go find Charlotte. More madness to indulge in. Crumble go find, he hears the computer, he smells your room, and something familiar stirs inside his little body. I see you. I've given you extension. You have cats. I am pleased. I'm sure. Crumble wants to find you. He howls. I want him to want you – I want anyone to share this outstanding pain. Crumble, go find Charlotte.

Any pets apart from the donkey, Mary? There is, after all, always a donkey.

Your room poses a problem and I've just realised why. It's holy. No, don't roll your eyes and laugh at me, and call me deranged. Hear me out. Your room is a familiar yet strange place. It's where two worlds now meet. This didn't used to be the case. It was then a little girl's bedroom. Your bedroom. Now it's clear to me why people call a child's room a shrine. It's not just because there's an abnormality to keeping everything like it is. Or the hope day upon day that the child will return. It's those things and also one other. What do you do with a place that's now, because of such an untimely event, set apart? It inadvertently becomes a place of magical strangeness. Because it's no longer what it was. To use a banal phrase, it's no longer fit for purpose. But it can't, without some kind of spell, become anything else. Because then a defilement occurs. I'm frightened of your room. And the fear is born out of the knowledge that it's now beyond my comprehension. I'm also fearful because I feel under attack by it. It drives me out. My life is narrow because of it. I can't use it. But I do give things from it, like holy water. I revere the items but give of them freely, to all. It seems vital to give any transaction no thought, but just to go with the flow, for anything moved or taken can't be undone. And then it's final. A necessary part of 'moving on'.

There will, I know, be a time that another place can be built on this holy ground. After all, isn't it the case that temples are built upon death or birth places?

Stuff is very difficult. It has and doesn't have meaning. Now let's take your Spanish book. What do I do with it? Oh I know already: keep everything until I'm ready to let it go, but just keep it somewhere else. I'm so resentful that you and, more so, I didn't get the reward for all your hard work. Is death a reward? I've spent three and a half years trying to make death, and premature death at that, sound good. Sound like reward. Sound like it means more than this we do here. *And wasn't there talk about reward being elsewhere, in a place better than this? This concept of Heaven.*

How long will I go through life wanting you and waiting for you? I look at your picture, and long as usual. And I'm sick of it. I'm tired of the continuous sadness that pervades my every waking moment and I can't help wondering, if I changed my environment in any dramatic way, whether then finally I could make something different. You still won't be here, though. There's no masking that. And why should it be masked? My love for you ran so deeply, searingly, I would have fought for you, died for you and now I find myself suffering for you.

You, woman of extreme suffering, tell me. Tell me how to stand the unbearable. Tell me how to wake up every day in the boredom of other life.

I'm waiting for you to come back from netball. It's Monday night. It's 9.30 and Lauren's mum is giving you a lift. Only she's not. I can conjure up the same feelings of anticipation for you and it's not even frightening. I'm capable of pretending, of separating. I sit on my bedroom window sill and I look. Finally, a car stops outside, and I know it won't be you. But I like to keep the pretence going for a little while longer. It's preferable right now to having a relationship with your death, or a new child. Well, the latter, really, doesn't ever enter into my head. I know that Lauren is a very big girl now and I don't need anyone to tell me that you aren't at netball. So why do I do it? I think I feel some comfort in turning inwards. It's like the childhood equivalent of holding a favoured doll very close and feeling that things are always going to be OK. In a way it's appreciating the safety and comfort of one's own sense of self. Is this mindfulness? Or maybe the trauma has caused my personality to split, but then I wouldn't be aware of it. Would I?

I can imagine how very lonely, isolated people could begin to have a strong relationship with memories and make believe, and then pathology slowly creeps in. I can see just from this how an individual not as sane as I could take a child, and force her to be you and hold her close. When your limits and possibilities are so closed down, you then fantasise and create something and become so desperate that you quite possibly ignore the consequences. I can imagine that when an individual thinks they have a right to such compensation, narcissism occurs, empathy goes out the window and evil is begun. Whoops, not for me. Gladly, I have a different kind of creative streak. You see, when certain creations are so disturbed or lost (Charlotte), one must forge a new one, to survive and keep motivated, by

226

any means. The human psyche seems very clever in this way.

OK, looks like it's all about separation after all. I mean the possibility of happiness with you being dead. Don't look at me like that. I have to be sometimes, and you are, aren't you, dead, I mean. If I live, then I have to try and live well, don't I?

Well, if I distance myself from you and am comfortable with the notion that I'm apart from you, then there are times now that I can be perfectly OK. It's usually after ovulation and before the onset of menstruation. So it's about one and a half days. But it's a start. And things have to be OK sometimes. They just have to.

I know what it is to be set apart, Mary. I know what it feels like to hold something, to have it close and to accept it and know that no other will understand; to hope for and seek the wise in order to share, and then ultimately to have to know that this gift is only yours to carry. I'm not talking about the gift of Charlotte or of Jesus, but the gift of suffering, the gift, if you like, of being apart, holy, just like that, of being beyond. I find it exciting beyond description. It seems like the ultimate in spirituality. If I died now, I feel I'll have achieved what it means to be beyond human, for that's what holiness is like. The idea of gift, surprise, material, achievement, wrapped, wanted, is all wrong. This is something, just received, not necessarily given, almost invisible, born out of purity, not necessarily virginity, but openness of a different nature, an asexual chastity that's beyond lack of sin, not competing with morality, not even integrity. It possesses all thought, all feeling, all mind and being. It encompasses everything and yet is nothing – the colourlessness comes to mind again. It's about the journey, the beyond, and the limitlessness, and not about the shoddiness, the limits of being human, and the failure of destination. It's everything and nothing and doesn't mind death but minds life. It is, but isn't, it watches but doesn't, it ponders. I ponder. You ponder. We both have lost and we both ponder in our golden aloneness of no colour, of all colours, insignificantly with significance. It continues to be a confusing paradox. A journey of journeys, of queens, a ride, encompassing places where no other would wish to go, but oh the light, the star, the force, the energy of that ride. Euphoric, almost reverberating, electric and flying, above the line, high on the cross looking down on the average. This is the experience of risk and joyful near-death after actual death. The freedom of life, the unbearable lightness of being. It's about being drawn into the vortex, the whirlpool, the black hole, and of allowing yourself to go, to fall, to fail and to know that the alter ego of vortex is peak, to be this friendly to destiny is to be faithful to faith without having any conformity to religion or a god whatsoever. It's to bear the marks of a spiritual queen. To be killed, and know that in that there's something and everything to be learned and experienced: the euphoria of metaphorical death.

It's Christmas soon. In about five days.

I've woken up with a slash across the right hand side of my torso. Is this the fifth wound of Christ? Oh shit, does that mean death is coming? Not so keen on the journey now, am I?

Charlotte, were you more like Mary? You were after all 14 or so and naive, chaste, and I, most like Him, have been crucified, or so it feels. Or are we all the same? Would you have come back from Harvard for Christmas, if you'd a better offer? Would you have been happy to leave me alone at Christmas? You would, wouldn't you? No care for me sometimes. I must often have been so miserable with your choices. Isn't it actually better to have lost you and know what my limitations are? Then I don't expect anything.

You were so cold in the water. When I'm that cold, I think about it. I feel it and want to make you warm. I want to go back to a point when I could have rescued you. *Do you think about it? The first nail? The second, the third? Do you think about the beatings, the blood, the eyes. Was there a point when it was too late? Too close to death and too far away from life? Do you go back to that point and want to make it different? With every moment that passes, and you miss His smell His smile His style, do you wish to go back to that point and want to change it? And then like me realise that you can't, you have to put up with it, yesterday, tomorrow and then again and then again, again and next week and all your forevers. You will live with this. You have to live with it – you can't die, because you have to live with it, the choice of not undoing history, of letting it happen and holding what you've made, a secret that could have been different. A desire even then to go with it, the experience, to have life after death, to have our real human resurrection. We knew. You and I could have stopped it. Anything is changeable but we went with the flow. We allowed a new dimension of history to occur, and now we have to live with the playful monster we've created, in your case Christianity, in mine, who knows yet, maybe in 2,000 years. Born out of a rock and a piece of wood, a sense of what is right. We did it, you and I, at different times, in different places, we did the same thing.*

I feel like I'm descending into the vagaries of vagrancy. I'm becoming a tramp. I smell. I wear fingerless gloves. I shake my head and my gaze is cast down. I'm paranoid. Whether it's the loneliness, the grief, the tiredness, the hunger now or just living with cats, or the panic of never working again or always working, I'm descending slowly into some kind of forlorn madness. Perhaps this has always been the case, a non-identification, a separateness. I distance, I observe. I'm not observed, however. I anger, I rage and in time will spit and hiss under a greasy veneer of body odour, blood and dried-on faeces. And yet if you washed me now and put me in one of Angelina Jolie's second-hand dresses, I'd look hot. So why have I chosen this to replace, beauty, sexuality, my androgynous uniqueness and individual wit? Because I can. I want to lose it completely. It's the way it is. When it gets bad, it gets worse and rolls along gathering momentum. Until presumably there's nowhere further to go down.

I am you, Mary. The stench has come upon me from our battered corpses. The dirt is smeared upon me from the lying. The shame is adhering to me for being human.

People promise all sorts of things, don't they, when they know you won't want them. But when you put them to the test, the door's closed. When it comes to it, they say, 'When we said "any time" we meant during office hours and when we said "anything" we meant only a little bit and then only occasionally and then only once and then only if you sign an agreement.' So no one, and I mean no one, will lend me any money and yet they seem to keep saying, 'Ask us if there's anything you need ever.' I just need not to work so hard for it, actually. I just want someone to lend me a few quid to tide me over. I'll pay it back.

When you've lost a child you're an inconvenience and a loser and a burden to those who haven't. They are, after all, intact and have a very long way to go to be as bad as you. When is anyone going to see me as someone from whom they can learn? After all, I'm astounding to have survived this internal holocaust.

It has come to me after certain encounters lately that religious people, men on the whole, can't stand having a partner with any individuality or sexuality. Women in religious groups seem to be bearers in all senses of the word. They bear the brunt, the lack, the nothing, the pain and the children, whilst the men who may or may not have any gifts, usually not, are permitted to shine.

This well-behavedness that I'm trying, and getting used to, could make me ill. I'm wondering if I should just descend into rage, once and for all. The trouble is then all the work containing myself that's gone before will be void, and I'll only be judged on how I am now. I've really set myself up, haven't I? Good behaviour, staying alive as an example. What on Earth was the point? I say that with no allusion to there being a point elsewhere – for example, Heaven. But nobody notices my good or bad behaviour, nobody's here or there to witness it. That's not strictly true, my legal team notice, my family, my true and good friends, and despite what I say, I do have some, quite a few in fact, and the newspapers. So yes, lots of integrity-orientated persons know who I am. And most of all, *I* notice. There'd be such a lot of notoriety if I misbehaved, not to mention a potential prison sentence.

Well, at least I had you even for a short while, and you were lovely. And you weren't in care. I'm glad, if only for that. I could have been the mother of someone horrible. *Did you compare Him to Barabbas, Mary? Did you wait while the crowd made their choice? You really have been through it, haven't you? They always seemed to want Him dead. Stress from the beginning, trying to hide him, protect him, all that anxiety, fear and grief; Herod, those wise people, meddling.*

Away in a manger, no crib for a bed, the little lady Charlotte lays down her sweet head.

I'm sorry. I miss you. Agony again. Why? Another Christmas. I get through. Always a noticeable absence. Grandma wants to go out for lunch. I wonder why? Without you it will kill me. Best and safest to sit in today. Let's not try and go beyond and replace. It's better to not mix with the big and feel small. It's like being thin: you should wear a small jumper not a large one that shows that you're thin.

I want to go to the school and put a crown of thorns on your statue and draw blood from your wrists and feet. You, the sacrifice, the lost one, the given, the sent. They don't deserve your statue. I'm angry again that I gave you to them, and now a statue.

Grandma touches me. I touched you. I don't know who's touching or being touched. I'm looking back and back again and not forward.

I respect myself and am thus respected. It's about grace. When no one knows how I feel about them and I behave well, their lack of knowledge of me, or what's inside me, is my power. If I'm still or appear to be still and do nothing, then any movement whatsoever is over there and not in me. If I confront them, then I declare my hand, I must be respected and respect myself.

That's it, I'm respected. They may not like it, or agree with the fact that I'm pursuing this case, but while I behave not improperly, then I'm good, sweet, and can have my hand shaken at the end of the inquest by the other side's barrister, as a mark.

There's no one left to die in my house so there'll be no more alarming phone calls or visits.

I've become fluent in my grief for you. It's what happens when one is forced to do something all the time, whether good or bad. It becomes second-nature. It's part of me. In some ways, therefore, you and it are more a part of me than breathing. It can only be internal. To say that it or you can be forgotten for a moment is a lie. I may not think about you, but you're a constant companion, like my beating heart.

There's no one left to die in my house. Does this mean there'll be no more phone calls or visits that cause alarm? Oh, I've already have said that. Does this mean also that I'm unattached? Am I free to roam from place to place, never really living, without attachment and without intimacy? Was I ever anything else? Can I change it now? Well, hold on a minute. I had you and Johnny and I'm as connected to my parents as I can be. 'Dum spiro, spero' again.

When it's bad I breathe and hold a very warm tea cup. That's what's always there, breathing and tea. So I can do that and then I feel calm, safe, stable. Nothing has changed, but my containment of it becomes calmer.

But sometimes it doesn't. And I feel sorry for myself.

I'm on red alert at the art class, in case someone hurts me. And they do. Three of them are talking nonchalantly about your school with the changed name. They're also talking about teenagers and, funnily enough, school trips. It all seems so obvious to me and I wonder how irreverent people can get. I'm angry. I want to talk about things that will wound them one by one, but there isn't the break in conversation that I need. I want to talk about soaps to annoy Steven, and boys who smell to upset Dodie, she has two, and boys who play truant, that will annoy her too, oh and maybe extramarital affairs, that will upset Steven more and may be why close friends commit suicide, Freya had one of those too. But I know even as I think it, that I am spiralling toward bitterness. And I dislike myself for bending towards the 'bad'. The trouble with bad stuff is that it has a knock-on effect. I do worry that life will get worse and worse and that I'll slip further and further into mental illness. And that sooner or later I'll imagine that everyone is against me, and judges me. I find myself constantly watchful like a persecuted animal or tramp.

Water, the very essence of life, what we're mostly made from, the very word causes me discomfort. Dark water, cold water, icy water, dangerous water, pitch black, all water leads to death, all water now leads to you.

Shall I slash my wrists and leave arrows and notes to blame and shame? Is this my crucifixion?

Am I the virgin upon whose lap the unicorn rests its head, like the pony on Dartmoor?

Oh my goodness, I haven't told you about the pony upon the Moor. OK, here goes.

233

Once upon a time a woman, that's me, went to dinner with her legal team at her barrister's house, where there were swans on the banks of the river, and in the river itself. This woman wore inappropriate clothing, wanting to impress, and was cold because the meal was in a marquee, but she soon relaxed, put on her cardigan, threw caution to the wind, drank loads of fine wine and ate the most lovely marinated lamb and was glad once again that she wasn't a vegetarian. There were many reasons for this invitation, and one of them was for me (have you guessed that I'm the woman?) and our team to walk upon Dartmoor as you did. I had to borrow Michael Powers's huge, bright green waterproof trousers, because it did then as it did before: it rained. And looking like an illegal immigrant in mismatched clothing, both in colour and size, I went.

I've never really seen Dartmoor, except at the end of the Ten Tors in 2008 when I welcomed your team back, so I wondered. It's bleak, wild, lonely, stunning, and as Michael said and I had thought, a fitting place to end your life. We were in a long line and Pamela, Michael's wife, seemed to be struggling, behind me. The strongest and most powerful member of the group was certainly Charles, my solicitor, avid map reader, and logical, with an amazingly positive attitude. Michael kept checking on me and I was so, so grateful. Our line continued like a caterpillar with lots of different colours. It was misty and slightly rainy, and then I think it happened. I saw a pony, a mother, just standing some distance away. From behind her a foal emerged, chestnut and white and dappled and moist. He bounded toward our line and went along sniffing, introducing, baying and breathing. Each person seemed to turn around to see him greet the next. And then he came to me. He stopped. He smelt me and looked. So much time seemed to pass and yet it was no time at all. He knelt down in front of me. Then he lay. I don't think I touched him, but I can't be sure. Most of the people were looking. I was overwhelmed. He got up. He walked beside me. And then he disappeared. Even now I'm not sure it happened, but others said it did.

Can anybody imagine what each transition is like for me? Every end, every beginning? The scavenging for meaning, like a slight, sorry bird in the frost.

What enables me to survive death, is it the same thing that enables me to survive life? Just going on and on and on, and then on some more.

You gaze at me across a crowded room. You're three. You love me intensely, fiercely, and I you. We're so connected across the space, inseparable. I cry inside because you look so beautiful and so vulnerable. You're a wise queen in a square pink hat and veil. It's the Nativity. We take photographs. Grandma and George are here. You have make-up on. It's all working. So how did it end like it is now at Christmas, with no turkey and people crying and these uncomfortable hostile feelings towards that school?

There's no more cloth left. I can't make you again. You're gone now. You can't return. Zoe is still coming back for Christmas. I want a child who is coming back for Christmas. Don't I deserve that? I want you back, only you. My old-fashioned child, thoughtful and unAmerican, not like the thumbs-up techno, speed junkie children today.

Christmas, the archetypal image of a mother and a child, yet one unprotected from the first. The scene, a bare, cold stable, the lowest resting place, the cheapest accommodation, for the highest human being. Those who give up life for others. You were the greatest of queens born in the most humble of places. He was the greatest of kings with the same start in life. I didn't mind when I knew, I accepted the greater good, the greatest philosophy, the bitterness of myrrh, competing with the promise of sweet-smelling incense. And still do I traipse on.

I'm inspired by a film, *My Afternoons with Marguerite*, where a woman I've never seen before plays a 90-year-old who kind of falls in love. This means anything can happen, anywhere, at any time, and not only bad things, actually good things too. Grandma's quote comes to mind, '*Dum spiro, spero.'* So I'm not going to commit suicide today. I'm going to see how it goes. And Christmas too. I'm going to make the very best of it. I can. Let me see, I'll take my violin and aim to play for them or with them. I'll take a cake which I'll ice and confectionery and lots of little fun presents that cost little. Yes, good, a plan, well done, Jen, good girl.

Have I kept you behind? You still haven't done your GCSEs and all your friends are beginning degrees. What happened? Your books are immaculate. It just doesn't make sense that you shouldn't have achieved, when you worked so hard and were so worthy.

How could I have lost you? I used to get into the bath and tell myself that if I could catch the top of my disposable razor as it floated under the bubbles by the time I counted to a certain number, then nothing would ever happen to you. You wouldn't drown. I always made myself catch it, so what happened? Where are you if you aren't here? Where are you if you aren't at University? Where are you if you aren't abroad? How do I contact you? How do I get in touch? Your books, they are here, we're waiting. We, the books and I want to get in touch. Oh, Jen, skating on thin ice again, wallowing, stop now, stop.

Those who disagree with my legal action haven't lost a daughter. If they have a daughter, she's not one such as you. I wish for them to let me be in my life without condemnation, as I do for them.

Liars, liars, go to church and then return cleansed but still dirty.

Being good can bring out the goodness in others, but only if they can receive the goodness.

I don't feel that I even have permission to laugh. There's no place for me.

Snow is coming. I wish for snow as I wish for war, in that people must come together and begin to know each other in such times. Life will become a level playing field, those with 4-by-4s must share, those with water must share, and those with heat must share. Those with daughters must share ... I know, just joking.

It's snowing and I'm stranded. Scarcity and awareness begin. Every possible entertainment becomes a delicacy. I can't go to The Plough or to a party. I don't want to ask Edward to use his 4-by-4 unless there's an emergency. So I think of ways to entertain myself and use the time wisely. Something I'm naturally good at. Is it time to play scrabble with Sybil, I wonder, and source morning coffee locally and actually get to know the neighbours? Or have somebody round here? I'm cooking a veggie spaghetti bolognese later – of course with dry soya mince. Remember, you always found them a little spicy? You needed lots of pitta bread to use as ballast.

We'll soon be sharing cars and doing stuff together in this village. Because we can't do anything else. We're forced down the climate change prevention road, but it seems that nobody sees it coming. And this is how it begins, on the quiet. I think people only understand change if it's delivered in the form of a lecture, like a declaration of war.

Forced to be holy! Not by choice. That's me, that's my world. *You, Mary, were you forced by untimely death or were you, as rumour has it, always holy, right from the very beginning?*

It's a full moon and with it comes certain lunacy for me. Do I have too much time on my hands? I go back, back to the beginning. And I see the bang to your head in the river as its force took you. I have a dead child. She wasn't small, she wasn't sick, but she's dead. My child.

Snow has fallen, snow on snow. So I'm snowed in alone. If you'd been here, we could have played games, done simultaneous equations, Sudoku, or whatever would have been timely. The sorrow is that I've lost touch with you. I've missed time. Like a doomed parent who has got fed up or been denied access. You won't know me now. So I'm watching cats in the snow and thinking of building my own snow person and reading. Maybe a homemade cappuccino later. Sounds good really. It's good to know that everyone's Christmas plans are fucked, not only mine. That's not graceful, is it? I have, however, in the scarcity realised that my entire happiness depends on an onion and then a tomato, oh and definitely garlic.

Sex, I need sex, intimacy, holding. Funny, isn't it? *As a bereaved widow, and losing an only child, I feel like I'm supposed to be pure, chaste, like you, Mary.*

Do I blame everyone? Do I think that everyone did this? Well, there's a sense that if someone is not on my side, for me, then they're against me. They must show a sense of allegiance, and I mean by this actually talking to me in a friendly manner and not blanking me. It's no more than this. Acknowledgement means they aren't against me. And I need so much of that. *Evil triumphs, remember, when good men do nothing.*

Sixteen years ago in this living room on Christmas Eve, there was a tree, and presents for at least six people. The worst problem I had was that at four o'clock the lights fused and I ran to Ferry's to get some more. I remember the panic at the unilluminated tree and how we'd have to suffer this for days if it wasn't rectified. And how somehow the lights on the tree signified the lights in our life. And the magic of the time. There was no question of going without them. They switched Christmas on, made it real, made it cosy and spiritual. And yet now there are no lights, upon no tree, surrounded by no gifts, and no people gathering here together. Just me and a memory. The lights joined us together, made us mysterious, and made me a part of something. I'm no longer that. You are the light that's fused, Johnny had already gone and the others are useless without you.

Am I brave? It's a strange word. People use it not knowing its true meaning. It doesn't mean heroic, in the sense that you run and shout and risk your life to rescue a cat up a tree or run after a thief, it means doing the unspeakable and not speaking about it. It means suffering and not telling. It means living and wishing constantly that the pain would go away.

The quality of endurance should make me a person warranting pilgrimage, an icon, rather than someone to be protected from or feared or managed. I'm not dirty; I'm clean, pure, light, bright and white even in the darkest of moments. And bravery above all is the manifestation of truth.

I wish I knew someone who loves you in the way I do.

Christmas Day is the only day people are pious, and even then it's only for a moment before the gluttony and arguing commence. Have people learnt anything? Has anything changed, is there any room at the inn now? My parents liked my iced cake. I wrote their names on it. I also took my violin, which I played sporadically. We pulled crackers from last year and had treacle pudding and custard – not the cat, don't worry. As soon as I arrived, the pressure to enjoy myself completely overwhelmed me and I burst out crying. It was the word 'daughter' that was the clincher, on Grandma's card to me.

Did they say the word 'son', over and over and over some more? My son? Were there any other Jesuses? Was there a my-son-Jesus everywhere, until there was nowhere to look? Until you had to look down in a kind of shame, at your own pain. Did they say it near you, to you, at you, by you, above you, 'my son, my son, my son', louder and louder until it was branded scalding upon you tender heart and soul and head and ear and flesh? Until your whole flesh became the bloody taste of baying, branded word of God, of name of Jesus, 'boy, babe, man, God; dead son, dead Jesus, your son, your son, deceased'. I bet you never got mail, though, did you, woman of god, I bet the postman didn't litter your porch of thatch with the word 'dead' or 'deceased' day in, day out. Now I'm competing with you, mother, competing with you. My misery is worse than yours, because it's mine and I'm here now feeling its dark shadow over my freezing body. I shiver.

'You become responsible, forever, for what you have tamed.' So wrote Antoine de Saint-Exupéry in *The Little Prince*.

The pondering had already begun. Is it the making of something great, that it begins slowly and without notice, and therefore has substance? No one batted an eyelid at the unremarkable Jesus in those early days. And I suspect that nobody batted an eyelid at unremarkable Mary either, slowly coming in on the outside like an unfavoured race horse in the spiritual stakes. Just as they barely saw you and now hardly freeze a thought upon me. I'm unseen, unheard and unremarkable.

Charlotte, were you an ordinary girl, made extraordinary by death? Holiness must surely begin when a young person dies before her mother. The familiar child meets the strangeness of early and untimely death.

I can't work out whether you were special before you died or after, or both, and whether there's connection between the two.

If I am OK, is it right?
And what is right anyway? And how long does it last?

Did you ever have a good day after Jesus died? People say it was different for you, that you were different. I don't believe them, and how can they know? It stands to reason that if you were a human, with a heart, you would have been broken and therefore struggled with any reality of happiness again, ever. Isn't that so, Mary? Tell us.

And so begins a new year, 2011, any hour now. Same shit, different day. I eat. That's all I do well, really. I love to eat. If my head was removed, then I'd really have to die. No mouth, see? I'm in Exeter with Frank. We're at a Chinese buffet, just us. I'm jogging along without expectation. This is the necessary. Do not wish, just see. We go back to his house and watch another film on his computer. It's midnight, Grandma and George ring. I lie about where I am. No New Year resolution about that, I see. I'm promising to stay alive, how about that? I eat some more.

Oh for God's sake, I'm lying. I do many things well. And now have at least two passions, which are two more than most people, so I must stop this overwhelming self-pity.

I'm at the eye clinic. With Grandma this time, might as well buy a season ticket. Soon the appointments will get to me, if I'm here that long and we can buy a family ticket, you know like the ones they have at theme parks?

They're calling you. 'Charlotte.' They're calling for you. Do you have an appointment? Are you here? I look around. Maybe I've gone back or sideways in time. Maybe you didn't drown. Funny thing to say, of course you didn't. I'm making it up again. I see it's another Charlotte, a little Charlotte, not like you at all. I make similarities. Oh, now she's screaming in the side room. A bit like you after all then. Just joking. I'm wondering if you used to scream and scream when you were little because you knew what was going to happen to you, to us, more to you. Charlotte, would your name sound different if you were at university rather than at a graveyard? I mean dead. Would it?

Oh, where did I go wrong? The answer to this is nowhere. It's a rhetorical question. It's not my expectation that I'll be told, one, where, and two that I actually did!

The trouble is, I think it's my fault for having and losing two people. It can only be that I didn't care for them properly.

You see, all I can think about is not that you fell then and died then because no one was there to protect you. Or that you were throwing a rucksack, or looking after Yasmin, or in the rain, or any of the links to the actual event, but more who you were or how I made you be the person who was doing those things, there and then. And actually, perhaps even then, they, and we know who I mean, should have looked after you especially well in that case.

I used to be the woman who lost her husband in tragic circumstances. Now, overshadowed by new events, I'm the woman who lost her daughter on the Ten Tors Training. There's even a spin on that. Not on Dartmoor or with the school, or on a school trip, but Ten Tors Training, a nice bit of alliteration that rolls off the tongue, memorably. So am I nothing else, not the woman who is beautiful, or the woman who is eloquent, or the woman who stopped a lot of people from smoking, when the ban came out, since that was my job. Or the woman who ran the first East, West Brasserie, in Putney, that was me too. Or the woman who walked alone to the Sistine Chapel in 2008.

No, I'm the woman whose daughter died on the Ten Tors Training. Full stop. That's all I am, that's all I say I am. But it's my fault. I use it to change people, to overwhelm them, to give them the pain, to stop them in their tracks. I need to be that for the secondary gain that I relish, oh my God, how unholy am I? Very. I actually want to dump this fatigue upon someone else whenever I can. It stands to reason, that the reason I am this is because I say I am, so it sticks. If I said I was a librarian or a pilot, that would stick instead.

Although if I was a pilot, particularly with my eyesight, it might cause more alarm than being 'Ten Tors Tottie'.

I'm sad today about Grandma. She was looking in a toy shop window at some little figures on horses. I asked her if she wished she'd played with those in Ceylon when she was a little girl. She was upset. How could I not have seen? She was recalling miniature figures she used to buy for you, each month, building up a set when she used to come from London on a trip and stay with us. I wonder if you'd remember those times now. They confuse me. Because times in the past and times of loss should be about the oldest, not the youngest, and certainly not you.

I witnessed for the first time in nearly four years both of us grieving in different ways for you, our girl, it was heartbreaking. She was so silent.

When she came to the hospital as you lay dying,I told her not to cause difficulties, not to speak, not to make things go wrong, not to alienate people. It was all too late. She was silent then. We were all three silent. And it was all too late. I think back to those times every so often. I don't know what triggers this: maybe discomfort or aloneness, like now on a Friday night at ten to six, when I feel that the world has left me behind.

There is always such volume in silence.

Do I deliberately seek pain? Sort of like the death instinct? Do I tease, it prod it, tempt it to come out. Do I make it engulf me? – sting me, envelope me like the predator it is, like a camouflaged sidewinder snake in the dessert? A reptile that hides under the hot sand with its eyes just barely upon the surface, cool and waiting for an unexpected idiot to waft past. By the way, I saw one of those on the *Deadly 60* programme. Is this another false kind of grief? It's as if I'm going along quite nicely and then … I indulge. The computer was on, you see, Crumble came in, he heard the noise, as if he expected you to be at its helm, but it's me reading. Now grief's eyes appear prominent in the hot sand, I poke. I call Charlotte, he howls, am I teasing him as well with his tiny brain? He stops on the bottom step, looking up, wondering. Does he think that you're there? Do I want to share my pain with a cat? I call again, 'Charlotte', I like hearing it, I'm teasing myself, I'm going back in wished-for time. The sadness rises from my diaphragm. I haven't time or desire for this indulgence today. I release Crumble and I release myself. I throw the metaphorical stick into the sand. And the deadly sidewinder, pain, disappears for now.

If I'm glad of the person that I am now, how can I not be glad of the means that brought me here – as they say, the journey?

Am I searching for you in the wrong places? I'm outside the cinema. There's hair here, hair that's freshly cut and falling on shoulders, just the right, exact kind of hair – hair upon athletic shoulders, with 14-year-old braces, screeches, pinkness, unpredictability, naivety. You mustn't be found here. You're 18, no longer needing childish things, serious, away with your friends, free, independent, choosing, few restrictions. You're 18 and gone, far away, scattered over many beginnings, making way for new lives.

If I just do what I did when you were here, would things be more acceptable? Should I get up at 6.30 and make you breakfast? And then produce a packed lunch and wait for the school bus, making sure you have everything for your day. Or would I then go back to that life in such a real way that I could then realise exactly what I've lost? Perhaps I need to make sense of what I had and therefore what's gone and then things will become more peaceful. I can't understand it – I think because it was so sudden and unexpected. You were there, healthy and alive, and then you seemed to be dying.

I know that it's quite late in the day to be talking about something so basic.

Oh my God, more horror. I wonder if they cut you up for a post-mortem. The question incapacitates me, and sends a seizure-like tremor over my person. Cutting the beautiful body of Noods is unthinkable, unspeakable. The probability has come as a shock to me and I'm frightened to know the answer. *Did you get any answers to your questions, Mary? Was there any need for a post-mortem for your boy? Did they know of such a thing? Presumably, if people were punished for crimes, then crimes even 2,000 years ago must have been committed. So there must have been ways of determining even in a very primitive and possibly shoddy way, comparing to today's standards, how an individual died? Physically, anyway, His body was in a state, wasn't it?*

Well, your body wasn't 'found' as such, so there wasn't much mystery about your previous whereabouts and even the adults who were supposed to be near you couldn't conceal what had happened, so I doubt, and don't wish to be corrected on this matter, that there was any need for looking. The hospital medical staff did, after all, spend much time trying to save you and would have known what led to this moment.

Besides, if they looked too closely at you, maybe they'd find that your body would be preserved and sweet-smelling for hundreds of years and then to come, or do I bestow upon you an odd motherly fondness? Possibly.

To think of the unspeakable, sometimes, is the healthiest thing. To manage and make sense out of the most unsavoury fear is to begin again.

Mine, Mary, is definitely what I'd find if I dug her up, and what I'd feel. You see, I'm ready to see her before I bury her now, a little late, apparently. At least you went to the tomb to wrap and anoint.

I know, though, that what lies below bares no relation to what happened above, and that there's no pain for Charlotte, just the confusion and sorrow for me. A confusion and sorrow that really do not connect the perfectly scribed exercise book to a prematurely decaying group of bones and skin.

The trouble with fingerless gloves is similar to the trouble with beards, when one is descending into tramphood. There are compounding problems. If wearing the gloves isn't bad enough, then try cooking with them, and eating with them, just slightly sliding up the palm of your hand. They become tinged with what you're doing. They connect with the colour and smell of what you're preparing or consuming. And just as with sporting a beard, the edges discolour. It's always an orange-brown kind of stain. This then makes other people wonder, what you have got on it, or them. It might be soup, or bread, or both, or stew, worse, or gristle, worse still, or bones, or entrails – you see, very soon if you wear a beard or fingerless gloves, you're practically a cannibal. But that notwithstanding, nobody will want to touch you, and in the case of the beard, or possibly both, nobody will ever want to kiss you or get close to you, in any way, except saints of course, who are always looking for, and revel in, the most undesirable kissers. You then obviously become a social outcast, which in turn compounds the fact that nobody wants you. Sad but true, as I examine the discolouration beginning on the red-and-white-striped former socks, which I have converted to fingerless gloves.

Why are most people so slow? And before you ask, slow in a completely ineffective way. Some seem to need to explain something utterly boring at least three times from the beginning and then again. What the hell is wrong with them? Maybe this is the redundancy of the retired and the old. Hello, if you have to keep your mind active, the answer is really in the question. Terry, from Bideford – he's lost a child as well, so we have that in common as well as the fact that we're both mammals, well, he probably doesn't suckle, oh wait he's warm blooded, OK, we're both mammals, right – well, he keeps coming round to check on my car. The cause of this? I asked him one ill-fated day on the Quay where to put the fucking oil. Now it will never end. He was explaining something the other moment about motoring, and then I just went, nothing to do with trauma, just complete and utter boredom, into a kind of trance. It's the speed of mind. OK, yes trauma, different, unrelated trauma, the trauma of stupidity.

Why do we want to crush an egg when it rests in the palm of our hand? Well, because it represents something alien to us. It represents paradox. It's fragile and vulnerable, whilst being perfect and strong at the same time. It's unknown. You and I, Noods, are like this. The combination taunts and beckons. It confuses, and in the end the desire to destroy is overwhelming. It says, Look at me, I'm so simple and understated. You are never going to be this, no matter how hard or how long you try. I am the example. I am real and happily imperfect and you hate what I represent. I am grace and resistance. I make you feel violence, without you even knowing that you feel it. You so badly want to destroy me, and for what, nothing, just because of my mere existence. But it's more than that. You want to destroy me because I make you feel less. And yet although I'm everything, I'm also nothing. I'm small and translucent and when crushed, I'm nothing. An animal will eat my insides and my shell will just become colourless extra particles on the earth. So why destroy me? Probably only because you can. And that's the appalling sadness of it all. You destroy me because you can. You destroyed her because you can.

Do I get everything wrong? Am I the person who goes to a Jewish fancy dress party dressed as Hitler? I feel like I might be. Yesterday I left my car to be serviced. I had one hour. I went, unusually, to McDonald's opposite. And I sat there at a table next to two mothers, seemingly and half a dozen children and also a family. Not too bad so far, me being on my own being the only difference. Well, how about this. Most of these people seemed to be partially educated. Now, I know what you're saying, Noods, how can I know? Well, they were playing I Spy, beginning with letters FT. 'Four tills' was a possible and then came the answer and not in jest, comically: 'Free tills.' Also there's always something wonky about the jaws of undereducated persons. So what did I have and do to make myself stand out a little more? I chose a vegetarian deli sandwich and I opened and read from a small bound volume of Katherine Mansfield's short stories, like a complete tit. Everyone looked at me as if I was sporting that moustache and slick hair and they were avoiding pork. I was mad, to them I was mad.

I ask again if I'm wrong to have gone along a litigious path, for the pain that it's causing me. But what is the pain? The same two parents are against the case. Well, four now. In fact, I'd rather not name them, because it sullies the page. They're so wrong, so unempathic. I can't believe that they're not supportive when they were so close to you, Charlotte. It leaves me with a choice, to let things unfold or be proactive. And then someone sent me a quote by Sun Tzu:

'Be extremely subtle, even to the point of formlessness.
Be extremely mysterious, even to the point of soundlessness.
Thereby you can be the director of your opponent's fate.'

Sometimes it can be difficult for me not to push.

Why do I have to wait for everything? It's too hard. Today it's too hard. I want to rampage and lash out. I have to wait for you, Noods. I have to wait for money. I have to wait for sex. I have to wait, it seems, for the other side's legal team, to find a pencil. And now I have to wait for people to decide whether they're on my side. I'm tired. In days of immediacy, waiting is a shock. I need a break. And that's precisely what I'm going to do. When things are a bit firmer, I'm going to have a weekend away, without any connection to the case or the other world. Result!

Your death leaves me with a necessary journey, a fight. I must find the truth beyond politics. I must encourage repair for loss, my loss and that of those around me. Above all, I wish to behave, and have behaved, impeccably in my example to other women. An example that's has been set by two others, with grace: one, they call Mary, the mother, and the other they call Charlotte, the girl. Stand tall and wait, ponder if you like, and all will be yours, women can fight and win and be supported.

A single woman, one woman, a mother, can do it, alone, here, now, anywhere.

I have a huge task ahead of me, grief, but like anything of a greater nature it can be broken down into smaller chunks. Beyond this is repair, separation and compassion, which will lead to happiness.

And my repair is conditioned by whether this is truly a problem, or just simply life.

It's a beautiful sunny day. The weather this weekend has been very different from what it was like four years ago on the Moor. I've cried, and I've filled my time. I've seen the people I cherish, and with whom I most want to share experience. And I've been to your grave. I've taken spring flowers.

It's 3.45, always. I'm close to crying always.

And that's as it should be. I'll want you back until my last breath, on the day I die. But as we stand in time, I'm unbeaten. And remarkably I can be excited. Now, right now, some things work. And that's enough.

Lightning Source UK Ltd.
Milton Keynes UK
UKOW01f0035181017
311164UK00015B/384/P